Praise for *Whispers,*

"Nancy Heart has created an eye-opening masterpiece that will linger in your mind for a long time. True incidents and real people are described in profound detail, which will enlighten the reader and create empathy for post-war hardships and their victims. Young Anna stands as a testament to the power of strength, resilience, faith, and perseverance. It is easy to be moved by young Anna's strength and know that it brings her triumph at the end of her dark tunnel. In *Whispers, Sinners, and Saints*, the author has poured out her heart and soul, unveiling the true essence of abuse and deprivation. Explicit language and graphic violence scenes add authenticity to the narrative. This is a superb read and, as readers, we owe it to ourselves to appreciate such a journey of self-discovery, faith, and personal growth!"

—Five Stars from Angelique Papayannopoulos, *Readers' Favorite*

"Nancy Heart's memoir *Whispers, Sinners, and Saints* is a must-read for those with parental responsibilities, therapists, psychologists, and non-fiction history enthusiasts. With vivid anecdotes, memories, and nuanced, evocative depictions, Nancy takes readers back in time, opening a portal into the life of a poor Jewish family in Hungary during the Nazi, then Russian invasion of the country, then into the miserable life of a child living with an abusive mother in New York City. Nancy's poignant, intimate tone allowed me to connect with her and experience the story emotionally. Both the details of the extended family's life in Hungary and young Nancy's life in New York brought me to the brink of tears. The witty commentary and introspective thoughts on the culture and behavior of Hungarians against the backdrop of heart-wrenching life encounters put a smile on my face. Nancy's extraordinary story has touched me. Her decision to be different from her mother and harbor no resentment against her mother is a powerful lesson for victims of abuse."

—Five Stars from Keith Mbuya, *Readers' Favorite*

"A true story that spans the distance between horrors and Heaven, all within the experiences of a mother and child—it will test your willingness to see the truth. What's interesting is how one embraces evil while the other holds on dearly to good. Good wins in the end, but getting there, wow! Whispers is equally spine-tingling, provocative, and entertaining. I dare anyone to read this book and say their heart wasn't moved!"

—William M. Beecham, PhD, psychologist and Christian author

"Characters and events within this memoir of survival come alive, gripping my emotions like a white-knuckle ride. While I pray for all beings, there are some I would never wish to experience in person and others I would welcome with embrace and applause."

—Denise Foster, minister, reiki master, and teacher

"These characters come to life with the use of their own vernacular and made me chuckle aloud. But even more than possessing a unique flavor-enriched knack of sharing this entertaining, emotional, and historical account, this book wonderfully reflects the inner goodness, innocence, and mystical feelings of a young girl navigating through a maze of darkness to miraculously survive a life that makes Mommy Dearest look like a picnic in the park. I enjoyed this book so much I can't wait for the rest of the series."

—Marc A. Rabinoff, EdD, professor, author, and columnist

"Whispers, Sinners, and Saints is a riveting account of true grit realness, offering insight into a child's life we would not think happens in America. Her immigrant mother arrives in America to live the American dream. What the author survives as a child is a living nightmare.

Being a thirty-six-year official in Colorado, I have dealt with every situation as head of a juvenile intake unit, and I commend Nancy for not being placed in 'the system' for murder and not falling prey to substance abuse like I have seen others do with far less stacked against them. How she endured and lived to write this book is a miracle!"

—John J. Hafer, sergeant and detective

Whispers
Sinners *and* Saints

Nancy Heart

Whispers, Sinners, and Saints
Published by Featherwalk Press LLC.
Denver, CO

The events depicted in this book are authentic and all people are real. Dialogue is a representation of what was spoken based on the author's recollections. Some material may elicit an intense, emotional response.

Names: Heart, Nancy, author.
Title: Whispers sinners and saints / Nancy Heart.
Description: Denver, CO : Featherwalk Press LLC, [2024]
Identifiers: ISBN: 979-8-9897927-0-2
Subjects: LCSH: Abused children--Biography. | Children of Holocaust survivors--United States-- Biography. | Holocaust survivors--Biography. | Holocaust, Jewish (1939-1945)--Hungary-- Personal narratives. | Resilience (Personality trait)--Personal narratives. | Divorced women-- Biography. | Spirituality. | LCGFT: Biographies. | BISAC: BIOGRAPHY & AUTOBIOGRAPHY / Survival. | BIOGRAPHY & AUTOBIOGRAPHY / Jewish. | RELIGION / Spirituality.
Classification: LCC: HV741 .H43 2024 | DDC: 362.7/0973--dc23

Cover and interior design by Victoria Wolf, wolfdesignandmarketing.com, copyright owned by Nancy Heart.

Featherwalk
PRESS

Whispers, Sinners, and Saints is dedicated to all those who experienced persecution and torture at the hands of another human and is especially dedicated to the heroes who found the strength and means not to succumb to darkness but instead rose to thrive with gained compassion and insights.

I also dedicate this book to my Big Mama Clara and to my past relatives I should have been able to meet but who were killed under Nazi persecution.

Note To The Reader

This book is intended for adults and contains explicit language and real-life scenes of graphic violence and childhood abuse.

Prologue

I CAN'T BELIEVE MY GOOD FORTUNE. Here I am, sitting on my rocking bench on my porch, facing the Rocky Mountains. I'm a born city girl, Manhattan to be exact. Mother condescends me even though she's passed. "I always told you! You're not a city girl. You'll be happiest living in God's country somewhere." Well, she was wrong about a lot of things, but she was right about that!

I have also lived in South Florida, Miami Beach, for starters, with my mother. I attended the University of Miami in Coral Gables and settled down with a husband and two children in Pinecrest. I moved to Boca Raton and Delray Beach when I was divorced. I had to move after forty-five years in Florida. The single best reason was to escape the haunting memories of those places. Out here in Colorado, I've had a fresh new start; my past doesn't weigh me down or pull me back. The "I have to move forward" attitude has brought me a new life.

I am a survivor, and through my struggles, I humbly thank the guidance from an intangible source "All Knowing." He was my trusty reliable source when I had nowhere else to turn. With a heavy sigh of relief, I must point out that if it weren't for me listening to the *whispers* of All Knowing, I wouldn't have survived. I wouldn't be alive to tell my story.

I have finally climbed the steep mountain of struggle, and *yes*, I have a lot to live for! I enjoy watching the changing mountainous landscape, depending on the amount of snow that's fallen, and all four seasons, especially after living in one forty-five-year-long steamy, hot summer in Florida.

I am immensely grateful for this fourth season of my life. I have gained so much growth and compassion through my first three seasons that I feel they have molded me into who I am today. I did not let my struggles make me into a bitter person. Instead, I'm a better person, and I am proud I have broken generational burdens, not passing them on to my children as was done to my mother and me.

In this last chapter of my life, I promised to write. I'd been taking mental notes since I was four, not only to make sense of the madness I sustained growing up but to give motivation, encouragement, and purpose to anyone who feels less than hopeful for a brighter future.

It is paramount to realize struggle is the opportunity for growth and to become a greater person through gained insights of lessons learned. None of us really knows who we are unless we are challenged. In the face of challenge, we see our true nature, our strengths and weaknesses, what we need to change, and what to hold on to dearly.

I was fortunate to survive a highly abusive, negligent, and Asperger's mother, who would not be diagnosed until she was eighty years old. I learned to listen to my All Knowing at five months old. I had no one else, and perhaps that's why I gravitated to Him so early on.

At five months old, I suffered through two rotations of shadows that occurred in the room where I lay in my crib. With age, I figured out that I'd experienced two sunsets and sunrises over two days without anyone checking on me or feeding me. Instead, I was left naked, hot with fever and pain, sloshing in my excrement on a plastic mattress in my crib. There came a point when my last attempt at crying to be rescued pushed me out of my body. I didn't recognize myself. I hovered above myself, wondering, *What's this blob?* All Knowing answered, "That's you." The shock thrust me back into my body. So, instead of seeing the negative of almost dying due to neglect, I see the gift of the precious union I accepted, treasured, and respected. All Knowing saved me throughout my whole life.

Only in the process of writing my bio for this book did I realize that my mother's story has a great deal to do with my story. The tragic atrocities she survived fell onto my shoulders to bear. This story comes from bits and pieces and chunks my mother told me of her life, and I don't hold back anything. Plenty of bad and ugly are woven into this quilt. Friends and acquaintances have inquired, "Are you worried what people will think?" Or they've commented, "You're very brave." Sadly, they missed the point. The words on these pages are to show by real example that there is no human excuse to harbor ill will and hate toward anyone, for that does no good—not only to the perpetrator but to all those in her midst.

My story starts with Mother's. The long whistle of my tea kettle whisks me back … to howling wind and New York City's frigid *air*—more biting than a hard apple, rudely welcoming its newest immigrant to hit its shores in the year 1957.

Family Tree

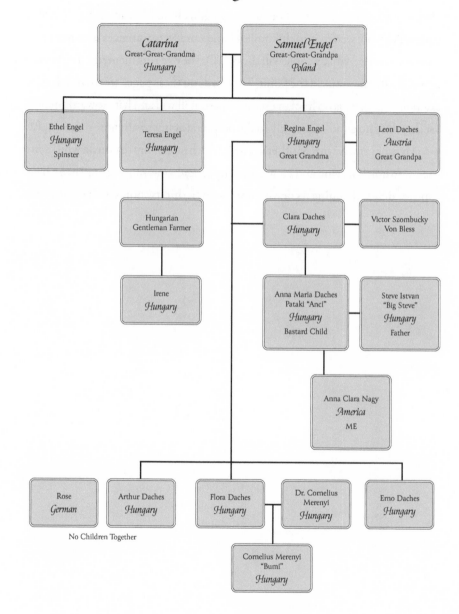

Catarina
Great-Great-Grandma
Hungary

Samuel Engel
Great-Great-Grandpa
Poland

Ethel Engel
Hungary
Spinster

Teresa Engel
Hungary

Regina Engel
Hungary
Great Grandma

Leon Daches
Austria
Great Grandpa

Hungarian
Gentleman Farmer

Clara Daches
Hungary

Victor Szombucky
Von Bless

Irene
Hungary

Anna Maria Daches
Pataki "Anci"
Hungary
Bastard Child

Steve Istvan
"Big Steve"
Hungary
Father

Anna Clara Nagy
America
ME

Rose
German

Arthur Daches
Hungary

Flora Daches
Hungary

Dr. Cornelius
Merenyi
Hungary

Erno Daches
Hungary

No Children Together

Cornelius Merenyi
"Bumi"
Hungary

1

GRINNING IN MISCHIEVOUS DELIGHT, *Wind* flirtatiously tussled Anci's brunette strands of hair caressed by the collar of her brown seal fur coat. *Good thing I borrowed this coat without asking Mutter Clara,* Anci thought to herself about her mother. *At least I have something to keep me warm. Heck, it's the only thing I own.*

Like an unwanted suitor, howling *Wind* crept his cold fingers up Anci's spine till the hair on the back of her neck stood upright. She adjusted her collar, but it wasn't enough to keep out the next brash gusts. Anci believed she was "as strong as bull's horns," like all Hungarians. *Wind* and Anci were a match—equally vain; neither was about to succumb to the other. In fact, even in that moment, Anci did well to practice her grandmother Regina's teaching: "Do not wrinkle the forehead; prevent future, unwanted signs of aging." She merely grunted a sigh and swatted at her tickled ear like a goat's tail shooing a fly. After all, the brown-eyed, twenty-five-year-old had her sights focused on the greatness America offered.

Anci walked in full throttle, the only speed her superhuman legs practiced, until she finally outraced the wind. In respect to Anci's strong constitution, *Wind* waved her on with a helpful brisk salutation. *Wow! In America even the wind pushes people forward with a helping hand, unlike the world of communism, where the iron fist holds everyone down.*

The stench of New York City smelled great. Anci preferred tear-filled eyes of black soot to the oppression she had fled back home. The stink and soot at least held exhilarating hopes of freedom. She'd heard she could speak her mind openly about world events without having to face radical punishment, like disappearing to a Gulag for two weeks … or worse, forever! Everyone knew somebody who disappeared like that, and if they didn't, then they were the one who experienced such horrible torture. How wonderful to be away from that!

I wish I could speak this English! Her mind resorted to a song she had sung many times in her head. If played or sung, it carried grave punishment back home. Testing her newfound emancipation, Anci decided to softly murmur Doris Day's hit that penetrated American radio waves the previous year: "Que Sera, Sera." She checked her close vicinity and noticed there were no repercussions. Celebrating her small victory, Anci amped up her volume.

Que sera, sera …

These words etched in her memory like a broken record. Hearing them sung with her voice was meaningful beyond words. She understood communist Hungarian ideology was the antithesis of "free thought." These seemingly harmless words were punishable. Under a totalitarian regime, individualism was forbidden, and words offering choice were due cause for a spy to turn the listener or repeater of such lyrics into the authorities. The authorities, in turn, had the right to whisk the political opposition away for interrogation.

Back in Hungary, adults, including little old grandmothers, prudently turned their radio dials to the right as they simultaneously mouthed, "The walls have ears," to drown out whispered words of suppressed anger, oppressed political views, and depression from miserable hopelessness and hunger shared among friends and family. Since Stalin sympathizers were everywhere, it was common knowledge that all homes and businesses were bugged. Communists heard everything! "The walls have ears!" was commonly whispered as the radio dial was blasted to full volume.

Communist mentality consisted of poverty jointly owned by the vast majority, the working class, while the small minority ruling class owned everything. But none of that mattered to Anci now. *America is my home!* she reminded herself, feeling the effects like an unclipped nightingale newly escaped from a cage. Singing the promising words "Que sera, sera" reminded the immigrant of the taste of her brighter future that already belonged to her.

Back home, fear was instilled by the secret police authoritatively conducting the "midnight knock," whereby they unexpectedly showed up in the middle of the night and seized someone from their home. There were no friendly neighbors—only nosy neighbors who acted in the name of serving the Communist Party. There was a quota imposed on each person to report suspects to the security police. The higher the number reported meant one was a more dedicated communist to the party. And for those "nosy neighbors," pointing one finger toward someone else meant they averted three pointing back at them.

Nothing more needed to be said to raise suspicion than, "They afford to eat a bologna sandwich," or "They have new shoes" or "a new hairstyle," which earned the suspected one a midnight knock. A cooperating comrade was one who was feared rather than lived in fear, or so he or she thought. Either way, the motivation to stay alive under the communist thumb was fear-based and fear-driven.

Tales from family survivors told of men in uniform torturing their captives for a minimum of two weeks; unlike James Bond movie scenes, this was real life. Family members were clueless as to who were the spies who reported them as political rebels to dangerous officials. And no one knew where the dungeon of the city was located, but everyone knew at least one person who was taken away. Worst of all, many knew someone who never returned.

BARKING BLASTS FROM city cabbies' horns rudely jostled Anci back to the present. She scurried on to the yellow-striped city curb for security, simultaneously releasing, "*Menj baszd meg anyadat,*" which expressed more than, "Kiss your mother hello!" In Hungarian, Anci literally swore, "Go f**k your mother!"

Waiting for the light to turn green at the busy intersection, she wondered, *How long did my mind wander? Wow, back home, someone would have told me I speak Hungarian very well for the words I just exclaimed.*

Anci grew up in Budapest, the capital of Hungary, but New York City was a metropolis like no other as far as Anci was concerned. It didn't intimidate her. She loved it, especially since she just learned she could swear like the worst of them, and no one was the wiser. Tapping her foot, anticipating her turn to jump into the hullabaloo, she appeared much like a child waiting her turn to enter a candy store. The thrill of plentiful, modern cars darting around pedestrians with disregard to red lights percolated her blood. In immediate love with the big city's zest for commotion—with taxis ready to run down their own mothers to catch a fare—Anci ingested car exhaust like an asthmatic did their inhaler. The madness filled her senses. *Yeah, I feel alive!*

Anci hadn't been in New York longer than maybe a couple weeks, but like sun and water to a flower, she thrived on the city's pulse. She'd paid a hefty price to finally arrive where those born on the shores of America took for granted, and not for a second would she allow more time to pass without sucking in her present environment. Ambulance sirens, honking fire engines, and constant construction sounds merged into one giant, clashing symphonic cacophony. The rapid heartbeat of the city streets became her meter.

At the next red light, Anci was in awe of the plenitude of lit signs promoting capitalism. She was swimming in a sea of advertisements featuring playhouses and movie theaters. Her remorse in not having enough money to attend either and her inability to speak English were quickly overshadowed by the incomprehensible notion of *how rich America is! No one worries about the electricity bills!*

There was a billboard with the Pall Mall cowboy blowing smoke rings, advertising cigarettes, and another billboard with a large Pepsi-Cola bottle cap. Chevrolet, Canadian Club, and Admiral Television Appliances took up prime real estate in the advertising since they were situated in the fork of the road between two avenues. Everything was larger than life, enveloping her 360 degrees around. The reputation of Times Square preceded itself. In addition to the freedom of one's will in America, Anci quickly found free money on the street. Like a crow, she spotted shiny objects some distance ahead. Slightly changing course, she ran to claim her prize with a smile. *People are so rich in America that they toss away small change. I must write about this to Mutter Clara back home.*

Anci referred to her mother by the German title for mother. She even called Mutter by her first name, Clara, probably because she grew up sharing living quarters with her grandparents. Her grandpa Leo only spoke German, while her grandma Regina spoke only Hungarian. As far as Anci's name, it is an endearing term for Anna. Everyone she knew called her Anci even though she was more bitter than sweet.

For Anci and the Hungarians she knew back home, it was a crime not to pick up found money, after which, one spit on the findings and said, "May the rest of your family follow," followed by another "puh" before tossing it into one's purse or pocket and, if necessary, her brassiere.

Anci couldn't believe that no one had beaten her to those coins. She practiced her learned superstitious ritual and tapped her pocket, proud of her accomplishment. Then, like a Doberman belled to dinner, she heard the sounds of her native language, which perked her ears to attention. Hunting for the exact location, she turned in one direction and then spun around in another. *Is it possible? Could I bump into a Hungarian so far away from home?* She spotted the loud and obnoxious fellow Hungarians oohing and aahing in excitement over their first time seeing the cowboy smoke rings and wondered if she'd had the same loud initial reactions. The Hungarians began walking toward her, continuously pointing at this and that, hypnotized by their bedazzling surroundings. They closed ranks with Anci, standing shoulder to shoulder.

Given a fleeting moment to act, Anci turned to them to ask, "*Magyar?*"

The Hungarians proudly hailed back with smiling eyes, "Hungarian!"

In the safe arms of America, the Hungarians were happy to comply, in respect to the shores embracing them into freedom, and reply, "Hungarian."

"How long have you been out?" Anci asked at the same time as the other Magyars.

"Two weeks," both parties answered with smiles.

The red light switched to green, and in a New York nanosecond, the Magyars were gobbled up by a sea of New Yorkers, whisking them away into a tide of blinking marquees along 42nd Street while Anci turned to walk Seventh Avenue again.

Anci easily kept New York City pace among strangers on all sides, including ethnically diverse people she was seeing for the first time. Hungary was a white, homogenous society except for gypsies and male athletes from visiting nations who played in soccer tournaments.

The nuance of items and gadgets sold inside and outside the stores in Times Square was somewhat of a time-travel experience, whereby she was suddenly propelled into an abundant future. Her eyes feasted on the cornucopia of plenitude as her head shook in disbelief.

Anci, born in 1932, was twelve in April 1944 when Nazis ordered the slum where she grew up to be the designated ghetto for all Jews to live, including her family. During that year, her family would all be gone or dead or deported to concentration camps except her grandmother Regina. The only clothes available to Anci were those removed from corpses or left behind by recently deported females on their way to the cattle cars for extermination. So, fashion and electronic gadgets in these American stores were amazing, especially since radios had been confiscated from those living in the ghetto. The variety of cameras displayed in one storefront window alone was more than she had seen in her lifetime. They were handheld and not her customarily seen clumsy objects, detachable in three parts and transported in large carrying valises.

Photographs were a big expense in Hungary. Mother had Anci's first picture taken before her second birthday. The town doctor told the family that Anci wasn't going to live long so they needed a keepsake. Mother always added that family said something about her head being too big and it was a sign of something. Apparently, the expense of that pocket-size photo made the family go even hungrier than usual that week. As far as those cumbersome cameras back in the old country, Anci recalled the blinding flash and the puff of smoke, and she chuckled.

She chuckled twice as loud and looked over her shoulder to see if anyone would rush to claim her sandwich that she'd magically retrieved without putting in any money, just by pushing some buttons on the machine in the Horn & Hardart automat. She didn't even realize that she had walked away from Times Square or what she was doing. Unconsciously driven by hunger, she saw food behind an encasement and started to manipulate the device, eager to obtain any of the goods caged within it. *This is easier than digging for food like I did in the rubble after an air raid hit a grocery store!* Anci grinned. Normally, the large machines had purchasable sandwiches on display through individual glass windows, and with the right amount of coinage deposited into a metal slot, a glass door opened for the removal of the purchased item. *America is a special place indeed.*

Caught up in the thrill of the city, she walked out of Horn & Hardart, on to 57th Street and made a left as she glommed down her sandwich, though careful not to drop a delicious morsel. Anci licked her fingers and wiped her mouth with a napkin she conveniently dropped on the street floor in front of Carnegie Hall on 57th Street and Seventh Avenue. Without missing a beat in her step, she turned left to head back to Times Square.

This time, dusk accentuated the lit-up marquees. Trying to read the vaude-ville act next to the large Planters Peanuts sign in the thick of things on Broadway, someone suddenly grabbed Anci's arm and swung her around. After the initial shock of an *unwanted dance partner*, the face of the *laughing hyena* zoomed into focus.

"Country Katy!" Anci exclaimed, giving her a bear hug. Country Katy was a friend from back home. She was a peasant girl, the oldest girl out of nine children. Her father had wanted a boy, and since there weren't any bequeathed him, he treated Katy as his son. Well within reason. He and Katy killed hens and chickens together, for the most part by breaking their necks with their bare hands. Anci, being Anci, outright called Country Katy "a peasant" to her face, quickly delivering a compliment in the same breath. "You are as sly as a fox," she added, as if the insult washed away the burn. Not to worry, though, because the two were as resilient to blistering comments as they were to the blistering cold.

There in Times Square, Country Katy stood reinvented: her drab brunette hair was Marilyn Monroe bleached blond and teased, her mouth painted in blaring movie star red lipstick. But most noticeably, Country Katy was dangling off the arm of a new man—like a howler monkey, she had swung onto a new branch. *Her laughter and happiness know no shame.*

Anci shrilled, "Ah, Katy, you big whore, how are you?"

The two of them bumping into each other was kismet. Into this scene, rushing to catch up, there emerged another Hungarian. Her name coincidentally was also Katy. Out of breath due to years of excessive chain-smoking, she finally joined the Hungarian huddle, exhaling her last puff of smoke to then glimmer her yellow smoker's smile.

"Let me introduce you to *Kiss, Steve* and Katy."

Steve's last name was Kis, meaning "little" in Hungarian, but no man wants to be called little. He learned Kiss meant a peck, as in a smooch, and preferred it. In Hungarian, the family name is always said first, before the given name. So that's how Steve came to be called *Kiss, Steve.*

Anci shook *Kiss, Steve's* hand but grinned at Katy. Unbeknownst to Country Katy, this Katy and Anci shared history as well.

"*Ay, yi*, I know Katy!"

She was a city girl, and Anci conveniently referred to her as City Katy to keep the two Kats distinguished from one another. They were old friends, as both City Katy and Anci had leaned on each other in their own times of crisis. City Katy, for the most part, was well known by all who knew her to smoke a cigarette over eating food. Given the choice between a cigarette and a roll, City Katy would snatch the cigarette and say, "You get fat!" No wonder she and Anci were good friends. Anci would shove the roll into her mouth so fast that proud Hungarian Houdini would have considered her for his assistant.

To think of it, the two girls had met at a dance hall. How else? City Katy was outside smoking a ciggy, and Anci was standing outside, trying to find a way to enter the establishment without having to pay. Most times, Anci's good looks and a smile caught an interested fellow to request her company on his way in, but not so far on this particular night.

While Anci waited outside, City Katy extended her ciggy and asked, "Hey, you want a drag?"

They exchanged meaningless conversation before City Katy delivered her icebreaking bold inquiry, "Are you still a virgin?"

Anci replied, "Yes," to which City Katy answered, "Me too." Then Anci, handing back the butt of their shared ciggy, decided to fess up and replied, "No," to which City Katy answered, "Me too," and they burst into a robust, bonding laugh.

One night, after their pained feet made the girls want to cry more than dance, they left the dance hall to walk home, taking a shortcut through the park. They were approached by a team of young men—literally, the Hungarian National Soccer Team. The girls recognized them, so City Katy immediately allowed her guard down. Stupidly, City Katy mistook their attentions as flattery. She was feeling special, especially after an evening filled with cocktails.

As a seasoned street rat, Anci's street smarts were otherwise alerted, and, as she phrased it, she could "smell a horse needing to relieve itself from a mile away," translating it politely. Anci motioned for City Katy to quickly follow her, but City Katy, too inebriated, didn't catch the undertow of mischief ready to bring her to her knees. The men circled their target, preying upon her like a soccer ball in play, ready to score. Anci took off running. When she stopped to take a breath and looked over her shoulder, she didn't spot City Katy anywhere. She hoped City Katy had taken off in another direction and was somewhere safe.

That was not the case. City Katy became the unwilling recipient of what each and every one of them had in mind to give her, until they deemed themselves done. Her cries tearing through the night air fell on deaf ears. Her body's defense mechanisms kicked in at some point, and she passed out. No one came to rescue her. She woke up where and how they left her: dirty and desolate. No amount of soap and water or tears could wash away her pain. In time, swigging the booze bottle was the only way City Katy was able to drown out her sorrow, self-loathing, and the horrific flashbacks. The raping bastards robbed City Katy of her sense of dignity. In turn, she turned each bottle into her newest best friend.

ANCI OPENED THE WEEKLY Budapest newspaper one day and found an advertisement with an opportunity she couldn't pass up. The master sculptor Zsigmond Kisfaludi Strobl was requesting Hungarian women to audition before him. He had been issued a government grant commissioning him to create a statue, a figure representing the strength of Hungarian women. Anci immediately thought of City Katy. It would lift her spirits. City Katy wanted no part of it; she was too depressed. But Anci finally persuaded her to at

tend the audition with her.

Grinning girlishly, Anci said to City Katy, "Master Strobl will have to make a choice between the two of us. Can you imagine if one of us is actually picked?"

Certain she herself would win, Anci thought, *There is no way City Katy will ever win with her plain looks.* To both their amazement, City Katy was chosen from the hundreds of auditioning women.

Maybe he mistook our names, Anci thought. So, she personally confronted the master sculptor and challenged, "You bypassed me for a lesser body?"

His explanation, "Her body was chosen to emulate in sculpture form the average hefty Hungarian body type of our time," was somewhat consoling to Anci's aloof entitled ego. *Katy is older than me by five years. Maybe that's why she is hefty even with all the smoking she does. I can't imagine what she would look like if she ate instead of smoked.*

The statue captured City Katy's youthful grace, and she'd made her mark in life. City Katy was now exalted like an Egyptian sphinx.

No matter the reasons, today the Liberty Statue made from City Katy's image still stands proud on Gellert Hill, Budapest, overlooking the Hungarian people below in remembrance of those who sacrificed their lives for the independence and freedom of Hungary. Perhaps her statue will survive among one of the few relics of our time, causing people to ask, "What great goddess is this, placed among the heavens by day and the stars by night? Who was she to be immortalized into a granite angel to guard the city below?" Only time will tell. City Katy's accomplishment meant only one thing to Anci at the time: "That should have been me!"

City Katy now stood in front of Anci in this unexpected reunion in Times Square, reminding Anci, *I never should have taken this one to the Strobl audition.*

"*Ay yi*, Country Katy, dear, and dear City Katy, imagine meeting you two whores together here! Hungary is the smallest country in the world, and yet here we are—us three whores. Who's left to whore in Hungary?"

Making their re-acquaintance in 1957 America at this juncture of their lives was comforting for each of them. There was power in numbers. The Hungarian revolt of 1956 against the Russian Communists—that lasted from October 23 to November 11—was based on it. They had successfully overcome their opposition and braved conquests—land mines, flying Molotov cocktails, and an unbearable weather crossing to where they now stood—and their feelings moved all of them in kindred spirit.

Void of words, the impromptu union of Hungarians huddled together closer, interlocking elbows to form a tight *Czardas* circle—their traditional Hungarian folk dance. Country Katy instinctively boot-stomped her foot and released a peasant "Whoop!" into the brisk air. *Kiss, Steve* began humming the first stanza of Hungary's national song written by Sandor Petofi, and being the proud people they were, the four stuck their chests out like roosters and crowed as loudly as they could their most heartfelt Magyar hymn. Although Country Katy was tone deaf, their voices carried pride, they smiled, and their entire bodies and souls sang into this moment of moments, pushing through their streaming tears of joy:

Magyars, rise. Your country calls you!
Meet this hour, whate'ver befalls you!
Shall we freemen be, or slaves?
Choose the lot your spirit craves!
By Hungary's holy God
Do we swear.
Do we swear that servile chains
We'll no more bear!

Funny thing is, their performance went unnoticed in the City of New York in 1957. Imagine! This was the first time they had been allowed to sing the hymn since Hungary's takeover by the Germans in March 1944, followed by the Russians who kicked the Germans out in February 1945. Hungarians learned to control their urge and desire to sing their national anthem in public or in earshot. Although behind closed doors and in the proximity of their most trusted loved ones, they dared to do so, but even then, they only mouthed the words or whispered them, at best. No one would chance being heard singing what they could now sing safely and freely, thousands of miles away from their homeland. Their declared feat was equivalent to astronauts sticking the American flag on the moon, and that event wouldn't occur for another thirteen years!

When done, City Katy added, coaching the others in broken English pronunciation, "Give me your tired, poor, sick and huddled masses."

These were the first American words they learned, after the "Que Sera, Sera" song, the title of which they later learned was in Spanish, giving the Hungarians something to chuckle about most of that day.

Anci pulled out a few pennies from her pocket and said, "Look what I found today. America! Can you believe this great country! What can I get for these three pennies, some chewing gum?" *I will keep quiet about my sandwich. That way I have a better chance of getting another free one.* They all laughed. Anci could never retell a joke, but she was funny when she didn't try to be funny.

Looking at her friends, Anci considered that this reunion was actually their second. They had spent time with each other while laid over in detention in Austria, before journeying to America. Their first reunion occurred in Vienna, at the Nunenhoff Hotel on Mariahilfer Strasse. It became Anci's home, courtesy of the Austrian government and American taxpayers, and allowed the Hungarians to move to the next step in the immigration process. Anci was among the first five hundred to arrive to this point of safety. Soon others, who arrived either by train or foot after Anci, were all infiltrated into the immigration process as well. The next step for Anci, if all went well from here, would be America.

At one point, all Anci knew was that her newfound family—the two Kats, City and Country Katy—were gone and on to their next juncture: Camp Kilmer in Piscataway, New Jersey, in the United States of America. They had departed by either a boat or plane—Anci didn't know which. Country Katy had been sponsored by a beauty salon on East End Avenue, Manhattan, to learn the trade. City Katy also went to Manhattan and really hit the jackpot with her credentials as the subject of a statue by Strobl. She was given an apprenticeship to refurbish high quality tapestry rugs for museums like the Guggenheim. In a relatively short time, both Kats would own businesses they were respectfully trained in, earning them the American dream: fists full of dollars.

2

MONTHS PASSED, and Anci, whose future was unknown, remained stuck at the immigration process midpoint at Nunenhoff Hotel. She did not understand how to acquire a sponsor or obtain a job to proceed to Camp Kilmer, since her skillset was secretarial. As she set out to learn more about what she needed to do, Anci bumped into a fellow named Steve.

Anci recognized him from the saloon he owned with his parents in the Old World. This Steve was *Nagy, Istvan*. Nagy in Hungarian means big or great. Again, the family name is always said first, before the given name. Istvan means Steve. So, Anci told him, "You best not refer to yourself as Istvan anymore." Then added, "You're Big Steve." They became familiar with each other while scheming to break out of what they called their "holding cell."

Big Steve was slender, non-Jewish, five feet four inches to her five feet five inches. They shared stories about how they had made it this far. He boasted that his parents' home literally bordered Hungary at the entrance and Austria at the side exit. That's what helped him cross the border effortlessly. Anci, on the other hand, shared that she had found her fiancé in bed with another woman and was so heartbroken she mentally checked out. When she regained her senses, she found herself among a large cluster of people making their exodus from Hungary.

Looking around, she noticed people carrying as much as they could, while all she had was what she wore, and she had nothing to eat.

Learning as she went, she found out that Hungarian escapees had to be careful to avoid checkpoints where their papers were inspected. Since the Russian Communists would not allow Hungarians to leave the country, any Hungarians trying to flee would be shot. Anci followed her own rule: When she was asked if she had made her destination by foot, airplane, or train, she replied, "I got to Austria the same as you. How did you go?" She would have a weird look in her eyes that confirmed she really had no clue.

Intermittently, in the most unexpected times, Anci would blurt out a new memory that came to her, such as, "I remember sitting under a tree, drunk, working up my nerve with others I met along my travels to face the mine fields we had to cross ahead of us." No one dared ask if she witnessed someone getting blown up by stepping on a land mine. She would have said what she remembered if she did. Perhaps the look in those far-off stares of contemplation already spoke volumes about her troublesome confusion, warning others of a potential meltdown.

Anci did tell of her undying perseverance fueled by "nothing to lose," based on the home life she'd left behind. Mutter Clara was married to Tibby, who shunned Anci. Tibby was a widower to Clara's best friend, Mootzy. Clara broke the bad news of his wife dying while they were in the concentration camp together. Clara felt guilty and indebted to Mootzy because the bullet meant for Clara by the Gestapo hit Mootzy. Clara cooked and cleaned for Tibby, and he married Clara on the condition that Anci was to live in a Jewish boarding home.

"Tibby was a cold-hearted man, a man not good enough for any woman, but Clara came back from the concentration camp and wanted to be married. She had me at seventeen and wasn't married. Somehow Mutter thought marriage would make her a proper woman. Tibby was not a man. He used Clara as his maid, and she still worked like a dog, standing long, hard hours six days a week as a bookbinder during the day."

No, Anci didn't have a good word to say about him. She probably resented Tibby for prohibiting Clara from seeing her. Especially since Mutter Clara and

Anci were miraculously reunited after Mutter Clara survived the concentration camp. Anci was considered a war orphan since she didn't know if her mother was dead or alive, and Anci was loaded onto one of the large open trucks in a convoy headed to the land of Zion-Israel. Her truck was last in the procession, and as it started to move forward, Mutter Clara showed up, frantically calling out "Anci!" Through the dry dirt dust, Anci spotted her Mutter's outline. The cloud of dust was blinding, the scene heart-wrenchingly hopeless, yet there was Clara again calling out, "Anci!"

"Clarika?" *Mutter Clara, that's you?*

The truck began to move faster, kicking up more dust. Thirteen-year-old Anci pushed her way through the sardine can of orphans promised new beginnings in a far-off land and jumped off the moving truck in a leap of faith, landing in Clarika's arms.

The joy of the reunion was short-lived when Tibby placed Anci in the most expensive boarding school for Jewish girls. As Anci remembered it, she wore tattered clothes and begged like a dog at lunchtime for morsels of food from the girls commuting to school. "They laughed and threw a salami slice on the ground. I would pick it up with my mouth and then lick their shoe in thanks. I lifted my leg like a dog, pretending to pee on them when the girls threw nothing."

Other than Mutter Clara, most everyone else in the family was dead. However, there was Aunt Flora who moved to Germany, which translated to "as good as dead" according to Anci. There was also Uncle Arthur, but Anci was never close to him since he had left the night she was born. There was no more than that to say. Mother did suffer from time to time, not knowing how she got from one place to another. Supposedly, one can liken that experience to driving on autopilot. The difference with Mother was that months would lapse before she realized she had been mentally checked out. She'd say, "I really don't know what happened."

The only tidbit Big Steve shared about his family was that his Uncle Imre was the Premiere of Hungary. Whether that was true or not needed to be checked out. Google was yet to be invented. His delusions of this relation to Premiere

Imre Nagy consumed his interests and conversation, as he kept abreast of the news from back home. Big Steve was born January 1, 1929. His small stature melded right in with the rest of the Hungarians during these undernourished times. After all, what were people going to grow on when starvation was their daily diet?

His personality was strong and direct, with a command of entitlement from his peers. Like all male chauvinist Hungarians of his day, he was not to be questioned. What he said was law. To his credit, he was a hard worker, believing in strong European work ethics. He believed women were created to serve men with a snap of a finger. The times were the 1950s, and the thought of a woman having her own mind was not even an idea. Women were *haus fraus*/housewives/slaves with a smile, anchored down by a baby. Women were married to the house as much as they were to their men, unless they worked at jobs as nurses, teachers, secretaries, and maids in America.

Germans and Hungarians proudly accepted jobs as maids. If people didn't have a family member to sponsor them to immigrate to America, then a job could gain them entrance into America and later put food on the table. Married, manual-laboring women had to still cook dinner and keep the home clean in America just like in Hungary, except Americans had a five-day work week while Hungarians worked six. Spinsters were a rarity. Culture dictated that women's purpose was to marry and procreate.

Hands down, the Hungarians bet on Big Steve's abilities to make his life a success. He goofed around with other detainees, showing off his "art of kissing American ass." He knew when and how to smile so it read genuine, when to bow with respect with "Yes, Madam" and "No, Sir" and "Right away, Sir" and a smile to higher-in-command bosses or wealthier prospective tippers, and when to extend his hand for the indication of his expected deserved tip. His body language said he was eager to please and proud to be given the opportunity to ascend the ranks. He hoped to gain employment in the hotel industry. He was ultimately the perfect example of why Americans allowed new immigrants into their fine country. He did the job other men raised in America found too menial and demeaning to do, and he conducted himself with pride and integrity. All he needed was the chance. His drive was great, and he wanted the chance to prove himself. His fellow Hungarians believed he'd become a millionaire in no time.

Anci and Big Steve did the best they could to fight the thoughts of possibly not crossing the American shores into freedom and opportunity. Borders to America were not open, so without a sponsorship or qualifications for a job, there was no entrance into America. In passing conversation, Anci recalled hearing that her Uncle Arthur from her mother's side had been living in the United States for a while. Big Steve persuaded her to contact him for assistance. Such a relative was worth gold as a sponsor! All Arthur had to do was vouch for Anci's character. Due to desperation, Anci went against her gut feelings, pleading in writing, "You are my only hope!" adding, "Won't you please help?" the second time. In response, Arthur wrote a bunch of empty words that filled a worthless page. "Pity, I wish you well," was the bottom line.

Arthur was out of commission for all intents and purposes as a CIA operative. Anci didn't learn about the real Arthur for another decade. At that time, she was complaining to a Hungarian friend who happened to be an FBI agent. "My retard Uncle Arthur Daches is a real good-for-nothing piece of sh*t. I am struggling to put food on the table, and he doesn't ever call to see how I am doing."

"What do you mean, Arthur Daches?" he asked. "Who is he to you, again?"

"He is my mother's brother and a real piece of sh*t, dumbass. Why?"

After making sure it was the same Arthur Daches the FBI friend was thinking of, he said, "Arthur Daches is the last person I would call dumb."

The truth unfolded in 1971. Unbeknownst to anyone but him, Arthur had signed up as an agent between Germany and England. He was on England's side, giving inside information to the British that he obtained from the German Nazis. His life was not his own. His German wife was the perfect cover-up. When the Russians overthrew the Nazis, Arthur relocated to America as a mole working against Communist Russia.

But at the end of 1956, Anci was clueless to all that. Big Steve counted on Uncle Arthur, saying, "He is family." Anci knew not to count on him. All she had heard from the family was that he'd left them and never so much as wrote a letter. She was ashamed of having such a piece of excrement for a family member, given the little she knew about him at the time. Arthur was considered a cold, ruthless bastard in Anci's book.

Luckily, Big Steve pulled a few good strings. His family business experience, along with his knack for the English language, earned him hire at the Waldorf Astoria in Manhattan with the help of the American Immigration and Naturalization Service employees stationed in Vienna. Big Steve was on his way to the Promised Land America via American Airlines!

Anci was alone, stuck in the Nunenhoff Hotel once again, but not for long. It seems Austria was overwhelmed by the cost of the influx of Hungarian refugees and asked other countries to step in and help. President Eisenhower sent American INS employees to Vienna to assist in processing those refugees who wanted to come to the United States. Two weeks after Big Steve left, Anci was pushed through to Camp Kilmer "to give way to others needing to come in," she later explained. She traveled to New York's lower bay by boat, passing the Statue of Liberty. This unforgettable moment brought tears to Hungarians as they placed their hands over their hearts and shouted, "God bless America! We made it!"

Upon disembarkation, awaiting buses transported Anci to Piscataway, New Jersey. After arrival at Camp Kilmer, she received a fresh set of clothes from the Red Cross. All this occurred even though she had neither a job nor sponsor to claim her. She complained plenty, waking up on a cot and seeing the last thing she wanted to look at each morning when she opened her eyes. Yet, there it was staring her in the face: a small, green, government-issued, cheap vinyl bag with the printed word REFUGEE in bold white letters. *Who needs a reminder of this situation? Do they think anyone here is waking up in the middle of the night craving* palacsinta, *with a sudden dose of amnesia, forgetting they're a refugee?* Palacsinta, a delicious rolled crepe with apricot jelly or a cheese Danish filling, was on her mind. With a lack of food in her belly, food was always on Anci's mind.

Time never went slower than the time she spent in the barracks at the refugee camp. The anxiousness of not knowing her fate made this highly impatient young female a bag of nerves. Her desire and pressure to start her life trumped her interest in the theatrical shows and television available for entertainment. Once she passed the inspections of her health, political party affiliation, and criminal background check, she received an identification card from INS and a social security card, leaving the final step in the hands of the Labor Department to match her skillset to a job.

Anci's problem was that she possessed no employable skills. Hungarian secretaries weren't valuable in America; Hungarians had forty letters to their alphabet in comparison to Americans' twenty-six, making their typewriters totally different. Nonprofit sponsors had become increasingly skeptical of their ability to place Anci. Her space was valuable to more than 120,000 other refugees. Feeling the stress to move on, she was glad others chose destinations like Australia or Canada to relocate. Her eyes were set on New York City.

"Don't worry. The answer to how you will make it happen will come!" Anci heard her friends tell her, though they were just a memory whispering fortitude. A month had passed since the Kats left her behind. Somehow, just when Anci's frantic nerves feared deportment, she was summoned to the office at Camp Kilmer. The official told Anci, "We have a solution to getting you released."

Ay yi, solution! I heard Hitler's master plan for the Jews was a "solution"! Okay, I guess they had enough of me and are sending me back home.

"Little lady, if you don't know what to do, the best thing for you ..." the official began as Anci braced herself, "... is to get married."

"Marry!" *I never thought of that!* "Marry who?" she asked.

The refugee camp official morphed into a masterful psychic and wheeler-dealer. "I have a man for you in our country. He lives in Ohio State in a city called Cleveland. I can introduce you two in an hour, after which you can get acquainted. You can take it from there."

Anci met the Clevelander within the hour. He was Hungarian. He asked for her hand in marriage after knowing her for only ten to fifteen minutes. Poof! Just like that, they were engaged. Next, her meager belongings lay in one clump in a pillowcase, tied at the top, outside the office door. Not thrilled with what was transpiring, she sat still in his Dodge. He spoke, and she stared dead ahead with those *stoic brown eyes* of hers, numb. *There's something wrong with this guy or else he wouldn't have to go to a refugee camp to find a wife.* She couldn't care less about his endless babble ... about some Hungarian part of Cleveland they were going to live in. Her mind screamed like burning rubber tires spinning donut wheels. Desperately trying to escape these pivotal moments, she shifted into survival mode, keenly readying for her available exit.

"There's plenty of *mak lekvar*/poppy seed jelly to make any Hungarian happy. There are plenty of storefront signs with Hungarian names like Molnar and Kovacs in the neighborhood where I live to make you feel welcome too," he added. Trying to be sly, he quickly slipped in, "The drive is going to be a long one, and a motel stop is evident." Clevelander didn't know who he was dealing with.

She exerted the brakes and pushed back cunningly, saying, "I will stop for food, but I am too excited to stop and sleep!"

To better pinpoint what she was dealing with, she noticed the Clevelander was more swine than human with his snotty snout, greasy acne-dimpled skin, slimy spit-slicked hair, and his body too hideous to take in without gagging. Anci's mind scrambled, *How do I handle this stupid situation?* Anci, resorting to past experiences for what to do, recalled her cracked-up relative Irene, who'd been booted out of her home by a Nazi and ousted to the ghetto. Irene dealt with life the best she could. She closed her eyes when she pissed in the street, saying, "Everything's gone." There is no dignity when one's fragile mind shatters from heartache and despair.

Anci was a child of the Jewish ghetto at the time, and there was nothing strange about anything that happened anymore. What people did to cope under duress wasn't the same as what they'd do under civil times. But right now, more than ever, Anci understood what Irene had done to escape her surroundings. Fancying the idea of making everything disappear like Irene did to escape her scary world, Anci turned to this method to cope with her predicament and closed her eyes to the grotesque-looking fellow driving her to God knows where to do God knows what to her. *I want to be in America but not like this.* Anci grasped what she had learned from Irene and announced, "Don't worry about me. I'm going to appear to be sleeping, but I'm listening." They drove for twelve to fourteen hours straight. She became increasingly anxious as the sun set. It meant they were closing in on their destination.

"Now I am hungry. Let's eat somewhere," Anci stated, buying more time before the newly engaged couple would arrive at his apartment. They stopped and ate then continued driving. "We're home," was the next stop "Lover Boy" announced. Once inside, he hurriedly slipped on a pair of black silk pajamas over his unwashed body, dousing himself instead in cheap *eau de toilette*. Anci gagged and darted behind him into the bathroom and managed to shut the door. These two had totally different agendas.

Anci noticed there was a bathtub and knew how she would turn this bad situation into a good one. She double-checked the locked bathroom door, ran the bath water full-strength, and peeled away her perspiration-drenched clothing. She immersed her naked body into the steamy hot tub, mentally escaping from the impending doom on the other side of that bathroom door. Her chin submerged level with the bathwater as she tried to recall the last time she'd had a decent bath. She poured in a hefty amount of bubble mixture and soaked.

There were bath houses in Hungary, a system for the masses to soak in mineral-rich pools from their natural springs bequeathed by the brutal five hundred years of Turkish rule, but other than sitting in massive baths that easily tight-squeezed five hundred to a thousand people, Anci could not remember a time she'd sat in a singular bathtub.

Anci slipped into a womblike slumber in seconds. With her eyes shut, the heightened senses of her tongue lodged loose a piece of scrumptious dessert from her teeth from dinner. The sweet taste transported her to a bittersweet memory with her much-loved cousin Irene, who she lost back in the peril of ethnic cleansing by the Germans. *Ay Irene*, Anci sighed, wishing she could describe to her the dessert she ate after dinner. Anci's eyes moved in rapid movement from side to side as she entered a dream state. Her recollection of Irene being thrown out of her upscale, three-bedroom apartment after her mother was dead and her Aunt

Ethel's whereabouts were unknown began an unraveling of difficult woven threads in time back home.

Anci was already living in the ghetto before the ghetto was called the ghetto. The family was so poor that seven of them lived in a one-room efficiency. In time, no one was left in the ghetto except Anci and her grandmother Regina, sharing a worn and tattered hay bed. Everyone else was gone, their whereabouts unknown.

Anci was hungry. Since there was no food to be found, she made her way, whenever possible, to her two aunties, Teresa and Ethel, and cousin Irene, who was Teresa's daughter. Her aunties managed to muster up for her at least a slice of bread during the hardest times.

Anci knocked on her aunties' door one day, hoping to get some food and company. "Das is schmutz!"

A Nazi general, oddly clad in men's boxers, black knee-high leather boots, and an officer's cap, exclaimed jarringly, greeting the twelve-year-old Anci and referencing dirt. Wide-eyed Anci thought the comment the general made was surely about him. He pulled out his revolver, and in the nick of time, with split seconds to spare, one of three prostitutes tactfully regained the general's perverted attention toward her own scantily clad body, while another charmed him back from the door. He was already taking eager aim at the frazzled child. Luckily, Anci escaped death yet another time, like a slippery alley cat with many lives, this time from a Nazi bastard in a drunken stupor with an endless need to demonstrate his pride and devotion to his nationalistic country by nixing another unwanted Jew. Anci swiftly summed up that the apartment absent her aunties meant they had either perished, been exiled to the ghetto, or deported.

Anci scampered the streets to look for her favorite, Irene, who she knew would not survive alone. Finally, she saw the crazed Irene in the street standing in front of a pastry shop, an unforgettable sight. With dirty, outgrown long nails among short-chipped ones, and scuffled and matted long hair like a stray mad dog, Irene stood in a once-white dress.

Drawing closer, Anci noticed Irene busily conversing with her reflection in the pastry house window while sloppily eating cake.

"My mama, Teresa, is dead," Irene murmured to her reflection.

Standing next to Irene and addressing Irene's reflection in the window, Anci asked, "So what are you doing?"

With her mouth stuffed with confectionery delight and her hands juggling two more pastries, Irene replied, "What's it look like I'm doing? I thought you were the one with the brains. I'm doing what Maria Antoinette did when there was no bread to eat."

In unison, they stated, "Eat cake," and laughed.

"Where'd you get the money from?" Anci asked.

"From Mama Teresa's money satchel kept under her pillow."

"What happened, Irene? I went to your apartment, and a half-naked Nazi nixed me from there. He pulled out his revolver and almost made me dance my way to death."

With crazed eyes, Irene whimpered, "I am all alone and scared."

Anci put the equation together after gathering some more details from Irene.

"The Nazi threw me out on the street. He said he spared my pitiful life. He spit on me. Luckily, I moved, and it went in my hair, not my face. He yelled something about how I should thank my mother for jarring a full cabinet of food for him to eat. It was the only reason he didn't shoot me. That bad man has enough to eat for a long time. He said, being a Jew, I would be smart to join my dead mother quicker than sooner. He told me to find the ghetto where I belong." And then Irene added in naïve seriousness, "You will take me to the ghetto with you, right?"

Anci tilted her head in a quizzical motion and sat Irene down. Masterfully playing her cards, Anci ran her nature's comb, her fingers, through Irene's hair.

"Irene, how much cake do you plan to eat?"

"I am eating all that this money can buy. I waited a long time for this. You want to help me?"

They had five pieces each, and for a brief moment, all seemed well in their chaotic world. They laughed and pretended not to be in their putrid hell. Anci went inside the establishment to clean up. She exited the pastry shop with their last piece of cake and the empty moneybag folded under her arm. Irene was urinating in the middle of the street in broad daylight.

"My Irene, where do you think you are?"

"Right, no one can see me?"

"Why is that?"

"Try it. Close your eyes, Anci. Everything is gone."

ANCI RUDELY AWOKE as the level of bath water trickled into her snoring, parted lips. Startled, she grabbed hold of the edge of the tub and simultaneously opened her eyes.

"*Ai yi.*" She remembered hearing stories of her exhausted Mutter Clara being salvaged from the bottom of the mineral pools. *I better watch it. Bathing is dangerous.*

Her body toweled dry, Anci had a newer quandary to deal with, namely, a disgusting man on the other side of that bathroom door. Giving herself a pep talk in the face of her latest adversary, she boosted herself with her previous accomplishments. She had made it out of repression, she had made it past bombings and land mines, and, cheating death, she had made it away from both German and Russian guns pointed at her. She had made it out of the ghetto, and she had made it past her rigor mortis grandmother who died in her arms one frigid night. Now, she had to make it out of this anxious lion's lair.

The warm water had played its trick on her. Tired and woozy, Anci looked forward to retiring into a real bed. Only in America for a little while, she'd already experienced a real bath, and now she looked forward to sleeping in a real bed. A real spring mattress bed was vastly different than the hay mattress she had shared with three adults. She didn't count the bed bugs. *America, I have to love this country!* She opened the door and considered that maybe with some luck, the lights would be off and the man she had to lay her body next to would be asleep.

Oh hell no! Lover Boy was at attention! *Great!*

"We are going to be married, anyway, so, how about it?" he challenged.

"How about what?" she challenged back, wanting to smack his perverse grin off his silver-toothed, swine-shaped face.

He oafishly slung his sloppy body—not on top of Anci, but over his self-designated side of the bed—to pull out a couple of cigar boxes as he grunted in his stretch. When he managed to pull his torso back up onto the bed after the awkward acrobatic dance, he placed his prized treasure boxes on the bed. With a deep breath needed because of his overexertion, and an extended one-sided grin, he dumped the contents onto the aged, off-white, bed sheet.

"Pick out a wedding band and whatever else you want," Clevelander said.

Having diverted attention away from his original plan, Anci made a conscious effort to follow the one rule passed down for generations: never wrinkle the forehead. She then automatically assigned her right forefinger to rummage through his generous offerings. Pushing the contents to and fro, she picked up a weird thing her finger stumbled upon; it looked like a bone with gold solder. Nothing was wrong with her eyes, but her neck jerked forward like an ibis thinking it sighted a fish. Anci raised up the strange item, drawing it in for a closer inspection. She sat frozen like Darwin's depiction of an ape holding a human skull in its hands while in mysterious intellectual contemplation. She realized she was holding a gold-filled tooth and knew immediately what this implicated. Her mind raced with horrid flashbacks.

She heard the screams of pain from those who had their teeth extracted because of their gold content when the Nazis pulled Jews aside and checked their mouths. Not to mention the humiliation of the Jewish men as the Nazis made them pull out their member in public to show they were circumcised, proving they were Jewish first. Was the victim of this tooth extraction alive? Was the person male or female, a mother, a child? Did this belong to someone she knew, perhaps even a family member?

Finally, her trembling hands dropped the gold tooth. She decided not to jump to paranoiac conclusions ... until she found another one. Within seconds, and in total abhorrence, her finger pushed on another oddly shaped gold thing. Anci unconsciously looked up at Clevelander with questioning eyes.

Picking up her inquisitiveness from the mirror, he finished his poor attempt at popping a nasty puss-filled pimple before nonchalantly licking his hand to shellac his stray, flyaway top hairs into place. Apparently, this was his habit when about to make a noteworthy comment.

"I was smart to remove the jewelry from the *JEDO*/Jew bastards before I killed them! Ha-ha-ha! They weren't going to need them anymore. Not where they were going. Ha-ha-ha!"

Rendered speechless, Anci anxiously waited for the crack of dawn. Sleeping with one eye open throughout the night, her first time in a real bed, after a fantastic bath, was certainly not as restful as she imagined it would be!

Finally, the crack of dawn arrived. She bustled about and convinced Clevelander she anticipated marrying him and there was no time to waste. She managed to buy his trust so she could buy herself some time to break away. She kissed him on the cheek and promised into his ear things she knew any man wanted to hear. Once he was out of the apartment, making necessary wedding arrangements, finding the gown and clergy, Anci seized her moment. She grabbed luck by the bullhorns and ran blindly to the first proprietorship with a storefront sign she reckoned as Hungarian. Problem was that in the wee hours of the morning, stores weren't yet open for business. She pounded relentlessly from desperation until someone finally came to unlock the door. Anci hysterically pleaded her dire situation and conveyed her fear for her life to the owner. Not knowing what else to do, the owner's wife called the Hungarian newspaper in town. Anci made news headlines, receiving her fifteen minutes of fame before Andy Warhol purportedly coined the phrase.

The good Samaritan Hungarian couple allowed Anci to stay with them "for a short while" until she "got on her feet." Only a couple days later, a nice old lady named Margaret was touched by Anci's story in the *Magyar Usag / Hungarian News* and offered the pitiable immigrant a job at her strudel factory with a place to stay in her home. Anci took the generous offer, but ten days of preparing strudel proved enough for Anci. Seeing strudel everywhere, even outside of the shop and penetrating her dreams, she quit the job in the name of saving her sanity.

Anci was desperate. She knew her friends the Kats were in New York City somewhere, but she didn't know their addresses or their telephone numbers, so there was no way to contact them. At this juncture of hopelessness, having been in America for two weeks and not yet able to obtain steady footing, Anci had absolutely nothing to lose. She took a gamble and fed a hungry corner payphone a bunch of nickels. With her financial investment dependent upon her trusty forefinger correctly dialing the number, she hoped her friend Big Steve could be located at the Waldorf Astoria, where he told her he would be working.

"Hello, I would like to speak to Steve Nagy. He works there."

"One moment, please. I will connect you."

Big Steve's voice came on. "Hello, Waldorf Astoria, how may I help you?" His English was good, but his accent was still distinctive.

She was thoroughly surprised he answered the phone; moreover, totally thankful he came to her rescue. To make things easier for Steve and to grab her golden opportunity, Anci told Steve she would meet him outside the Waldorf the next day after his second shift.

When she arrived the following day, she figured she had conquered the most important task needing to be accomplished and decided she deserved to see this famous place: Times Square. *I have only been in America two weeks and look where I am!* Anci proudly acknowledged.

Like dominoes, her life was clicking beautifully now, for it was that same day she reunited with the two Kats. She finally collected their addresses and home telephone numbers. The Kats left it up to Anci to reach out since Anci's new life was still in the making.

Steve kept his word and met Anci, and they subsequently reached out to Country Katy to see if she knew of a place that would accommodate the two of them. This task was a no-brainer for Country Katy, who quickly arranged for Anci and Big Steve to have a great rental apartment in the same building where she resided, in Westchester, New York. Unbelievably, the place came fully loaded with furniture. The couple could have lived a hundred years in Hungary and never have accumulated so much. Anci and Big Steve were ecstatic with their good fortune.

"Already, the seeds of this wealthy country are bearing generous fruit!" Anci said.

They should have spit or knocked on wood or even bit their tongues after expressing their happiness to insure their luck from being jinxed. Within the following two weeks, the Immigration Services Department had two representatives knocking on their door to conduct a "friendly visit."

"You've been reported for committing a violation!" one of the authorities said, and they flashed their intimidating badges.

Anci sensed trouble and said, "One moment," as she closed the door on the two inspectors. She nervously scurried to Big Steve. "*Na*, what 'Yenta Patrol' gave them the right to meddle in our business?"

Big Steve rushed to get dressed. "Keep your big mouth shut, leave this up to me, and squelch your spicy Hungarian paprika temper," he yelled at her and then proceeded to open the door in quite the opposite manner, greeting them with a pleasant "Hello."

"This is a *N I C E* country, and people don't just live together. Here, people get married first!" one of the deputies explained.

The other deputy, holding a clipboard and continuously tapping his badge with his pen, added, "We'll ship you people back to Europe if you don't behave."

Decades later, Anci would finish retelling this snippet with a smile and add her humor, saying, "Rules in America sure changed over the years. Does this mean America does not qualify as a N I C E country anymore?"

On February 13, 1957, a small-town newspaper featured a captioned picture of the Justice of the Peace marrying "two Hungarian escapees," as they put it. The groom was Istvan (Steve) Nagy 28 from Szombathely, and the "radiant" bride was Anna (Anci) Pataky 25 from Budapest. The couple was noted to reside at 8 Hartsdale Road, Hartsdale, Mt. Vernon, New York.

Although Anci smiled in the Hungarian newspaper for her wedding picture with the judge, accepting the meaningless kiss her husband gave her on the cheek, something told her, "A person doesn't have to be psychic to know something isn't as it should be." This extended to more than her misspelled maiden name. Specifically, her Catholic, anti-Semitic husband, Big Steve, did not know his wife, Anna (Anci), was a Jewess.

3

MORNING, NOON, and night, nausea consumed her. Nothing being ordinary, Anci's life wasn't going to change anytime soon. The only prenuptial agreement Big Steve demanded, though verbally, was: "There are to be no children until we are financially stable."

Big Steve wanted to make sure his life was stable, economically well-founded, before fathering children. His words were commendable, but Anci couldn't care less about his words, his desires, or any of his good common sense. Why should anything change? She never cared about what anyone else wanted. She believed her aging body clock was frantically ticking and dismissed a possibility of ever getting pregnant. She diagnosed herself infertile. And if, by chance, she did become pregnant, she was certain she would keep her child. She convinced herself that economics was not a deciding factor, her ovaries were.

Besides, Anci figured since there was no written prenuptial agreement in their marriage, she was legally safe. She couldn't be sent back to Hungary because she was pregnant! That was ridiculous to entertain. As well, Anci was sure the man who spoke about "giving his baby everything when the right time came" would not be disappointed if they had a baby. She was also, though, not thinking.

"The time has come to tell you ..." she practiced in the bathroom mirror aloud. Barely finishing her words, she stuck her head into the toilet bowl in the nick of time. "Guess what time it is?" Nope, nothing sounded right. She would have to do better than that!

She didn't know how to tell Steve her secret. In this time of uncertainty, she knew they had great sex, which had nothing to do with her not being "in love" with her husband. Save the tears, a relationship void of emotions is the only way Anci operated. The woman emotionally remained detached from her partners. Her heart was hardwired not to be empathetic. To Anci, surrendering the mind and body to the act of sex was one thing, but giving the heart, her soul, was impossible. "I never want to love anyone," was her motto.

Anci was scared. She knew she could lose her husband if she chose to have the child. Big Steve shared Hungary's zero-birth-rate mentality. "Babies are a burden, another mouth to feed when there isn't enough to eat among the existing family."

Steve's foresight made good sense. God only knows why Anci wanted a baby. Again, the woman was incapable of love. What was the purpose? Was primal need for procreation that strong? No, that wasn't the reason; Anci just wanted to have a child so she would have someone to take care of her in her old age. "Someone's got to wipe my ass when I can't anymore," is how she'd say it.

ONE DAY, WHILE STILL CONSUMED by her dilemma, Big Steve came home and enthusiastically pointed out the window. "Look out there! What do you see?"

Anci didn't understand.

"What do you think about the car outside?" He pointed to a new Dodge.

"It's very nice."

"That's good, it's ours!"

Her mind went snow static white from anger, like a malfunctioning television screen. *Not once did he ask if he could buy a car with the blood money I earned scrubbing houses and waiting tables!* The inconsiderate manner her husband had sprung the news of his brand-new Dodge, with whitewall tires, infuriated Anci. *He must be joking. He borrowed the car for a day to tease me or he is pointing at a stranger's car to see how I react.*

Reality set in hard when he turned the key in the car's ignition and drove away. Any trust Anci had in Steve was now broken.

In reaction, she snooped through his belongings. *Where did he get the nerve? Who knows what else he is up to with my money?* She went into the bank. There was zip, zero in their account. *There should have been funds remaining after this careless car purchase! Where did my money go?* Anci was a frugal wife. She watched what she spent, depriving herself of anything extra, to the point she ate a can of sardines every day for lunch while juggling two full time jobs a day. She had no idea where the money had gone.

Normally, how well the couple interacted depended greatly on the time of day. Their relationship was topsy-turvy. In the morning, Anci's clumsily clanging dishes in the kitchen drowned the sounds of Big Steve's rustling newspapers. Oddly, there was limited verbal interaction between the couple whose bodies intertwined in loud, mad sex during the night. It seemed, as the morning sun rose higher, the space between them grew further apart. They were like two completely different couples by day and by night.

Their typical mornings went like this: Big Steve sat at the breakfast table behind a separating pulled curtain of newspapers, waiting to be served like a king in his castle. There was plenty to know about in the matter of world affairs concerning their Old Country. While Anci did her best in domestic duties in the kitchen to serve her husband, Steve opened the floor of communication with his greatest obsession outside earning his first million dollars—specifically, Hungarian politics.

"I left my parents behind in that communist mess," Steve said, flapping his newspaper.

"I left Mutter Clara behind," Anci said, equally curious about what might have happened in their Old Country.

"So! Anci, listen to this. I'll only share the highlights." Steve put down his newspaper and started rattling the timeline and events that occurred back home from some list of notes he accumulated daily to better understand what had happened while they were still in *Magyarorszag*/Hungary until 1956. The communists never reported the news. So, no one really knew what was happening, other than the news that first the Germans then the Russians occupied their country.

"Here we go: 1951, Religious freedom was forbidden. Thousands of worshippers were jailed or deported to concentration camps.

1953 brought the death of Stalin at age seventy-four.

"And today I read and added to my notes: 1956, Hungarians cry, Imre Nagy to the government! Russians go home!"

Steve picked up the newspaper again, but this time with greater fervor, appreciating this clarification in their shared history and the mention of his Uncle Imre Nagy. He then read on.

"Wow! Thousands of people knocked Stalin's colossal steel head off his statue and dragged it through the streets of Budapest. Thousands of students joined the fight against the Soviet Army. Children flooded the streets with soapy water, causing the tanks to lose their traction. Boys and girls snuck up to the disabled tanks and finished them off with a grenade or Molotov cocktail." Steve peered over the papers.

"Anci! Did you ever see anyone throw a Molotov? I saw one thrown into an army tank. The kids were young and sloppy. The gasoline they poured into the empty bottle spilled all over their clothes so when they lit the bomb they were going to throw, it wound up exploding them."

"Jesus Maria, I witnessed that too. I had a very good friend … hmm …," Anci couldn't find the words fast enough and just added, "a charred rigor mortis body I can't un-see."

Steve went back to his notes and interjected: "October 24, 1956, Imre Nagy appointed as Premier of Hungary."

Anci, perplexed by Steve cutting her short with such a serious recall and his constant obsession, challenged him, "What do you care about this Imre Nagy, honestly?"

"What do you mean why do I care so much? Are you stupid, woman? Imre Nagy is my father's brother! How could I not care? Why do you think I was a Freedom Fighter ... for nothing?"

"What kind of Freedom Fighter were you? I saw you busily scratching your numbnuts in the same stinking hole I was in. I saw the fighting you saw. Steve, you smoked cigarettes and guzzled booze you won playing cards, for days on end. There was nothing else a person could do if they prized their life, but that's not being a Freedom Fighter."

"Keep rambling, you big-mouthed woman with an unthinking head taking space on your shoulders!"

Anci became sidetracked from telling her husband she was pregnant. She wished she knew for certain if Big Steve was actually related to Imre Nagy. Imre Nagy was a huge political figure. One day, he would become historically revered as the revolutionary grandfather of a democratic society in a communist world. Anci didn't know if she should be proud or worried. Should she be proud because her husband's uncle was a great man or worried because her husband had cracked up and was perhaps delusional?

Steve Nagy and Imre Nagy shared the same last name. *Who knows,* she thought. Either way, Big Steve remained buried behind his Berlin Wall of newspapers, which Anci had to somehow tear down in order to issue her own flashing news bulletin.

Big Steve was consumed with the historic events. As much as breakfast fed his belly, he hungered for the world's translation of what he and his people underwent battling communism.

"The Rakosi regime ...," he began as he stood up, slamming his fist on the table and conducting an oration more appropriate to a group of fellow rebels huddled together for safety in a bomb shelter. His words were wasted on all four papered walls of the tiny kitchen and his wife's deaf ears. "... came into power August 20, 1949, and it was the direct beginning to the Hungarian Revolt. I fully agree; see, I told you that dog penis was the one! Rakosi headed the *police of terror,* best known for the phrase *midnight knock."*

"Okay now! Enough! Sit down and read it to yourself," Anci ordered.

"I sure wish the Magyars could see this print!" His fist slammed down on the kitchen table again, sloshing his orange juice. His reddened head was filled with fury as he saw hated images of his Hungary inundated with Soviet propaganda, hammer and sickle signs, rifles thrown over soldiers' shoulders, Rakosi's bald-headed statues, and that godforsaken Soviet Red Star on official uniforms and building apexes. "Hungarians don't approve of the Soviet way, yet Hungarians bowed to its way." Not knowing why he was on his feet, he made like he was reaching for the utensils for his breakfast, placed far from him, and he sat himself back down.

But he didn't stop. Holding the newspaper, he flailed his arms, announcing his demand for attention, and continued reading: "October 28, 1956, Premier Nagy demanded the Soviet troops withdraw from Budapest immediately. Furthermore, the security police would be dissolved."

This was four days after Steve Nagy's uncle was appointed to office. Steve read and reread every printed word, licking his fingers to turn every anticipated juicy page as he had done every morning since he and Anci first cohabitated.

But this morning was different. Anci's mind was working up her nerve to announce, "I am with child." *Maybe I just tell him the same way he delivered his news, pointing at our new car only he drives. Hey, see this? Congratulations! I know. I will cook Steve a lip-smacking meal. A full belly might work as anesthesia to the blow immediately after.*

"See ANCI! God and everyone know those *hook-nose vultures* were the start of all the world's problems!" Big Steve blurted, pounding the table simultaneously.

What did he just say? Anci remained quiet.

Tension ... there was plenty. Anci had listened to her friends and her husband divulging their true feelings about the Jews, yet managed to keep quiet. She knew better than to speak up, as every day, she saw the true nature of people.

She had lived in the living hell of the ghetto. Her family had been made to walk in deep snow or transported in cattle cars on their way to Auschwitz, or they were shot. Anci was left behind to fend for herself and her ailing, feeble grandmother Regina while Mutter Clara was marched off to the concentration camp.

The sight and smell of the toast she burned flashed a vision, and she was taken back to the two rigor mortis bodies she saw charred by a Molotov cocktail. Her mind skipped to a time when she walked with the only other survivor she'd encountered, left behind in the ghetto to work grave detail. He was Jewish like her. This man's assigned detail was to discard the corpses of his fellow Jews away from plain sight. Anci sometimes walked alongside him around the ghetto, strictly to have contact with the only other living human being besides her grandmother and herself. With her aunties gone, days of leaving the ghetto were meaningless, unless Anci was scavenging for food.

Anci needed real human interactions other than walking over and around dead bodies, wondering where the living people had gone. She bent down and saw a scarf on a dead Jewess. As was done to all Jews, the woman was marked with the yellow star sewn on her garment. Without any hesitation, Anci whipped the scarf off the corpse's body like she'd won a prize and wrapped her neck with it for a touch more warmth. Her action was no different than the time she knelt to remove a Nazi swastika pin from a dead Nazi soldier's lapel and placed it in her pocket. The cheap tin metal cross would serve as concrete proof she wasn't experiencing a nightmare; she was experiencing the pits of living hell on earth. Rotting cadavers were piled in the store window. The sign ironically and brazenly read "BUTCHER."

The stench from decaying carcasses receded as the smell of brewing coffee brought her back to the present and the breakfast she was preparing. Her nausea caused her to gag.

Ay yi, it was good she was planning to tell Big Steve she was pregnant—but how?

Big Steve read aloud, "Two-thirds of Europe's Jews, including 1. 5 million children, are dead." Then he added, "Anci, what in dog's dick are you doing? Horse's dick up your ass, come here with the coffee today, not tomorrow!"

"I am busy here making you a wonderful breakfast; I can't stop right now to discuss politics with you. You want good eggs or good politics?"

The condescending names Big Steve called his unsuspected Jewish wife and her Jewish people, her challenge to prepare breakfast, and her need to announce her pregnancy proved to be too much for her to tolerate. As it was, Anci suffered from being helplessly uncoordinated and clumsy and commonly lost patience over her lack of abilities. Owning an inadequately constructed nervous system and a lack of self-control, all due to her undiagnosed Asperger's, Anci took the meal she had prepared, which looked more appropriate for the kitchen garbage, and sloshed his food onto a plate.

Anci nastily snatched the newspaper from Big Steve's hands, released a disgruntled roar as she rumpled and ripped his reading material, and tossed the "goddamn" printed words aside. She lunged toward him, elbowed his ribs, and slammed his burned eggs and toast on a dirty dish in front of him. She then served him his freshly brewed, but stinking, coffee. The table was a sight with more liquid contents on the table than on his saucer, and even less in his cup.

"What kind of crooked dick have you got for a brain, woman?"

Big Steve's scolding of Anci was short-lived. She was not about to be interrupted. With one hand on her waist, bent over so her mouth kissed his ear—like she had seen Leo do to Regina—Anci shouted, "Hey, Mr. Big Shot, I am pregnant! What you got to say about that?"

The chair sucked in Steve's slight stature, digesting him, as he ingested his slosh of food without chewing. He wiped his mouth and inflated his chest, allowing his deep, deliberate breath to help him sit up tall. Steve puckered his mouth sideways to display his distaste for her, and when his head began to slouch, he remembered, *Be a man,* and tilted his chin up. As if his coffee cup were a gavel, he lifted it upward. He knew the suspense he was creating with his collectedness was killing her.

Seizing the moment, he relished in issuing torture to his disobedient partner. He added the use of his tongue against his teeth to loudly chirp sounds of his disdain over this newly presented information of becoming a father. The final verdict was about to come down, but he added a few more theatrics first. He gulped his bitter excuse of coffee as if there were more. Locking his squinting, snarling eyes with hers, he slammed his coffee cup gavel down and sternly issued his executioner's sentence.

"Get rid of it!" He stood up, reached into his pocket, and coolly pulled out a wad of bills. He counted to a designated number in his mind and pressed it into her hand.

"Get rid of it!" he proclaimed once again.

Grandma Regina told me Papa Leo gave her the same orders, "Get rid of it," and Erno was born, Anci recalled.

She watched from the kitchen window as he drove away, her mouth clenched tight, knowing his judgment was final. Until now, she had waved as he drove off, but her hand, anchored down by his command, proved too difficult to lift. *No one ever got away with telling me what to do!*

Those words, "Get rid of it!" and the look on his face repeated in her head. *What does he think? I am garbage or what I say is unimportant?*

She counted the money. There was $300 in her hand. *I didn't even know we were so rich!*

Over the next few days, Anci held on to the money but did nothing. When the topic "Get rid of it!" came up again, Anci yelled back, "I don't know a doctor!"

Big Steve backhanded her and bellowed, "Don't worry, I'll find one!"

A few more days passed without any further discussion about the pregnancy. One morning, Steve kindly announced, "Let's go for a drive." Anci mistook his actions as Big Steve's attempt to make peace with her and her pregnancy. But instead, he pulled in front of a building, reached across, opened her car door, nudged her, and declared, "Go get rid of it. Call me when it's over! Inside you'll find the doctor who is the same doctor all the Hungarians go to in order to remedy the same condition."

"How convenient for you!" she yelled as she slammed the door and kicked it before he pulled away.

She proceeded into the building where she signed in and took a seat in the waiting room among a half dozen other women. Sitting and waiting felt like an eternity. Most of her family had been killed and, here in the United States, she had nobody. Now, she was going to, by her own free will, kill her baby? *Why should I kill the one precious gift I can call my own? Who is going to take care of me in my old age? What am I, brainwashed? Does my opinion as a woman not count? No, no one tells me what to do!*

Abortions in the 1950s were not legal. What was Anci doing, sitting in a room like this in this *N I C E* country? She thought of her own mother. *Mutter Clara did not do away with me*, she reminded herself.

Anci noticed the reading material in the waiting room but instead of picking it up, she decided, *I better think this abortion thing through right now. I'm always too busy working with my tongue hanging out to take a moment to think.* Anci started at square one, looking back at her life as she tried to figure out her next steps. *What the hell am I doing here? I am going to look* at *my life from another person's point of view in order to help me see things clearer.*

4

AT FIRST GLANCE, Anci was nothing special as a child, with her brown eyes and brown hair. But if one took a lingered moment, those piercing brown eyes burned right through a person to sear guilt into one's soul for daring to miscalculate her as nothing extraordinary.

Anci experienced more hard knocks in her young elementary school years than others would in a lifetime. Yet, the slight-framed child stood strong and proud and without complaint. Her great sense of being prettier and better than everyone else served her well, even though she knew she was also the poorest. Anci was not to be underestimated as a meek child based on her small stature. Her grandma Regina often said with gleaming amazement, "She's not typical; I just want to live long enough to see what becomes of this resourceful child. No matter how she is dropped, Anci will land on her feet. She is a survivor."

Grandmother Regina referred to Anci as the family provider, regardless of her young age, and rightfully so. In the time of the Great Depression, when only the rich afforded coal to heat their furnaces during the brutal winters, Anci found a way to save her immediate kin from frost. She organized and robbed a coal truck with a gang of boys to provide a warming fire for her desperate household members.

"God knows where the good Lord found Anci; she's an amazing child. She saved my life that winter," Regina often recounted.

Anci forged her scrawny body through a crowd of desperate and hungry people to scavenge meat for Regina to prepare in a "good soup" for the family. The accolades Anci received from Grandma Regina fueled her heroic acts more than food. "Little girl, what would we do without you?"

Anci was not like the rest of the women in her family. As Anci put it, "I am not mush, made of jelly, diarrhea!" Indeed, Anci faced her undesirable life with indifferent eyes. She was not privileged to know there was a better life. Growing up in the most indigent part of the city, Anci became more and more seasoned by the mean streets. She surpassed mere survival. She ruled the streets with the toughest neighborhood boys.

Unlike other girls who remained within the safe confines of their homes like cooped-up caged animals, Anci preferred gallivanting unsupervised in her neighborhood. "No way do I want to be stuck inside the stinking apartment." As a result, Anci's shocking colloquialism and mannerisms did not befit a proper girl. Her vernacular and gesticulations clearly indicated her rough-and-tumble harshness. With no one around to correct her behavior, her innate air of entitlement, bossiness, and brazenness overshadowed her slight stature, and the boys gladly accepted her as "one of them."

Anci's survival was innate. Her hands busily stole, and she cursed, spit, and kissed without the need to speak a word of the crimes she committed. Anci lived in an area where impoverished street-rat children ran and played in open sewers alongside rats swimming in the open drains.

The grim structure that Anci called home was shared with 150 other single-room apartments, and within each, an entire extended impoverished family dwelled. The whole building shared one toilet. Prison structures in the United States were less imposing. With only one bathroom for that many cohabitants, Anci accepted as commonplace that men exposed themselves to piss against the nearest wall and that piss flew out of windows from emptying piss pots.

Cold gray and pale yellow were the hues of Anci's world. The bitter cold weather, the concrete buildings, and the hearts in disrepair were all lifeless gray. The inhabitants of the dismal gray world with sickly jaundice complexions were as pee-pale yellow as the snow next to her building. The harsh cold environment penetrated and sat in her bones. Anci's empty belly and threadbare clothes did not help her desperate situation.

Budapest had the metro to transport people for the right amount of change, making everything accessible. There were plenty of nice places to see in Pest, Hungary, where one could visit the largest Jewish temple in all of Europe, the Parliament, the Basilica, and more, but Anci didn't live in *that* Pest. Anci lived in the part of Pest that was behind the ghetto's wooden barricade wall demarked by a large condescending Star of David, where the doormen were Nazi Jew-hating soldiers whose slobbering laughter was worse than hungry wolves. Although she could walk by the fancy places, she did so hurriedly; her presence screamed that she did not belong. Her wrinkled, faded clothes with missing buttons and letdown hems had been handed down so many times that the original owner could no longer be traced. Anci was the end of the line of benefactors. No one accepted her hand-me-downs. Nothing got thrown away in Hungary, but her clothes were a tattered mess of disrepair!

As hunger pangs remained her unwanted, loyal companion, the closest Anci reached to eating a delicious bologna sandwich was in her dreams. In some countries, people count sheep to fall asleep, but not in Anci's world. At one point, Anci lay her head on her makeshift pillow and her aching hungry stomach on her hay-filled mattress that she shared with her mother and grandmother on one side and her aunt on the other. In place of sheep, Anci imagined alternate ways to place deli slices of meat on a roll. On one side of a halved Kaiser roll, she placed bologna, and on the other side of the Kaiser roll, she placed winter salami. The child's preferences changed from night to night. One night, she favored folded meat slices, and the next night, she desired her slices of meat neatly laid flat. No matter the arrangement, a heap of butter was spread on the roll first. The accustomed pangs of starvation ran deep, making it difficult to fall asleep, even when her body was weak from the lack of nutrition.

Memories of starvation never escaped Anci, even long after she was settled in America. If she desired a piece of cake, she recalled her bellyaches from childhood and justified her indulgence. "You don't think I am going to deny myself after what I have been through?" she challenged. In this way, Anci kept a promise to the child, her former self, as she lay in bed hungry: "One day, if I ever get lucky to never suffer from hunger again, I am eating until my heart's content."

No doubt, the color of the cold concrete building structures of her ghetto neighborhood was the same stone gray as the hardened stone hearts around her. From the time she was born, Anci was scorned. Mutter Clara blamed her daughter for her own conception. "It's your fault!" Mutter Clara scolded her angrily through tightly pursed lips and gritted teeth. Anci was an illegitimate child, conceived on January 13, 1932. She was the byproduct of two people whose societal ranks clashed.

Unfortunately, in a time when a young girl's welfare was prized and protected by villagers, that protection didn't extend to poor folk. Clara, "too good for her world," worked for an unsavory flower shop owner who easily pawned Clara for her own proprietary gain. Clara, blindsided, loved the owner as if she were her own mother. That was Clara's first mistake!

Clara loved easily—the naïve girl had a sweet disposition with the face of an angel. For anyone playing matchmaker in Hungary, fixing up a boy with a girl was a lucrative enterprise. Payment for the find could be as little as a winter salami or a few golden coins, depending on who was paying.

The shopkeeper took full advantage of the situation and Clara's blind trust. Conscience didn't feed hungry bellies. The proprietor shrugged as she tucked the reward of her gold coins, spitting on them for good luck, safely under her right bosom.

Without exaggeration, it can be speculated that Snow White, as characterized years later by Walt Disney, was his animated vision of Clara. Clara's jet-black hair glistened against her porcelain white complexion as her big, beaming, believing blue eyes smiled, as if to say, "I really am the essence of sweet and innocent." Like Snow White, Clara's operatic voice was that of a nightingale. Despite her hard life, Clara sang almost all the time. Sparrows and squirrels thanked Clara's welcoming, loving energy by paying her ample visits. In turn, Clara graciously didn't let her friendly visitors leave without a morsel of bread, even though her gift deprived her of food.

When the bourgeoisie titled *Szombucky* Von Bless, Viktor, showed up in his horseman-led carriage, as preplanned, the flower shop owner waved Clara to attend to the person beckoning for her to come inside.

"Go on, don't be a stupid little thing. This is your big chance! Go!"

The eloquent royal's calculated, threaded words whisked away the breathless, naïve girl. The pure, dreamy-eyed girl ate the heaping portions of magical good fortune that the shining, lying prince falsely promised her. Had she known to do so, Mother Regina would have served Clara well to have warned: "Careful, little girl, snakes might be pretty, but after they finish shaking their tail, their venom is deadly."

Clara had loved her little world before Viktor, but now she loved the universe for all the new possibilities he promised. Szombucky Von Bless, Viktor came from a long line of royals he claimed stemmed from Queen Maria Teresa of the Austro-Hungarian Empire. Most likely, he lied about his bloodline, but his royal title, *Szombucky*, his financial status, and the family's palatial home caused no one to question the family. Viktor exposed young, innocent Clara to the finer things in life and made promises she was all too willing to believe. Soft-spoken words are so easily believed, especially when the heart already desires to believe that dreams can come true.

The two were from total opposite spectrums of each other's reality. Clara figured she had nothing to lose; she materialistically owned nothing and was socially ranked below nothing. Yet her words were her honor; they were "as good as gold." Viktor, on the other hand, had material social status to lose if he were disinherited. And because his class was superior to most, Viktor used Clara as a dispensable object. With ease, he spoke unconscionably manipulative words to obtain his targeted prize. Yet, Clara was a reward he did not deserve.

Had she confided her secret rendezvous to her Orthodox Jewish father, emergency flags would have flailed alert signals. Papa Leo would have pulled the reins so tight on the budding relationship that the so-called "prince," in Anci's words, "would have had a dog's dick shoved up his ass sideways—better yet, a horse's dick!"

Clara's father, Leo, was a piece of work. He had a temper like no other! For once, at least, Leo could have directed this demeaning characteristic in the right direction, but his opportunity to act as supreme father by standing up for his daughter would not come in time.

Among Viktor's worthless empty promises, he swore to remove Clara's family from their squalor and into his palatial mansion. Bellies would never sleep in a blood-sucking bed or know hunger again! Furthermore, Clara fantasized about the new and extravagant clothes that would adorn her body. Their children would have the best schooling, and she would experience a magnificent wedding day. Her naïveté was pitiful. Miss Pitiful Snow White truly believed she was moving into his royal family's residence, as well as everything else he told her, never suspecting that his true intention was to do her dirt.

Caught up in the whirlwind of wishes, Daches, Clara gave Szombucky Von Bless, Viktor her virginity on the day of her sixteenth birthday celebration. Clara gave away a woman's most precious value on that day. Ten months later, Daches, Anci, the bastard child, was born. Anci's Mutter Clara was *proli*/proletariat, while her father was bourgeoisie—a union that would never continue. As usual, the female was left to carry the burden of their brief unification for the rest of her life, while the male proceeded in his life without consequence. When the young, unmarried mother walked down city streets with her child, people, knowing the situation, crossed to the other side.

Women whispered to each other, as well as to their children, saying, "There's the stupid whore with her bastard," sometimes under their breath and sometimes openly. On the occasions words went unexpressed, daggering, sneering eyes did the snarling. Men reacted differently. Men sped up to pass them or they shunned them with their backs, as if their mothers or wives were watching. Others smirked at them perversely. Clara learned the hard way: a woman's honor is something of valuable consideration regardless of social status. Scorning people spit *on* Anci and Clara.

"A woman with child is not the problem. A child born out of wedlock is a problem! A child born out of wedlock to a Jewess is a curse!"

Seems like spit carried a great deal of weight in Hungary. If a person found something, like a coin, they had to spit on it before placing it away; not doing so jinxed the person from being lucrative and fortunate. As well, "I spit or sh*t on your luck" meant a person was truly wished good luck. Wishing someone to "fall into a lake of diarrhea" was even better. But "I wish you good luck" directly translated into a jinx. Also, a person spat or knocked on wood when they boasted about having good fortune in order to keep their good fortune. Spitting in another's eye or on someone demonstrated personal disapproval. Finally, sh*t was good to step into, albeit it had to be by accident.

That being said, apparently, Clara didn't step in enough sh*t or was jinxed. Her life catapulted into a living hell. When Clara became pregnant, she was sixteen and unemployed. She scurried to correct her desperate situation and settled on taking the only job offered: punching in at two in the morning in a bookbinding factory. After Anci's birth, her work schedule remained six days a week, standing for a grueling twelve-hour shift, leaving her not much oomph at the end of the day to entertain the idea of spending quality time with Anci.

As she grew from baby to child, shrewd Anci was no dummy. She knew Mutter Clara didn't have the strength to deal with her. Constantly unattended, Anci ran wildly in the mean streets. This lifestyle suited her fine. Anci did what she wanted, and she wore the attitude that "no one can tell me what to do" as her invisible crested emblem for a chipped shoulder badge. Misbehaving and worthy of punishment, either for goofing off, bad school grades, or answering back to her Grandma Regina, the cunning child utilized to her advantage the household's rule established by her Aunt Teresa, Grandma Regina's sister, that "no one wakes a sleeping person" in the Daches home.

Each night, Anci kept one careful eye on the clock that told her when Clara would return home and then quickly scooted her body under the bed covers, pulling the sheet up to her neck so Clara couldn't tell that Anci neither washed nor changed from her street clothes. On some occasions, Anci went into bed without removing her shoes. Again, Anci enjoyed pushing the envelope; she got away with a lot. No one called Anci a stupid child—just heartless.

What Anci, as a child, didn't recognize was how content people were when she was sleeping, even if she was faking. No one could stand dealing with the "mean little bastard," as she was referred to by her mother and grandmother. The power needed to force Anci to comply was more energy than any of them could afford to expend. The family was undernourished and overworked, so they saved their much-needed energies for themselves.

Anci prided herself on her defiant attitude, restating, "No one can tell me what to do!" and "What do you mean you can't make people do what you want them to?" Hearts toward Anci were as cold and bitter as the non-ending winters outside, and Anci seemed to have been born without one.

Concerning school, Anci sometimes did well reciting poetry. Those years correlated to Anci's ability to recant lengthy literary works from rote memory in front of her grade in the auditorium. Anci received high praise for her ability to remember every word of the lengthy assigned prose, which made her feel recognized and smart. As she got older, she remembered every word she had recited, every poem she had read, and the words to songs, including the national hymns for Germany, Russia, Hungary, and even France. Rote memorization was one of Anci's geniuses. Anci was safe as long as feelings were not discussed.

Anci was unable to comprehend feelings past the obvious ones of happiness and sadness. Since Nazis and communists did not permit feelings to be discussed, she was innately lucky in that regard. Her inherent inability to understand emotions, as well as being unable to read others' facial expressions due to her unknown Asperger's condition, served her well during this time. Sensitivity was truly a luxury one could only afford to possess in a highly civilized society, and this was not the world in which Anci grew up.

JUST AS ANCI EXPERIENCED years of acclaim for her school recitals of poetry, there came years when she couldn't do anything right. Anci disliked following instructions, another Asperger's trait unknown at the time. She proclaimed, "I don't do well with authority!" but that sort of individualistic thinking in the late 1930s wasn't well received, especially in Eastern Europe.

One story involving Anci not following orders took place in grade school. Anci's teacher announced to the class, "Anyone with outgrown shoes and dresses that will fit Anci needs to bring the items to class tomorrow. We need to help out the indigent among us."

Anci, standing amid her classmates, was humiliated. As if public insult were not enough, the teacher sat down and commanded, concurrently lifting her outstretched leg with her pointed foot, "Anci, pull off my boots."

In full respect, all the other students had been given the same command on other days, and all humbly complied without hesitation. Unlike any of them, however, Anci refused to be told what to do; she was too good to remove someone's boot, especially after being humiliated. Anci's aloofness had nothing to do with being raised on the street or with feeling prettier than the rest. She was born with a brazen attitude, another Asperger's trait. No amount of imported soap could ever wash it away!

So, Anci pierced an evil glare back at her teacher and, with one defying hand on her hip, retorted in the voice of an encapsulated devil, "Pull it off yourself. What's wrong with you, are you crippled?"

Every last child in the class gasped at this unprecedented behavior. Consequentially, Anci earned a tug on her ear and a challenging order: "Tomorrow, report to class with your father."

This was potentially the most embarrassing dilemma yet! Everyone had a father except Anci. The child who'd gloated for "putting the teacher in her right place" was now left to contemplate, "What father?" Anci was afraid Grandpa Leo would tear the teacher's head off and then death grip Anci by the throat. Since Anci's objective was to reduce the amount of backlash she had to face, Papa Leo wouldn't be good advocate on her behalf.

Disheartened and worried sick, Anci expected to face another round of degradation the following day at school. With her chin downward and her body slumped over, Anci dragged herself home. She lifted her head momentarily when she approached her front door and discovered that Uncle Erno was there. Since stepping into feces is good luck, Anci immediately thought, *I must have stepped in sh*t on my way home!* Erno was rarely ever home. Thank goodness he had lingered outside their apartment. *How come I never considered this uncle?* she thought. Craftily, she quickly went to work. She had to persuade Erno to help her. "I love you like a father," she told him, finally convincing Erno to role-play Anci's father.

Uncle Erno's hefty size at eighteen was promising in making him pass as her father, but she knew it would come down to the right attire to make him look age-appropriate and right. Anci was now relieved to think her teacher wouldn't uncover Anci's secret—that she was *a bastard child.* Anci coached her halfwit uncle to dress in his brother Arthur's one suit after he washed. Arthur's hat would be the cherry on top. The next morning, Anci led Erno to her school, never letting go of his hand, and respectfully introduced the "halfwit" as her father to "the rude 'devil f**ked' teacher," putting it in Anci's terms.

Erno, the one "halfway there," didn't have a clue what was going on. The teacher blabbed and purged her complaints to her heart's content. Erno sat, as instructed by Anci, with his hands in his lap, listening without uttering a word. In those days, his silence was interpreted as paying utmost respect to the instructor. Thankfully for Anci, a report of the incident was never given to Clara or Leo, who Anci feared would beat the living crap out of her. Although, the truth is, Mutter never laid a hand on the child.

Anci and everyone else loved Erno. He was endlessly available and never spoke about anyone's business. Regina Mama, Erno's mother, asked him the same question every day: "How is everything, Erno?"

Given the chance to snitch on Anci each day, he simply responded with the same slow, slurring words, "Yeah, Mama, everything is good; everything is in order, never better."

Regina learned from trial and error not to ask anyone else in the family about how day-to-day life was; they would tell her the truth, especially when it came to her cooking.

"God bless you, Erno," Regina Mama would say, wiping her fallen tears.

5

BECAUSE LEO ONLY SPOKE GERMAN in the home and Regina only spoke Hungarian, their children understood both languages. However, they mostly spoke Hungarian in their home since Leo was hardly there. Leo hated Hungarian. The only time Regina laughed with Leo was when he attempted to speak her language, saying something other than his intended phrase. Leo had a mean streak and enjoyed pointing out the absurdities of the language.

Regina's laughter at Leo always ended with him exclaiming, "Dear God, who made this Magyar? You mispronounce it slightly differently, and it takes on a whole new meaning!"

A frequent example was when Leo raised his dinner water glass in a toast, intending to say "*egeszegedre*/to your health," but he mispronounced the phrase and comically altered it, saying "*egy a seggedre*/one on your ass!"

Indeed, Hungarian was the type of language where mispronouncing "Shakespeare" as "*seg spear*" twisted a dignified name to mean toilet paper. The embarrassing idiocy of the language would have Leo cry out, "Good God, this is a stupid people's language!" and then recite Shakespeare into his piss pot.

Leo wasn't mentioned without his family picturing a roaring lion. Family could only speculate on what ignited Leo's rage. Every evening, he returned from Café Gerbeaud, a stylish coffee house where the aristocratic and elite rubbed shoulders. "I am working! I am socializing with the elite in hopes of being commissioned work," he would tell Regina when questioned on his where-abouts. But could caffeine have been the reason for Leo's uncontainable outbursts of lunatic portions? As women sometimes do, Regina explained away Leo's rampages as "being due to frustration facing failure as an artist." Others blamed his temperament on "not having a better life."

Family legend goes that Anci's Grandpa Leo behaved with all smiles, debo-nair and very well liked, in his frequented coffee house. He was a talented artist; his paintings were exhibited in the Hungarian Museum of Art. He sold few and "wouldn't stoop so low as to paint houses," to feed his family. He insisted with a standoffish sense, "These artiste hands creating my brilliant brush strokes of genius are not to be compromised by menial labor." On occasion, Leo became lucky as a commissioned gold leaf master for several churches, like the Matthias, and official buildings and ceilings of stately estates, like Vajdahunyad Castle.

The monetary reprieves from those jobs, however, were short-lived. The magnificent painted masterpieces he created and intended for sale in order to feed his family's bellies hung tauntingly on display in the unworthy pauper Daches gallery. In other words, all four walls of their paupers' flat were covered, from top to bottom, with Daches's masterful works. The art coordinated stylishly well with the gramophone and the books, but not so well with the peasant décor of furnishings licked and trampled by scurrying cockroaches.

Stress mounted with jittered nerves as if everyone walked on land mines when Leo was at home. They worried that Leo, the human ticking time bomb, would detonate. When Leo exploded, everything previously glued together went flying again off the fireplace mantel in one clean arm sweep. Sadly, Leo broke Regina's inherited treasured figurines so often they became too splintered to repair.

Wretched mother Regina surrendered the pasting projects to Clara, who worked patiently to restore the trinkets, serving as feeble reminders of Mother Regina's better days as a luxuriated young lady.

Before the days of crazy glue, Clara proudly regarded her recipe and ability to glue an art form. The ingredients and measurements consisted of one pinch of flour and a few drops of water added to a pound of patience.

"My good Lord, Leo's failures are entirely my fault!" Regina would cry out, scolding herself aloud in the midst of her nonstop bawling. She mumbled and had full-on dialogues blaming herself for the family's despicable plight—all because Regina's family disinherited her as Leo's calculated meal ticket.

The family tale unfolds with a young, promising artist named Leo visiting a gentleman farmer friend in Austria. Leo fell in love with a young woman's painted portrait that hung on a grand wall of this estate. "The mesmerizing beauty," the host explained, "sits as a model for many splendid paintings." Leo could not get the image of the beautiful girl out of his mind. And so, in poetic fashion, Leo searched for this bewitching creature in pursuit of marriage. His determination navigated Leo to successfully find the woman, Regina Engel, residing in Hungary.

Regina was the most revered beauty of her day, and later, so was her daughter, Clara. However, there was one great difference between the two. Regina, unlike her daughter, Clara, was not born into poverty. Regina's parents, Catarina and Sam Engel, owned the one and only, and first, general store in town, affording the family everything they needed to live comfortably. Sam Engel started his young adult life by traveling between Prussia and Hungary on horseback, fulfilling orders for goods to the people he met in the villages and towns along the way. One day, his horse died in Hungary, and he decided to stay. Sam married the prettiest girl in town, Catarina, and they had three daughters, Regina, Teresa, and Ethel.

As far as Regina, she was headstrong on not marrying anyone but her childhood sweetheart, Karl, whom she'd known since grade school. There was one catch. Regina's mother did not approve of Regina's choice. "Karl simply does not have the financial capabilities to maintain Regina in her accustomed fashion. And damn, there is always something people want that they can't have!" Catarina declared.

Without dispute, the best prospects called on Regina, the prettiest girl in town, for courtship. But Regina obstinately declined these best, suitable suitors from near and far. In turn, her girlfriends loved her, for they did well to take her discards. Slowly, one by one, her friends all married and graciously crossed thresholds into reproducing offspring. Naturally, suitors requesting to court her dwindled as she aged. Still, neither parent nor Regina claimed checkmate. Then, at twenty-eight, a spinster's age, word reached Regina that "the love of Regina's life, Karl, married another." Brokenhearted and in total contempt for her parents for never allowing her to have her true love, Karl, Regina swore she would marry the first man who requested her company in courtship.

Soon thereafter, Leo Daches, artiste extraordinaire, entered her life. At six feet eight inches, Leo and his handlebar mustache towered over everyone. Leo cleaned up well and wore a suit befitting a top-notch gentleman. Comfortable in his courtship attire, he rapped on Regina Engel's door with one hand while holding a photograph of Regina in the prime of her youth in the other.

The female who answered the door was *not* the bright-eyed, long-haired girl Leo expected. With remorse, his gut questioned, *When did this butterfly turn into a moth?* But once invited into the Engel parlor, Leo's interests reemerged, viewing the aged Regina as a monetary prospect.

Initially, Regina's parents were grateful to consider this prospective emancipation from their spinster daughter. After all, her two sisters, Teresa and Ethel, younger than Regina, were already long gone—an uncomfortable societal faux pas mother Catarina did her best to keep hush-hush. Back in the 1800s, there was a progressive order for girls to leave home. Since Regina was the oldest, the younger sisters should have remained in the family domicile until Regina accepted a marriage proposal.

However, because Leo was an artist, and artists mostly had a reputation for being starving artists, Mother Catarina was quick to warn her daughter, "Once you leave the nest, there will be no financial purse strings attached to assist you two in any way." Regina should have known her parents were more stubborn than a double-headed bull. Mother Catarina had never conceded to allow Regina to marry Karl, so why would she believe that her mother would help her financially if she needed it in the future, especially since Mother Catarina clearly stated she would not. Ultimately, Regina's promise to herself to *marry the first courter to come around*, her desperation to get away from her family home, and Leo's promises of a great future outweighed her parents' threat of no future financial help.

Indeed, Leo twirled his mustache in shrewd, manipulative thought as much as he twisted Regina around his finger. He banked on the Engels to step in and assist them in future financial crises. Leo believed there was no way the Engels would let their precious, spoiled daughter suffer in abject poverty! And Leo had big dreams of living the high life as an "artiste extraordinaire." He was aware his paintings did not earn him enough to afford him the cushioned high society life he wanted, so he schemed to obtain this dream by marrying Regina. *Her family will be thankfully generous for marrying their last remaining daughter at the age of twenty-eight, and I will be set for life!*

Two weeks after Leo knocked on the Engels' door in 1912, Leo convinced Regina there was no need to wait to start their life together, and they eloped. Leo rented the first apartment available, as miserable as it was. He was certain they would be out in no time. *Surely, Regina's parents will see this* drecksloch/sh*t hole and move us to a suitable place on their *forint/Hungarian currency.* The next day, the Engels received the telegram of the newlyweds' announcement, their new address, and a request for a visit.

Two days later, the Engels paid the new couple a visit. Before they entered, their help delivered and hung Regina's beautiful dresses into the Daches's shabby closet. Little did Regina know that these items would have to last her the rest of her life, meaning she would never afford to buy anything for herself again.

Once the help exited the Daches's slum apartment, Mother Catarina took two steps past the threshold. The Grande Dame closed her eyes as she took a deep breath to control her disgust. When she opened her eyes on exhale, Mother Catarina's eyes speared bone-chilling contempt into Regina. Her look of great disdain would sear this life-altering moment into Regina's memory forever. Mother Catarina's next words were even more deadly. "We will never return! You are disowned. I meant what I said. Once you left the nest, there would be no financial purse strings attached to assist you two in any way."

The embarrassment and shame of Regina bringing down the family status was the Engels' greatest fear. Regina, whose name meant queen, was certainly about to live a life of irony. Her parents, but more so Mother Catarina, refused to permit the Daches squalor to tarnish the Engel name or the prosperous business of their general store. Without removing a coat or taking a seat, Mother Engel projected her voice and distinctly pronounced every word: "Regina Daches, you are permitted to call only after you have bettered this disgraceful situation; until such time, this shame is not to extend to us."

Lack of assistance from Regina's parents and Leo's poor work ethic anchored the Daches couple to remain stuck in their louse-infested, and therefore "louse-y," apartment. Time rolled on, and the Engels kept true to their word. They nixed their daughter Regina out of their life completely.

Worse yet, word of Regina's true love, Karl, seared Regina's ears by way of small-town gossip. The man her mother deemed "not good enough to marry" became an entrepreneurial success. Speculatively, the harsh truth of Regina's upside-down, inside-out world weakened Regina into suffering a bottomless pit of severe depression.

Leo, on the other hand, had to live with the fact that he married an older woman for her money only to realize his manipulative plan backfired. Left with a sickly older woman, untrained to keep an organized household, duly enraged him. Their union couldn't have been worse. Neither person bargained for the other. The added burden of children quickly came. First there was Arthur, then Flora, then Clara, then Erno. Arthur was born in 1913—it was said "at first coitus." Flora was born in 1914, Clara in 1915, and Erno in 1923.

Along the busy Daches procreation timeline, there was one stillbirth in 1922, the year prior to Erno's birth. The tale attached to the lost fetus was buried with the baby, but the surviving siblings often heard their mama Regina cry, "It was the lucky one."

Unquestionably, Leo hated being in the house as much as the family hated his presence. Like many nights in the passing years of increasing disgust for his life, Leo returned home glassy-eyed from the consumption of odious amounts of coffee spiked with rum. Regina was never wise to the smell of alcohol on Leo. She had a perpetual cold and hacking cough, which today might be speculatively due to severe allergies, bronchitis, or asthma.

Long before Anci was born, one night in particular in 1921 would stand out to the helpless bystanding Daches children who were all below the age of nine. A highly intoxicated Leo wrongfully threw his pitiful pregnant wife under him, not in love but in savage rape. In the darkness of the one-room apartment, bloodcurdling screams, violent beatings, and slurred degradations penetrated the souls of everyone present. It wouldn't be the last time. It was the first time in what became an endless cycle of assaults and physical abuse.

The horrified children witnessed their crazed father unjustly and repeatedly punish their mother. More times than not, the Daches children awoke exhausted and in the same position—clustered together under a cloaked sheet of fear. From yelps that were not hers, Regina knew how Leo educated his dependents about his massive power behind his six foot eight inch stature—not by physically laying a hand on them but by the fear he instilled in them with his willing and capable hands reserved for their beloved mother. On occasion, Mother Regina martyred herself, throwing herself in front of Leo to buffer the blows meant for her children.

Mama Regina knew their helplessness in being unable to protect her churned a growing unifying hatred against him in her children. Each insane episode justified the children to angrily declare, "God, I hate Papa Leo," behind his back. After a specific night of abuse resulted in the stillbirth, witnessed by the entire family in their one-room dwelling, Regina never corrected her children regarding Leo. As a conscientious, loving mother, Regina did not want her children respecting their controlling monster-father. Such action would be doubly wrong and conducive to rearing a dangerous brood of children who would repeat their father's behaviors. "One insane person in the household is enough to tolerate," Regina would mutter.

Papa Leo's evening ritual of assault against Regina grew in intensity: each time, he repeatedly shouted into the woman's ear while physically defiling her,

"Everything that is wrong in our miserable lives is your fault!" She heard it so often that she was brainwashed and believed it. So even when Leo was out of their *drecksloch*/sh*thole, sweet Mama Regina unjustly placed Leo's wrongdoings upon her own shoulders, mumbling through her sobs, "Good God that keeps me alive, what did I do wrong?"

Ironically, Leo was religiously devoted. One side of Leo devotedly prayed to God for salvation from his other side, the worst damned monster within himself—very much like Dr. Jekyll and Mr. Hyde.

To battle his fear of losing control, he turned to his books of Orthodox Jewish prayers. He prayed without fail first thing in the morning with the rising sun, during the day, and once before bed. But religion did not stop Leo's uncontrollable temper.

Leo was a tortured soul, and as he suffered, the family starved at home. His release of pent-up anger found Regina in bed at night much the same way he left her. She was so weak and beaten from his brutal evening onslaughts that she slept all day. Unfortunately, she became pregnant again, and this time, Leo became crazier than ever.

Leo hollered, "Get rid of it! Go! Keep jumping off steps until you lose that thing!" as he forced himself, fully, inside her. His large, mean, controlling hand pulled her hair as he yelled, "Go and keep jumping off steps until you lose that thing." Leo's tormenting rants drowned his children's whimpers of fear. Her sick husband's slobbering mantra, "Get rid of it! Go! Keep jumping off steps until you lose that thing," sent her over the edge. She snapped.

Regina went missing. Luckily, their oldest son, Arthur, acted upon his instinct when his mother didn't return for many hours. Arthur said to his concerned siblings, "She never leaves the bed, let alone the house! There's something wrong with sweet Mama that she is gone!" Arthur set out to find her.

When Arthur found her, his mama was a sloppy, inconsolable mess. The image of Mother Regina holding her purple-welted body, shimmering in colors of black and blue that only a crow should wear, was unforgettable and unforgiveable! Her bodice trembled as she cried, and she said, "I ran so you wouldn't see me like this. I can't do this anymore." Sobbing heavily, she repeated over and over, "I can't do this. I can't ..."

Arthur escorted his desperately needed and beloved mother back home, swearing all the while, "One day I'm going to beat that cursed one until he walks like a scrotal sacless dog!"

But payback time would have to wait. Clara was only six, and Flora was seven. Arthur, the oldest, was nine and nowhere near Leo's height.

Despite the odds in the midst of so many brutal beatings, Erno was born. His name means determined, as in *determined* to live. His arrival made the crowded living conditions in the small, miserable Daches apartment even worse.

As Erno aged, his hindering development became more apparent. Erno's siblings sadly agreed and openly stated outside of his earshot, "He paid a dear price for Papa Leo's act of madness against him while swimming helplessly in Mama's womb." That's what they meant, anyway, when they said in various ways, "That f**king lowlife bastard we call Papa beat the sh*t out of Regina while she was pregnant. It's amazing Erno is alive. Poor thing ... he is not all there. You know that's what made Erno different."

Erno was slower than others; he was the type of child who would never grow up and leave his mama's house ... not willingly. And as far as Mama Regina was concerned, "I love all my children, but if I were only allowed to pick one, I would pick my Erno. He is the reason for my existence." Although they knew Erno was Mama Regina's favorite, the Daches children all adored their mother.

MAMA REGINA SIGHED as she thought that Leo was God knows where and the reason money was tight, while she struggled over what to serve for *Shabbat*/Friday night dinner. The children were still little, so she hoped her emphasis on lighting the Shabbat candle eighteen minutes from sunset would deter them from the lack of food. She covered a bread basket with a cloth to represent the challah bread that she wished they had. Next, she placed a Shabbat shawl on her head for a scarf, placed her hands over her eyes, and said the *Motzi*/

Shabbat prayer. She and the children then sang, "*Shalom Aleichem*/Peace Be Upon You."

Clara's uplifting voice was already beautiful at that young age. Mama Regina commended her by saying, "You have the heart of an angel, Clara, and it resonates through your voice." Their stomachs didn't have much to be thankful for, but their togetherness would be enough. After saying "Amen" together, the congregated family gathered around the table and ate their boiled potatoes instead of *latkas*/potato-pancakes since they could not afford the butter needed to make latkas. "*Baruch Hashem*/Blessed be the Lord," they expressed in unison.

AT EIGHTEEN, ARTHUR REACHED his full height of six feet two inches—six inches shorter than his father's six feet eight inches. The time he quietly spent anticipating standing eye-to-eye with his father never came. So, he decided to retaliate when he felt he was strong enough to have a winning chance. The next time his father, Leo, caused his mother, Regina, to hide behind a chair for cover, Arthur would earn the meaning of his name, strong as a bear, and assertively intervene.

Sure enough, like forecasted tumultuous weather, Leo's mighty roar of thunder surged. In the dark of night, Leo's big hand was plummeting down like an executioner's chopping ax. Arthur intercepted the blow, grabbing his father's arm in midair. Then Arthur morphed with the strength of Thor, the Norse thunder god, and hammered down on Leo—just as he'd sworn to his mother, just as he'd sworn to his siblings, and just as he'd sworn to himself he would do. He repaid his father for the years of unpunished rages—the brutal assaults against his mother too numerous to be tallied. Arthur didn't stop until *he* was exhausted and felt *his* vengeance well served. With open mouths, the rest of the family—who'd hoped the day would come but never believed it actually would—witnessed the event. Specifics about the blows delivered by Arthur were never mentioned. What was mentioned is that "Leo behaved well for a while after that."

With good conscience, Arthur was filled with remorse for turning into a predator like his father. But Arthur was torn because he didn't want his mother to fall victim to his father any longer. So, for the time being, Arthur continued to steadily enforce his father's good behavior with threats of physical punishment, as if Arthur were the adult and Leo the child.

6

ALTHOUGH THE NAME of this middle child literally means flower, Flora's name came to refer to her as "the least attractive of their bunch." Apparently in Flora's instance, flower was a misnomer, unless one meant a wallflower.

Flora was a great seamstress; no one could slight her abilities from behind a sewing machine. In fact, she sewed the finest garments commissioned by the aristocratic women in her town. The young, industrious Flora charged her clients extra and recreated the same garments for herself at no cost. Dressed like a high-class lady, accessing a gamut of the finest ladies and homes, including the King's Castle and the dignitaries of the parliament, Flora obtained an education refining her taste and mannerisms. She carried herself with distinction at work and out by day, and humbly returned to reality at home.

Others in her class were known to meet their future spouses while commuting to and from work with public transportation. Flora openly called people who met their life partner at the rail station "undignified people with low standards." Flora looked down on her own class, thinking she belonged among those she visited on a daily basis, no differently from the corner bank teller who feels rich handing out money all day. Flora, as plain-looking as she was, decided, "I would rather be alone than keep company with a loser. I don't need to perpetuate

Mama Regina's and Sister Clara's committed mistakes." Had Clara heard Flora's comments, she would have probably commended her by saying, "A smart person learns from stupid's mistakes."

One day, Flora found a ring. Where she found it is a mystery. She told no one other than her trusted brother Arthur. "It's my ticket out of this litter box!" she declared. But Flora waited for her opportune moment to move out.

In the middle of Flora's plans to exit and Arthur's actions to keep Leo in line with his clenched fist came a marked day in Clara's life. Two months shy of her eighteenth birthday on January 13, 1932, Clara was breach-birthing her child in natural childbirth, almost losing her own life in the process. The Daches family could not afford a midwife. Clara was on her own. The screams of agonizing childbirth had continued for two entire days. Clara's increasing moans and groans due to the tears of birthing the baby's feet and hips first constrained their small living quarters even tighter, pushing Leo and then Arthur into the brinks of insanity. As she worked to birth the baby's shoulders, Clara's shrilling cry penetrated the cold winter night through the cracked windowpane. Agitated neighbors yelled back, "Shut up and give birth already or close the window, goddamn it! It's been two days of this sh*t!"

That remark was the strike that lit Leo like a bomb. "Regina!" he yelled through gritted teeth. "Do something already!" He grabbed Regina at Clara's bedside by the back of her hair with his left hand and crazily started to throw punches with his right. Arthur, now twenty, took hold of Leo to stop his father's madness and beat him like a drum with his thundering fists. Both men and their curses and grunts intertwined with Clara's groans as Arthur threw his hardest blows. At one point, Arthur picked up Leo from the floor to stand him on his feet and shoved him into the wall. Leo, grappling with his balance, knocked into his prized gramophone. Its arm scratched across the playing record. Other than absent Erno, the record received the least damage out of any that night.

Suddenly, Clara, known to sing like an angel, emitted the darkest, deepest sounds from the devil himself. The sound jarred everyone away from their madness, and all eyes turned to Clara bearing down with everything she had left. The head, the last part, was finally out. Where Clara's devilish howl trailed off, the baby's steaming body pierced its first sound into the frigid air. Clara, half-dead, muttered, "It's a girl." The newborn named Anna (Anci) Maria was anything but what her name meant—God favored or beloved, like the dictionary claimed—for she wasn't met with cheers and was considered nothing more than another unwanted mouth to feed.

"How are you doing, my dear Clara?" Regina asked, wiping both their brows and tending to the new mother and child.

With an escaping tear and a hard swallow, Clara replied, "Everything is perfect, just as it should be, Mama," having learned from Erno that Mama Regina only wanted to hear the positive.

Arthur couldn't resist hammering his fists of rage with one last final blow right after Clara's announcement. Arthur, seething with hate, sternly glowered into his father's beaten eyes and exclaimed, "If your breath travels my way or if you even think of harming our mother, I will make my grown man strength pain you, my aged father!"

With that, Arthur grasped Leo's limp head in his gripping palms and dropped it to fall with a thump onto the floor. Arthur stepped over his father's beaten body, pulled on his coat, and walked out the door. The same way he couldn't stand idly by, watching his papa abuse his family any longer, Arthur likewise knew he couldn't control his own fists from pounding his papa, even if his intent was to keep Leo civil.

Flustered, Flora followed him. She walked a considerable distance on the path in front of their "litter box" before she ran out of breath. At the point she could no longer keep stride with her brother, she stopped and uttered her tear-filled "goodbye." Arthur did not stop for a moment. Pumped with adrenaline, he kept walking. *Arthur never thought of waving bye?* Flora thought to herself. She would never forget standing there, watching her brother dissipate into a black moving speck, before disappearing into the rest of the gloomy, gray background.

"It was as if the devil was in our house that night," Flora would say, retelling the story in years to come.

Clara wondered, *What kind of jelly diarrhea leaves after I birthed a child and doesn't ask if I am all right or say goodbye? He must have felt he had to go, or he might have killed Papa.* Clara's summation: "The cacophony of events that night was one of the family's greatest tragic operas."

Later, Flora wondered, *How did Arthur afford to leave? He had no money, no training, nothing to fall back on.* Holding her breath, the frenzied woman searched for the ring she had proudly shown Arthur, which was to be her "ticket out." *The rotten whore animal, Arthur, stole my idea and ticket out of this litter box, and made it his own!* Flora was furious; Arthur vanished with Flora's hope of gaining a future.

PERSONALLY, ERNO was Anci's favorite family member in their slum apartment. She thought, *It's funny how Erno can sleep on our ironing board held up on one side by the bed and a chair on the other.* Mostly, she loved having Erno walk her to school on the slim occasions when he did. Sometimes, she would fake being tired and he would delight her in a ride to school, high on his strong, thick shoulders. On those instances, she felt privileged to experience what it was like to be a normal kid escorted to school.

As for Anci's mother, Clara, her nerves were shot. Six days a week, ten to twelve hours a day beginning at two in the morning, Clara's days and nights were flipped, out of sync with her daughter attending school. Clara's bookbinding job demanded she stand on her tired, swollen feet, shut away from daylight, in a dark, cement-gray bookbinding factory. Her fingers were constantly paper cut and sore. She had no social life. Her one companion was a mouse she played with for fifteen minutes before clocking in to work, and even its attendance depended on the rodent's mood. Not permitted to sing at work, the varmint was the only recipient of her songs before punching in her time card.

She was young, but instead of being able to unwind in the company of a girlfriend or boyfriend or a husband, her responsibilities returned her home at the end of her work shift. Too tired to do anything after house chores, she retired to her worn hay bed shared with her sister, mother, and child. Single girls were forbidden to talk to Clara. Married women shunned her, and no man approached her since she was raising a bastard.

Clara was embarrassed of mothering a child out of wedlock. Her circumstance complicated the simplest situations, like trying to explain to recordkeeping officials why everyone in her household shared the same last name. Forms were constantly returned. "Read the instructions more carefully. Don't just carelessly apply pen to paper."

Aggravated, Clara decided to take assertive action. "If money can take care of a situation, then it won't be easy, but it is not a problem." Clara's objective: acquire a different last name from her parents'. Marriage was the usual way a woman changed her last name, but this option was clearly not available to Clara. No man was interested in her total package. So, Clara had to become more creative. Through networking, she found a man willing to sell his last name in exchange for paid gambling debts. Hungarian gentlemen farmers and royals sold their family titles in exchange for cleared gambling debts. Clara didn't invent the process, but her solution to an embarrassing problem was genius because of her twist: a poor woman buying a name without a title. Clara added hours onto her shift for an entire year before she pooled the funds needed to attain her goal.

Funny thing was, Clara obtained more than she bargained for, and in a good way. She inadvertently befriended a coworker through the transaction. When Clara met Mr. Pataki, the man whose last name she would acquire, Clara recognized Mootzy, her female coworker, at his apartment. Mootzy was casually sitting at Pataki's kitchen table—in a man's apartment without the company of her husband. The sight of Mootzy immediately alerted Clara that Mootzy was having an extramarital affair with Pataki. When Pataki left them alone to search for a pen, the two women promised to keep each other's secret and thereby solidified the beginning of a long-lasting friendship.

"Now, let the donkey heads at the registrar's offices find someone else to amuse themselves with. No more Daches names across the board. From now on, we are Pataki, Clara and Pataki, Anna (Anci)." Every Hungarian recognized another Hungarian by the meaning of their last names. Daches was a German name meaning roof, but it didn't mean anything in Hungarian. Pataki, on the other hand, was the name of a river or a village by a river in Hungary. Either way, the name was good; Clara would gain respect with a married name and double respect for being Hungarian, which was better than German or Russian during these times.

The next goal on Clara's agenda was to obtain baptism papers for herself and Anci. The year after Anci was born, in 1933, Hitler rose to power and the Hungarian government worked to create an alliance with Nazi Germany. In 1938, anti-Jewish legislation cut out 80 percent of the Jewish professions and participation in the economy. In 1939, being Jewish became a racial group, not a religion. In 1940, Hungary allied with Nazi Germany. Fear of the Nazi thumb among the Jews spread like a disease.

All this turbulent change struck strong urgency for Clara to use their new, proper last names to go before a priest and request baptism. Everything took time and patience. Numerous times, Clara tried her best to buy baptism papers but did not succeed. Nevertheless, knowing the importance of the document, Clara continued to try even harder. She knew that baptism papers for at least her Jewish child would save Anci's life in case war broke out.

The power of money eventually and effectively found a priest willing to exchange money for the child's document in a handshake. However, the priest told Clara she was "too old to convert," and his words were final even though she offered double the money. Clara worked extra hard, back-to-back shifts a few days a week for six months, to earn the funds for the monumentally important white baptism paper. The name "Pataki, Anna" hand-printed in black ink by the priest on the baptism certificate would prove to be worth *life!*

7

IT WAS 1941, before Hungary decided to join Germany in the war against the Soviet Union, and Clara asserted to conquer yet another objective with her newly purchased name. She ordered her nine-year-old Anci to wash and dress and accompany her on a small journey into town. According to Anci, Clara led her in a gripping vice on, "an endless expedition to a place behind God's country." They traveled with a number of bus changes before Mutter Clara and child then began walking into an exclusive area built for the well-to-do. Clara stopped in front of a set of open, fancy, iron gates with a family crest. The number on the house matched Clara's cat scratches on her folded paper. After a deep breath and a quick adjustment to their clothes, Clara motioned with a waving hand, "Anci, go; knock on the door."

Anci did so, in stomping protest and defiance. Anci stood at the door, impatiently waiting for it to open. When she walked back to Clara, Clara marched the two of them to the door. They stood together, daughter in front of mother, with Clara's steering hands firmly controlling Anci by her shoulders. They waited, without any response from the other side of the door. After a few attempts at lifting and dropping the doorknocker, they finally heard the door locks turn. Clara gulped. A white butler's glove pushed the door open. Clara, in anxiousness, vice-gripped her daughter's shoulders tighter.

The uniformed butler spoke, "State your business, woman."

Clara's knees buckled. The woman who stood on the doorstep with child had so much she had wanted to voice for so long, but she went speechless. Clara did not expect to deal with the rush of emotions she was experiencing. The door to the palatial home opened wider. Naturally, Clara transfixed her eyes on the many exquisite items inside. Clara felt cheated. She felt entitled to having only brown-eyes among her family members constantly reminding her of her regretted union with Szombucky Von Bless, Viktor. This rich Von Bless family was sitting pretty, with pinkies in the air, sipping tea, while Clara slaved her best years away in a gloomy factory. Clara's life would have been different if she had known brown-eyed Bless, Viktor made promises he wouldn't keep.

Mother and child weaved and bobbed around the butler, who purposefully stood to block their inquisitive inspection. The Von Bless home looked like a wind-up jewelry box filled with opulent richness: polished marble floors, high pillar marble columns, and Viennese crystal chandeliers—the stuff of fairy tales. Shamelessly, the Bless gramophone played sweet operatic overtures in rhythmic meter to Clara and Anci's grumbling bellies enticed by fantastic aromas of butter-baked goods that escaped past the hungry pair standing in front of the open door. In finale, they both almost passed out when a flow of fragrant perfumes swirled around them, further boggling their keen senses. Clearly, Clara's mind overloaded from a fog of confusion.

With another big gulp, Clara attempted to state her business. In a meek, crackling voice, she uttered, "Good day, good man, *Pataki, Clara* requests the presence of Mother Bless herself, on a personal matter."

The butler in tails coolly directed, "Wait outside."

The door shut in their faces. They stood outside waiting. Determined to speak to the matriarch, Clara parked her ego and stood facing the door.

"Come on, Mutter, let's go. They don't want us here."

"No, I am not ready to give up." Clara clutched Anci's arm to stand firm, no differently than she clutched her purse.

Others in the private, multistoried, single-family home pushed aside their posh curtains and peered at the two below, sneering as if they smelled a foul bowel movement. Clara remained in position, standing unscathed. The locks turned again, and the butler showed himself. As instructed, he shooed the two desperados like rotten garbage.

"For the last time, good woman ..." Mother Bless, Royal Bitch, interjected with an authoritative tone over the butler, "tell the lowly peasant we are not in the business of interviewing flower girls for maids here. She need go elsewhere for a handout!"

To Anci, the need to get washed and dressed in their best and take that arduous trip made no sense. "Mutter, what do you want with this old sour face?" Anci pulled her hand away defiantly from her mother's boa constrictor grip.

"This is where you and I belong. This is where your father lives. This, all this, is what was promised me. This is what made you and broke me."

The trek home was twice as long as the trip to that godforsaken, Bless-ed place they visited. Anci was miserable, with Mutter pushing and tugging on her. The entire way back Mutter cursed Anci, their existence, and the whole world. Clara's determination returned the unwanted pair to the same location every week on the one day of the week Clara had off. Anci didn't want to go where she wasn't wanted. *If anyone cared to ask me, I would rather live it up as a street kid than be all dressed up sitting pretty.* Clara was not satisfied, until at long last, there was a breakthrough, a verbal agreement drawn between Mother Bless and Mutter Clara.

As a result, Anci washed and dressed in her best hand-me-down dress and waited as directed: downstairs on the street for the horse-drawn carriage coming for her. The sight of a fancy horse-drawn carriage visiting the mean streets of the slums would be strange and unusual. Anci, perpetually early, rushed downstairs and waited ... and waited ... and waited.

Two hours late, the modern mode of transportation afforded only by the elite, the Blesses' private coachman-driven horse and buggy finally arrived. The coach door opened. Anci was motioned to step inside by two gloved ladies wearing hats and sitting prissily. Anci was quickly shooed to take a seat across from them. Their grimacing faces and body language distinctly exclaimed their clear intentions: she needed to keep her distance. They didn't talk to her. Instead, they chose to stare and talk about her behind their fanning fans, as if she were a mangy dog.

The horse's reins were pulled to a stop. They all stepped out. The elegant ladies decided, "We can't possibly go any further. Necessary adjustments are in order before being publicly seen with *this one*." They marched her into a clothing store and turned her over to a store attendant, instructing, "Befit *this one* with clothes for the Opera House, return her upon completion. I don't care what you do. Make her right and make it fast."

After Anci was attended to, washed, combed, dressed in new attire, and with the approval of her appearance granted, the three re-embarked the horseman's carriage. "Coachman, onward to the playhouse!" the ladies instructed. The coachman cracked his whip on the hind legs of the horse. The horse whinnied in pain and retaliated with a jerked response and a running gallop. Anci, not quite sitting, was knocked to her boney rump, erasing any contemplation of the right way to sit in her new clothes.

Opera attendees wore fanciful plumed hats, dresses, and shoes. The pomp and stance of the rich pretending not to give a hoot about being noticed, while vying for attention, was most peculiar. As in any show, the masquerade was great, but all Anci wanted to know was, *When am I finally meeting this stuck-up grandmother or father of mine, already?* The day passed without meeting either one. Yet arrangements were made to pick up Anci by the Blesses' stagecoach once a month for the time being.

ON ALL OTHER DAYS OF THE MONTH, Anci hung out on the streets of her neighborhood. She preferred running around the street as a street rat. *I can be who I really am instead of sitting in some itchy, frilly frock, not talked to while being talked about.* Friends and neighbors mentioned seeing her enter a horse-drawn carriage. Their teasing caused uneasiness. Anci wasn't very good at understanding a joke, and in this case, she interpreted the jokers to be jealous. "Trust me, I would rather be out here with you dirty pricks having a good time than with the sorry sourpusses called relatives who don't want me," she stated. And Anci meant it.

Unlike her jesting street-rat companions, Grandpapa Leo treated Anci to momentous favorable memories upon her arrivals home by carriage, easing the disappointment that she hadn't yet met either her father or her father's mother. On one occasion, Leo stood alone, at attention, waiting for her as she entered the apartment. He was wearing his dusted-off courting suit, which transformed him into a different Leo, one Anci didn't recognize. Gentleman Leo was more pussycat than lion on his best behavior. Anci didn't know where everyone went or what possible arrangements were organized for Grandpa Leo and Anci to be the only ones in the apartment. Leo placed the gramophone needle onto a record in the same easy, graceful way Leo's gifted hand commanded a paintbrush to kiss canvas. Likewise, Leo gently motioned Anci to stay and join his company in a magical dance.

Leo, in elegant German, prefaced their waltz with a small introduction. "The Daches house may have empty stomachs, but we are culturally rich. We enrich our minds with classic literature, our ears with musical masters, and our eyes with my masterpieces, thusly nourishing our souls." Leo slowly and deliberately scanned his masterpieces that wallpapered their walls, quietly demanding Anci's respect. "Yes," he continued, "our bellies are starving, but our senses and hearts are full."

After his short narrative, Leo once again gently laid the arm of the phonograph onto the round spinning vinyl he'd preselected for their pleasure. The violin in the Viennese waltz strummed the stresses of their dismal lives away. Proceeding toward her, Leo lifted his chin and squared his shoulders, transforming before Anci's very eyes into a distinguished, aged Prince Charming. Standing toe-to-toe with his granddaughter, Leo respectfully tilted his head and addressed her as, "Little Lady." With one arm behind his back, Leo clicked his boot heels twice. He bent at the waist for his blue eyes to look directly into Anci's bewildered brown eyes, and regally stated, "Request the honor of this dance, Miss."

The tiny girl's grin stretched from ear to ear. The excited child smiled so hard her cheeks never knew such blissful ache.

"I take this smile as a yes, Little Miss. May I?"

Anci jumped up and down in excitement, and before she touched the ground on the second leap, Leo caught his granddaughter at his elbow and kept her perched there for their enchanted dance. Worlds of hurt whisked away as the ground underneath her feet disappeared. Such wild fantasy exhilarated Anci in sheer happiness she'd never felt before. Smiling, Leo looked at her, twirling her in perfect time to the music faster and faster, then slower—all in correct waltz tempo.

He counted out loud, "*Schritt eins, zwei, drei, hoch, und umdrehen*," which was German for step one-two-three up and turn, explaining, "This is the dance of aristocrats and dignitaries."

He expounded on how the women dressed in lavish gowns and doused themselves in unforgettable fragrances while the gentry fancied presenting themselves in long coattails and bowties, a world Leo had once known. The needle came to the end of the record, but their moment lived on forever as Anci's favorite memory. This version of Leo that no one saw at home would become the reason she would continue ballroom dancing four days a week until she was eighty-six years old.

ANCI WAS PRIVILEGED TO WITNESS how the other half of her was entitled to live. No matter what she said, Anci looked forward to the delivered dress—packaged in a box for her to wear to the family-arranged outings. Each time, her anticipation was high that she would meet her father under formal introduction. But her father, or grandmother, she soon realized, would *not* attend the playhouse excursions. Distant female relatives picked her up instead. After a while, Anci was collected by coach but no longer taken to the playhouse. She had a feeling something was up when no box was delivered with her order to be downstairs on a certain day and time. Confused, Anci didn't know she was being transported to *the Von Bless house.*

Now unaccompanied for the first time, Anci was undistracted and concerned herself with happenings outside the coach. The bustling streets from her elegant ride gave her a new perspective of her motherland.

She knew the horse-drawn carriages were for the bourgeoisie, the upper crust, but the difference between that and the open-aired, horse-pulled carts for the peasant-poor farm villagers and gypsies was still a class better than that of poor city dwellers like Anci, who walked or utilized public transportation.

All men, regardless of class, proudly wore thick handlebar mustaches if they could grow one. Many wore their facial hair to extend to the middle of their cheeks, while other mustaches reached past the widths of their faces. These stashes were stylishly worn, vigorously twisted, and curled and waxed.

The biggest difference in people's dress was between the city and country people, otherwise referred to as peasants. Peasants had dressed the same way for at least a century, whereas the city folk wore suits. City men and women wore hats, while peasant men wore caps. After a certain age, peasant women wore scarves, a black one with a long black dress and black shawl if they were widowed, regardless of age.

Another noticeable difference between the two societal classes was their use of soap. In particular, while laborers needed to wash themselves and their clothes most, they were too tired to do so, and thereby, washed the least, according to Anci.

Upon entrance into the Von Bless home, Anci was directed to sit on the parlor's sofa. The couch was nothing like the one in the Daches home. This couch did not need a sheet to cover up the worn spot that swallowed her whole. The housemaid set a small dish of cookies and the tiniest teacup of milk on the table in front of Anci. Fumbling with what her next move was to be, boggled by obediently wearing white gloves, her bulging, hungry brown eyes transfixed on the cookies, not knowing what to do. *Am I supposed to wait? I'm starving! What are three cookies going to do? Can't they spare a piece of bread and some meat? Miserable bastards, every last one of them, that's what they are!*

Her stomach growled, speaking its mind: *What's your problem? Feed me!* Anci bit into old, dry, and tasteless yuck! *These cookies are just like the old, dry, and tasteless people here. Knowing these cheap bastards, no one ever eats these cookies. Rich people can afford to buy cookies for display.* She shoved the cookies in her mouth, like a ravaged untamed animal, without any knowledge of how to do better. *Great, now I'm choking. Did they really think the tiniest thimble of milk was going to be enough?*

Horrifically, the child noticed all brown eyes on her. *Hmmm ... everyone at home has blue eyes. Now I see why they comment about my devilish brown eyes, which must be like my father's.* Initially, when Anci was first seated, she didn't allow herself to get too bothered about being highly scrutinized by judging eyes. But the constant scrutiny of her every move without approaching her was now agitating. She wasn't a fish in a fishbowl!

The longer Anci sat alone, as stiff as a board with nothing to do but think, the more the smart child questioned the purpose for her visit. Her grandmother Bless came out of her boudoir on two occasions. Both times, Anci immediately straightened her slouched spine, anticipating the grand introduction. But no, the Grand Lady merely remained at the top of the marble stairs and greeted her guests as they entered her home below. They walked up the stairs to join the waving matriarch, and together, they gawked at Anci as a spectacle, like the family science project gone wrong.

Her mind was confused as to what they expected or why she was there if they weren't going to approach her. Her anticipation of finally meeting her father and grandmother never occurred. No one even spoke to her. This day was nothing more than hard, cold rejection for Anci. In response, her mind turned off, and she didn't remember anything else that happened while she was uncomfortably positioned on the Von Blesses' sofa.

Anci's mind switched on once she was looking out the coach window on her return home. She caught herself gaping open-mouthed in bewilderment. Dusk was setting a magnificent overshadowing on all else that had occurred earlier that day. Gas flames flickered, illuminating the walkways alongside the Danube River, and delightfully danced in rhythm to the gypsies' violins serenading passersby. Anci was entranced. Surrealism set in.

In order to absorb everything introduced in this new world, Anci changed her position from sitting to kneeling, since no one would correct her in the coach. The brilliantly illuminated gothic-style parliament building was doubled in grandeur by its reflection on the Danube, making it look more storybook than realistic. The sounds of horseshoes trotting against cobblestone streets around the baroque-style King's Castle and the old medieval style Byzantine Matthias Church whisked her imagination to wonder how fantastic life might be as a royal. *They don't go hungry, and they definitely don't go dirty, with everyone kissing their ass clean.*

Suddenly, in an epiphany, the ingestion of Hungary's breathtaking sights made clear to Anci her mother's intentions of meeting her father's family. *Clearly, Mutter wants me to see the world outside of our miserable sh*t box. I didn't understand why Mutter insisted on me meeting my father and his mother or them meeting me. But I did see a lot I would not otherwise have seen. There is a bigger world than the one where we live, where rats run in our open sewers.* Her homeland appeared to be another country entirely. Budapest was grander than the four corners of the slum she called home.

Life had a way of working things out. The Von Bless family would become the least of Anci's concerns. After five visits, the Von Bless clan conveniently exited Anci's life as abruptly as they had entered, and Anci was fine with that. Somehow, the family in their slum apartment and Shabbat dinner had more meaning to Anci now. The cold austere of the Von Blesses' life awakened her to notice and appreciate such things as her Mutter Clara, who sang mostly opera that she had learned from their gramophone. It seemed everyone in the family carved their own niche to serve a purpose in their family. Leo was the baby maker, Regina the kind mother, Anci the provider in the worst of times, Clara the Shabbat dinner provider, Erno the external protector and Anci's father figure at school to present to teachers. Flora, however, was a very different ingredient in the mix of Daches *goulash*/Hungarian stew. She kept to herself and didn't contribute monetarily or in any other way. She ate the food provided and saved all her earnings for herself. *Flora is a selfish bitch,* Anci thought.

Anci looked forward to Shabbat dinners more than she did getting her hopes up to meet her father, who she never did see. Arthur had been gone for a while now, so no one even mentioned him anymore. Regina's remaining children were bigger now, and while Leo claimed to be at Temple praying, Shabbat evenings to the others in the family represented the one meal in the week when there was something of substance both for the belly and the soul.

Mama Regina always led the ceremonial lighting of the candle for Shabbat dinner right as dusk began. As she did each week, she placed her shawl over her head, lit the candle, covered her eyes, and then said the *Motzi*/Shabbat prayer. This night, Anci contributed the heel of a *challah*/egg bread—that no one asked how she obtained—into the bread basket. Regina happily tore the heel of the rare treat to share among Erno, Clara, Flora, Anci, and herself.

"God bless this child who works miracles in times like these," Regina said with a gleam in her eye.

Then Clara unwrapped one smoked white fish no bigger than her hand that she'd bought to share among the five of them, while saying, "Mama, I am unwrapping this fish like a groom his virgin bride."

"God bless you, Clara. You never forget us on Shabbat. Not like Flora and that Arthur who used to live here."

Flora said nothing.

Clara jumped in, "Tonight, we have a feast. Normally, we are not this lucky, unless Anci removes a stolen Kielbasa or winter salami from her coat sleeve."

Regina said, "On most occasions, I am left to be inventive, with little to work with than potatoes," taking her share of food and handing Flora her portion last.

"We sure are tired of potatoes every night," Anci said.

Clara pinched Anci hard under the table while she scolded Anci with her eyes. Clara then beckoned Regina, "Pass those potatoes, Mama."

"The trick in cooking is not making something but creating something from nothing, and that is culinary genius!" Mama Regina said.

Flora, Clara, and Anci rolled their eyeballs with their heads down in quiet response. Erno, however, was so good to their sweet mama. He truly was the only one to ever bring her consistent happiness. The halfwit taught them all a lesson: truth wasn't always what counts. "Yes, Mama," he said. "Your potatoes are the best."

"Amen," they chanted, honoring Erno for his kindness and Mama for her hard efforts before they dug in. Thankful for their food and each other, they sang the hymn, "God, Master of the Universe." Clara's voice outshone the others while they all basked in the joy of praising the King who reigns over Kings.

"*Beruch Hashem*/Blessed be the Lord."

STRANGELY, AS INFERIOR AS THE LIVES of the Daches-Pataki home were, their days together were the best they would collectively share. It was now 1944. Times were changing—as if the earth had tilted off its axis. More importantly to Anci, her world was changing like dirty diapers. Jews were being blamed for everything. Anci returned from school and found out her mentally challenged Uncle Erno had been collected by authorities. Thereby, a family link fell off Anci's family chain.

Shortly after Anci had left for school on the morning of his departure, Mama Regina mustered words from her bed and asked, "How is everything, Erno?"

Wearing his uniform and proudly saluting his mother, Erno, in his customary slow drawl, replied with twinkling, smiling eyes, "Everything is fine, Mama, never better." Before Erno shut the apartment door for his final time, he belted, "I will be home soon for dinner. Mama, I love you."

"I will wait for you, Erno. I will wait ..."

Regina's wailing cries continued for days. Then the wailing stopped, and the tearful cries continued. When the tears stopped, the cries continued.

The second Regina would hear the house key in the door, she'd yell, "Erno, is that you?"

"No, Mama, it's just me" got the best of everyone's nerves. So, members of the family trained themselves to knock on the door at the same time they announced themselves to avoid Mama Regina crying out, "Erno, is that you?" She whimpered herself to sleep nightly, her last words being, "The good Lord only keeps me alive to see you, my Erno, come home. Wake me when he gets back."

The impoverished Daches family had been living in the ghetto for years prior to June 1944, when Nazis, drawing a red circle on the city's map, designated where Jews were to be collectively separated from the rest of the population. The Daches family could not afford more than the slums. The whole idea behind Jews being persecuted because they owned everything certainly was senseless to poor Jews like the Daches family.

Anci's baptism papers served as her freedom passport. The small piece of flimsy paper allowed the child to maneuver around the armed ghetto gates. Anci managed to find Erno, and not too late. She was with him when he was issued his last meal: a single small roll.

Kind-natured Erno asked, "Want any?"

Anci grabbed the roll out of his hand and shoved it down her smiling mouth like the crazed wild animal she was.

"It was not any kind of bread; it was crispy on the outside and soft inside. Butter would have made it great!" she would later describe.

The next day, Erno boarded a train. Grandma Regina knew only what she was told. "He was sent to fight in the war." But most likely, "Erno was not fighting in any war," Anci would overhear Clara and Flora whisper to each other outside of Regina's earshot. In upcoming days, Clara and Flora repeated, "He didn't go to war, but where he went, I don't know," as if some new information would form out of thin air. They took turns starting their short dialogue.

"I think the issued uniform was an easy way to rouse Jewish young men away from their families without suspicion."

"Anci said Erno was taken away in a railcar."

"I don't know what that means, but something tells me that's not good."

Events wouldn't become clearer until sometime in the future after the Russians overthrew the Nazis in 1945 and the Jews learned that cattle cars deported Jews to killing centers. Not knowing whether their beloved Erno was dead or alive or being tortured was unnerving.

Jews were under tight restrictions. They weren't permitted to walk outside their ghetto anymore, except for Anci. Anci had to admit that Clara did a Godly service foreseeing and obtaining the lifesaving, white baptism paper for her. She knew Clara was not able to acquire a baptism paper for herself. She'd worked herself hard to earn the money, but the priest only accepted Anci with the excuse, "She is a child." It wasn't fair. Anci knew she should have been a better daughter, and she had put her Mutter through hell, not being the easiest child.

No matter what, Mutter did not abort me!

It was at the very moment when that thought crossed her mind, as she was sitting in the abortion clinic, that Anci made her decision. *I choose my baby over my husband's wishes! Grandma Regina didn't "get rid of it," and she had Erno; Mutter Clara didn't "get rid of it," and she had me, no matter how hard things got! My mind is made up!*

With her decision firmly set, Anci picked herself up and proudly walked her spreading ass out of the doctor's office. Rubbing her belly, she glanced at her watch and realized the only things getting killed that day were the extra hours before she called her husband to pick her up, along with any notion of telling Big Steve her decision.

8

ANCI WALKED AROUND during the remainder of her extra time, allowing her mind to float back to incidences she had deliberately shut away in the past.

With Arthur and Erno gone, Leo's rage grew to a new boiling point. Nerves were shattered. One night, a hard, persistent banging on their door shook them from their sleep. Flora, Clara, Regina, Anci, and Leo just about soiled themselves. No one was bravely stupid to answer the door, especially in the middle of the night. Everyone knew of the midnight knock.

Jewish persecution had spiraled. Buildings were demarked with swastikas, and stores and possessions were stolen from the Jews and handed over to the Jude haters. This was the mad order of the day. All fighting-aged men in the ghetto were deported. Everyone in the apartment was convinced the Jew haters were coming for the only remaining man, old Leo. Under Nazi law, the Jude Yellow Star was mandatory for all Jews to wear. The Yellow Star of distinction made Jews target practice for the gentiles who openly spat and cursed them on their forced exodus from their homes to their ghetto imprisonment. No matter what, the Daches family stuck together; no matter how crazy Leo was, they didn't want him taken. Their numbers were already dwindling. All they had was each other!

Regina whispered to Leo, "Who the hell is banging on the door?"

"The copulating Nazis are here to take one of us!" Leo said. "One of us may never come back," he added timidly, clutching his heart.

"Who do you want?" Flora shouted to whoever was on the other side of the door.

"Flora!" a man's voice exclaimed.

Flora recognized the voice and rushed to unlatch the door. Everyone else— Leo, Regina, Clara, and Anci—gasped, afraid a spray of officers would greet them. The door opened to a highly decorated military Nazi official. Still holding his heart, Leo collapsed into the whole of the sofa, which was his bed. He wished he could run and hide like the rest of the Germans, when the light switch turned on. Oh, but those were German roaches, not people.

Where the Nazi official Kornelius and Flora first encountered each other is a mystery. What is known is that he asked for her hand in marriage right there, and then within five minutes of his knock on their slum door, Flora realized, *This is my ticket out. I am going! So,* Flora said, "Yes!" Without a moment's pause, she put on her coat over her nightgown and got into his car, leaving her clothes and everything behind except for her small bag of incidentals that contained a toothbrush, creams, and other personal items. Only later did she tell Anci, who went and tracked her down at a fancy hotel where the couple was staying, that there was a backstory Flora herself had recently learned.

Apparently, Kornelius's Nazi occupation as a medical doctor assigned him to head up the operation that dug through all medical records in Hungary to identify the Jewish population for the purpose of Eichmann's "final solution," extermination. Kornelius was shocked and disturbed when he uncovered that his own mother, the biggest anti-Semite he had ever met, was actually born to a Jewish mother. Highly troubled by what he felt was his mother's betrayal, he sought vengeance against her in a way that would devastate her the most. His knee-jerk plan was to marry the ugliest, poorest Jewish girl he knew. Flora came to his mind, and, hence, he knocked on the Daches' slum door. Anci was proud of Flora for having it so good, from what she could see at the hotel room visit.

Flora wore silks and satins, stockings, a feather in her hat, perfume, and a new watch. *Not bad for an ugly girl. I guess luck is more important than beauty.* That luck would all change, but no one would know until it did.

ANCI CHECKED HER WATCH and called Big Steve from a pay phone.

"Okay, come and get me." She wrapped the three hundred dollars meant for the abortion into a paper tissue and stashed it into nature's purse for safekeeping—in her bra under her left bosom.

Big Steve pulled up in his car, reached over the passenger side, and swung the door open, smiling. "So, how we doing?"

"I don't know how we are. I am sh*tty but proud," she answered, guilt-free with her morals in check.

Big Steve called the doctor the next day. He knew his wife better than Anci thought.

"The doctor said he never saw you in his life!"

"Don't you remember this is a N I C E country? What do you expect? Sure, the doctor is going to deny anything! He doesn't want to go to jail!"

Weeks and months came and went. Anci skipped all necessary prenatal checkups. The pregnant woman had a difficult time believing her offspring would not be born "as strong as Hungarian bulls!" While buying time, Anci played her role as the obeying wife, preparing both their lunches for their workday and taking care of other household chores to the best of her abilities.

Suspecting nothing unusual, Anci placed a call to Big Steve's employer when she saw he had left his lunch on the kitchen counter.

"Let Steve know he didn't lose his lunch. I didn't forget to make his lunch. Steve left his lunch at home."

"Steve Nagy? He hasn't worked here in two weeks, Mrs."

"*What?*"

"Sorry, Mrs., I don't know what Mr. Steve Nagy is doing. I can only assure you the Steve Nagy I know hasn't punched in for the last two weeks."

The lied-to pregnant mother fumed in anger. Anci grabbed the newspaper Big Steve had left in the kitchen as if she were grabbing his neck and wrung it with both hands. She then tossed "the son of a bitch" newspaper in the garbage. Onto the kitchen floor, a smaller newspaper had floated out from the larger newspaper. Anci's seething eyes scanned the print prior to throwing it away.

"What in mother's Lord's ass is this?" Anci yelled at the top of her lungs.

The only English word she comprehended was *races*.

"His mother's stinking vagina. Big Steve is gambling! I know horse's penis about this man! He is lying. The only thing he is working is *me*! I'm not anyone's fool!"

Anci was a hot-tempered, crazed Hungarian. Once her mind was set, nothing, but *nothing*, would alter her conviction. She carved her own laws on mountains of megaliths, not just stone. Stone could be moved, even tossed, but a mountain named Anci couldn't be budged. Anci drastically decided, "Big Steve is *out*!"

She changed the locks to their apartment. She sent half his belongings flying out the window. Each toss traveled with an order, the least hostile mentionable. "Tiny Napoleon bastard needs to crawl back to the dirty hole he came from: his mother's stinking vagina! *Kiss my ass*, you bastard, and rot to death!"

Every ending is a new beginning. Every exit is an entrance. Steve exited Anci's life, and Country Katy entered. Purely by coincidence, Country Katy contacted Anci with news of her own the night that coincided with the day Anci discarded Big Steve. Country Katy had thrown out her Steve too. This Katy was the type of woman who found men to be as easily dispensable as expired milk. Katy was as much butch as her husband was effeminate. She needed a man more solid than her, not someone she blew over like a hurricane by merely raising her voice. Country Katy called Anci out of desperation. Katy hated nothing more than being alone.

Friendship between the two gals grew, almost as fast as Anci's belly. In her last trimester, absolute panic and desperation set in. Suddenly, Anci's reality hit her like a good kick in the ribs.

"Everything is going to be all right, Anci. There is nothing for you to worry about. You will give birth to a child in America. Imagine that: a born American!

You will be giving the greatest gift God can give. Already, you are a wonderful mother. Think of everything we had to go through to be a part of this great nation. Your child will just be born into luck," Katy told Anci.

"Peasant Katy, you are made out of some special stuff. You know how to roll the right words off your tongue. You make people happy to perform circus tricks for you."

Deep down, Anci felt Katy had her back, and if her friend didn't, the pregnant woman still had nowhere else to turn. On this rationale, Anci packed her small closet of thrift shop-acquired clothes and moved in with Katy the next day. Much would happen before she gave birth to her American-born child.

FRANK SINATRA and Elvis Pelvis Presley were among the popular song artists at the time, hitting the airwaves that bobby-socked girls swooned to. Chuck Berry's "Riding Along in My Automobile" spoke directly to the privileged young American. Back in Hungary, automobiles were few and far between and afforded only by government dignitaries, rich royals, and visiting foreigners.

Emulating Jackie Kennedy, American women wore white gloves and little pill hats when they stepped out of their homes. They wore brooches, white pearl necklaces with matching pearl stud earrings, and wind-defying sprayed hair. All city women wore a skirt or a dress with their prized stockings. At night, ladies placed their heads down on silk-encased pillowcases to keep their hairstyle in place until they revisited the beauty parlor in a week. Bonnet blow dryers were cumbersome, good enough for the young girls in the family, but grown ladies wouldn't dare do their hair themselves!

In the morning, the women prepared a breakfast feast, kissed their husbands, and handed them their bagged lunch as they headed out the door to work. Silver spoon-fed babies were well cared for by mothers, and older siblings toted their lunch boxes and carpooled to school. On errand day, husbands' shirts were dropped off at the cleaners to get starched, in between the grocery store and a slew of other stops, like the pharmacist and the shoe cobbler. Many housewives even had maids take care of household chores. Usually, those same wives found a way to fit in a weekly martini lunch with their girlfriends.

Pretty much, that was the scenario Hungarians imagined American house-wives' lives entailed. Songs or movies of the day did not represent any part of a recent refugee's existence. Anci and her friends could not identify with the American way; they only dreamed of it.

Two unrelated women cohabitating in this N I C E country in 1959 was appalling. Women like Anci and Katy living together were like hydroponic plants, seedless watermelons, lunar landings, rollerblades, mobile telephones, automatic vacuum cleaners, calculators, flat-screen color televisions, computers, or electric cars—they were unheard of at the time! Unrelated women didn't live together, and they certainly didn't stand up to men in those days. Not in America. They didn't have to. Not the white women, anyway.

White women were well compensated for giving birth to their white children. Chances to obtain an easy lifestyle for this privileged group were greater than any other. Everyone in America did their best to copy the infiltrated images portrayed in magazines and billboards and television programming. Not all lived up to their societal expectations, but the demands were nevertheless openly stated and out there. For that matter, people stayed married for better or for worse, no matter how bad the worst became. That included well-to-do wives who looked the other way when their husbands cheated. Jackie Kennedy was the perfect example for women to follow. After all, most women depended on their husband's paycheck because they didn't have work experience to fall back on that would afford them their accustomed lifestyle.

Country Katy was the big sister Anci always wanted, and Anci was the company Katy needed.

"We would make a perfect couple if one of us was the opposite sex," Katy would say.

"We make a perfect combination like a good kielbasa sandwich: one the bread with butter, the other the sausage. One provides the money, the other the hot spice," Anci would add. Then they both laughed.

Katy lost her beauty parlor job and became a draft person in an architect's office. Luckily, the place of employment needed another person. Katy vouched for Anci, and she was in. Being an American professional in the same workplace, Country Katy was just Katy from that point on. "Anci" was an endearing way of saying "little Anna" in Hungarian. At work, Anci was called her Americanized name, Ann, which was not confusing since Anci's birth certificate stated that her first name was Anna. Humbly grateful, Ann lived and worked with her best friend, relying on her more each day as her stomach stretched to enormity and fatigue increasingly consumed her.

Since Katy did Ann's job at work, Katy attempted to teach Ann cooking skills. Katy hoped Ann would be good for something. Katy was dreaming!

The more I can do, the more Katy is going to make me do. I can't do what I can't do. Why do I have to be so smart? Ann thought to herself.

After throwing away a few burned meals, Katy resorted to delegating kitchen cleanup detail as Ann's household contribution. *Surely, if one can't cook, one can clean.* No matter how hard Ann tried, though, she failed. Something more was happening with Ann that no one understood. Sadly, she wouldn't be diagnosed with Asperger's for another fifty-three years. Consequently, no one around her was familiar with Ann's set of hindering circumstances. And no one had the time and patience to teach Ann a task requiring eye-hand coordination. On top of which, growing up hungry in dirt-poor squalor and the hard conditions she was exposed to back in her old country did not help Ann become a socially finessed human. Most of us would have perished under her experiences, but she graduated valedictorian from Hard Knocks U.

Cleaning the kitchen after dinner, Ann broke half the plates. "The first two by accident, the others because I am so damn frustrated doing this sh*t," she admitted. Her excuse: "I don't do well with authority," as in, she couldn't take Katy telling her what to do. The woman worked with five thumbs on each hand, rendering any task impossible. In the kitchen, Ann broke more dishes than she put away. Katy remained calm. She laughed off the mishap while, unbeknownst to Ann, Katy cleverly calculated the charges to be added on to

Ann's portion of the next rent bill. There were consequences to be paid, just like in life.

In response to Katy's laughter, Ann's temper cooled in the kitchen. Katy had the patience of a mother with her young, something Clara did not have the strength to exert on Ann's strong will. Katy was a "shrewdie-pie," and she questioned if Ann played her. Regardless, Katy handled Ann best.

Not giving up on her friend, Katy attempted to teach Ann how to clean a house. Handed a broom, Ann lifted the rug and swept the dirt underneath. Katy, on to Ann's game, folded the rug and hid it under the bed. Ann, in response, still did not utilize a dustpan and simply swept the dirt under the couch or the bed. "It worked for Mama Regina. Good enough for us then, good enough for us now." Old habits die hard for most. But that idea is heightened for those with Asperger's. Add not taking authority well and that led to Ann doing as she pleased.

"No, Ann, that's not how things work. Maybe you didn't know any better. Around here, we do it only one way—the right way."

Ann replied, "Isn't it time you take a bubble bath, Katy, you old whore? I will make you one now."

Katy, overwhelmed by Ann's thoughtfulness, began readying for the act of dissolving the day away.

"It's good, yeah, Katy, you are soaking?"

"Yes, Ann, wonderful."

Gloating, Ann lifted the rug and swept everything underneath it. *What Katy doesn't see, she doesn't know,* Ann thought with a smirk. *I outsmarted her.*

ONE NIGHT AFTER BRINGING groceries home, Katy directed her useless friend to put them away while she soaked in her bubble bath. Upon her return to the kitchen, ready to prepare a meal for them to eat, Katy thought she had lost her mind. Half the items were nowhere to be found.

Frantically, Katy yelled, "Ann, I am pulling out my hair. I have to go back to the grocery store!"

"What in the Lord's ass for?" Ann called out.

"Anci, I must have left a bag there. Half the f**king items I bought are in my mother's vagina ... that store!"

"What are you walking around doing, looking like an idiot child only a mother could love. Katy, what are you looking for?"

"Ann, where are the retarded sardines? I bought a half a dozen devil f**ked cans of sardines! What did the stinkers do, swim up some rotted father's stupid, f**king penis?"

"Come here, next to me, my Katy," Ann said, not budging her pregnant self, lying in bed.

Katy walked closer to tell her friend she was hungry and was not going to bed without eating. As Katy neared, Ann turned to her side, lifted her pillow, and exposed all the canned food Katy was looking for under the money satchel Grandma Regina used to keep money in.

"Katy, it is all here."

Ann laughed; Katy laughed harder. Katy laughed at Ann for her childhood innocence. Ann laughed for the sheer joy—she had done something right, without much effort, even if only to make her friend laugh ... until she cried.

Until then, Ann didn't have a clue that other people didn't have the same customs as her family regarding food as money. Anything worthwhile went guarded under Grandmother Regina's pillow for safekeeping, where the woman, incidentally, lay most of her life away. Regina practiced what she preached. Her motto was: "If you have enough time to sit down, take a load off, put your feet up, get comfortable." This motto would be passed down for generations.

9

DEPRESSED, TIRED, AND FEELING sorry for herself on her routine route to work, Ann couldn't resist rummaging through a heap of discarded clothes she noticed tossed onto a curb. The pile was an entire layette of baby clothes! Ann was so happy she took a seat at the curb, next to her newly found treasure, and cried. *Now, I understood why I had to make these treacherous long walks in the cold and snow.* Not to jinx her good fortune, she spit on her two forefingers and managed to mouth the words, "Thank you, good God," through quivering lips. She missed God's reply, *"Don't thank Me yet. You still have to carry the goodies to work and back home."*

Before long, Katy discovered something sweet for herself: a sugar daddy named Adolf. Adolf compensated for his infamously shared name, and his old age, by spoiling Katy with expensive toys. A brand-new car, for starters, was a marvelous gift to convenience Katy's life. The materialistic gesture earned Adolf a title, as Katy pronounced it in the worst kind of broken English, "a sweet-hard."

"I thought about that, Katy," Ann said. "A sweet-hard ... isn't that a sucker? What a perfect name."

Adolf told Katy he could give her everything but his last name ... he was married. He was ugly, too, but Katy didn't care; when she did what he wanted, she turned out the lights. Adolf, "sweet-hard," was another one of those bald-headed men with a closely trimmed, horseshoe-shaped haircut. Like all men of that era, shaving hair completely off was not an option. Mr. Clean, an animated figure, was the only shiny bald man allowed to be sexy. To Adolf's benefit, he dressed very well, drove a fancy car, and dined Katy and Ann at dinner clubs. Attractively to these two young Hungarian females, Adolf didn't leave until he spent the wad of money he came with, and his time never extended longer than a weekend. Best of all, he only showed up once a month. Adolf "sweet-hard" was tailor-made for Katy.

"I could use a sugar daddy like you in my life, Adolf," was all Ann had to say.

On Adolf's next visit, he planned to bring along his friend Sidney Zucker to introduce the "two hot Hungarian dames." Sidney didn't mind that Ann was pregnant because, according to Ann, "I am thirty years younger."

Katy told Ann what she knew about Sidney before Ann was introduced to him. This way, there were no secrets. American-born Sidney didn't speak Hungarian, was married with grown children and currently contemplating whether he should begin divorce proceedings. Up to that point, Sidney was an admirable son of a rabbi, and he had lived his entire life in Flatbush, New York. Sidney, honorable and faithfully monogamous to his wife for over thirty years, suddenly decided he wasn't happy.

He described his adult years as one long sleepwalk. He was in a cold sweat, sitting on a fence otherwise known as a midlife crisis. As a young man, he bought into and followed America's indoctrination: "the American dream." He married his high school sweetheart, mortgaged his life up to his eyeballs, raised two children, and always kept a dog. If Sidney didn't mind that Ann was more than eight months pregnant, she wasn't going to mind that he was old and married.

Zucker means sugar in German. Put that together with Sidney, and he would have been more age-appropriate for Ann's mother than her, which would make Sidney, literally, Ann's sugar daddy. Ann preferred older men; she found them to expect little, while they were safer and more forgiving of her antics and more generous. *Old farts quietly understand they have to percolate—buy and do—if they want a young chick-a-dee like me.*

Plenty of others idolized Sidney's life. Many men had sacrificed their lives and failed to obtain Sidney's achievements. Many also tried and tried again to provide for their families the way Sidney did. Yet Sidney was ready to discard his pleasant suburban life, calling his successes a waste of time. His claim slapped many men in the face, saying they were blind sheep following society's doctrines. But he couldn't fight how he felt.

His head and his heart were in two different places. George, his brother—who had a metal plate in his head—owned a conscience and nicely pointed out, "Yeah, Sidney, you can't see all you have because your head is stuck up your ass." From Sidney's perspective, he had gravitated away from his wife. Her life was the children; his life became the job. Sadly, when the children left, except for seasonal visits, he and his wife discovered they didn't know each other anymore.

Like other men experiencing a midlife crisis, Sidney translated his peaceful humdrum existence as nothing to live for. He didn't want to *just* age gracefully. He wanted more. Sidney wanted Father Time to set the clocks backward. The sixty-plus-year-old wanted a second chance. He wanted fun and excitement, and finding a young woman was his first objective in fulfilling his goal.

THROUGHOUT THE DAY PRIOR to meeting Sidney, Ann had an awkward hunch. *Something's going to be different today!* She hoped she liked the "fella" Adolf was introducing her to that evening. Adolf had a New York accent, and "fella" was how he referred to Sidney. She hoped she wouldn't regret wasting her time.

When Ann was introduced to Sidney—a pink-skinned, freckle-faced man who wore his brash ginger, wavy hair severely parted to the side—Ann thought he looked like a man who didn't forget to wash behind his ears before buttoning up his white collared shirt. His tie wasn't bad either. *I am a European woman who appreciates that Sidney did not just slap on cologne to cover up any dirt and smell.*

Katy and Adolf sat watching television with Ann and Sidney on their first date. The two Hungarian girls each interpreted the programming differently. They agreed on only one thing: There would be as many interpretations of an American program as there were Hungarians who watched. Each interpretation was as diverse as fingerprints—no two were alike.

Other than owning one pair of decent shoes, Ann owned the worst case of intolerance. She was also sensitive to the slightest high- or loud-pitched noise or flashing light from the television. It was enough to bring attention on her for acting differently. The best way to explain Ann in social situations was the awkwardness others felt in her presence.

Within minutes of the men's visit, Ann decided Sidney was more than her nerves had bargained for. *This one can leave now* was all her mind kept ordering. The agitated, aged redhead, shaking his ice in his scotch-and-water glass, was testing Ann's ability to maintain a civilized composure. Movements on the nonstop black-and-white talking box, the popping gunshots, people talking over the noise, and the *American gibberish* she didn't understand, all layered one on top of the other, were pushing Ann's nerves to the limit. Ann's world was progressively swirling out of control. As a rule, needing control and the threat of losing control caused Ann to become dangerously out of control. On top of it all, the continuous sound of Sidney's ice hitting the sides of his empty glass progressed from being a wrecking ball to a jack hammer.

This one shakes that glass like a bad baby shakes a rattle, for godsakes! Coincidentally, Katy and Adolf were seated directly behind Ann, laughing out loud at the joke being told on the television program they were all supposedly watching. Ann misconstrued the timing of events. *Are these degenerate imbeciles laughing at me? I am confused! Only their stupid moron mothers, who bore them, would know.*

Her thoughts spiraled further out of control. *Sidney's foot thumping like a scratching dog has to stop!* Ann could feel she was about to lose her cool. She was like a pot of boiling water, ready to overflow and make a mess. Attempting to stop and control her environment, Ann clutched Sidney's rattling hand with one hand and his shaking leg with her other hand. For help, Ann yelled to Katy in Hungarian,

"Godforsaken one is shaking like he is a toy wound too tight. I have to make him stop. If he doesn't, I am afraid I will give him a shaking he will never forget."

Not understanding her words, Sidney simply smiled and said, "Aren't you a doll! Yes, I am due for a new one." Obviously, his understanding of her actions was different from her intention.

Fortunately, Adolf did the translating between English and Hungarian, smoothing out Ann's words. Ann was glad when he removed Sidney's glass from his hand. Only a millimeter of a second spared Sidney from having Ann shove ice cubes down his throat.

Unfortunately, no one was in the clear yet! The television box still blasted. Katy looked over to the couch from the kitchen where she was refreshing beverages and noticed Ann's eyes bugging out of her head and her hands covering her ears. Ann was cursing in Hungarian and nodding her head vigorously back and forth.

Katy ran up to Ann and pulled her arms down away from her ears. "What the hell is with you? How are you acting? We are in company. You look like a mother's stupid child."

"Turn the noise of the f**king television down. What, is everybody deaf? I can hear this God f**king crap from the neighbor's apartment! All New York got free radio for godsakes!"

"Okay," Katy laughed. "You know these old farts are deaf; they have earwax and hair growing in their ears."

"You don't know how close I got to beating the pulp out of this *fella* jerking off the glass. If these old turkey vulture necks don't watch it, I will pull every last hair out of their donkey ears and their rat noses too, so they hear. Then I will pluck every last hair out of their head and shove the entire mess down their throat so they can't say anything because they will be choking. That ought to teach them not to laugh at me, and that will really give the redhead a reason for him to shake his hands and legs. I will make him feel like a dying cockroach on its back. It's taking everything I have to not kick him in the *kartoffelwurst*!"

"My sweet Ann, no one was laughing at you. We are laughing at the funny show, not you."

"No one was laughing at me? Your mother's a dirty whore! Don't lie, Katy!"

No one was laughing at Ann. Overstimulation caused by the noise from the television, the rattling ice, and meeting Sidney proved to be too much. It certainly would have been helpful for everyone if people were aware of Asperger's symptoms in these times.

Katy, practicing the constraints of a saint, asked, "My sweet dear Ann, what's a kartoffel-whatever?"

"Kartoffelwurst is German for potato sausage, *Katy*!"

"Okay dear, we will buy some kartoffel and slap it on a plate to eat instead of looking to kick Sidney. Everything will be fine now. I won't give anyone any more troublemaking ice."

Katy prepared more drinks, one for Sidney and another for herself. Water poured over ice was Katy's customary drink to uphold appearances, as if she were imbibing. However, hoisting back vodka was Katy's medicine to deal with Ann's rare form tonight—rare, that is, for anyone else but Ann's usual self as Katy had learned from living with her.

As Katy poured herself another shot, and this time added it into a glass of water, she grappled with what to say next to Ann. "Keep the boys entertained, Ann," she shouted, thinking, *I hope Ann understood that I mean to behave ladylike with a smile on her face and sitting pretty. At the same time, I hope the gentlemen know they are not being neglected. I just have to calm myself.*

The television's rapidly moving action frames jumped into scrolling, blurred horizontal lines, which triggered Ann to turn her head, cover her eyes, and yell, "Oh my God, bad for the eyes. Bad for the eyes! Make it stop! Turn off this whore f**ked television! It is making me *crazy*!" Her hand rose to block the painful view of the television. She squinted her eyes shut and sat down.

Katy ran to Anci and crouched down. "What in Jesus's mother's f**king God are you doing again? When I told you to entertain the boys, this is not what I meant. You are going to scare these nice men away."

"Katy! This television is killing me."

"You are a real piece of work, Ann, you know? Now sit still, Ann, and behave."

Sidney adjusted the TV antenna with tin foil, and the programming resumed without any more jumping horizontal lines.

Katy handed Sidney his refreshed drink with a smile. "Sorry, no ice, darling. Ann likes you."

"Yes, Katy. Adolf told me Ann is very nervous. She hasn't dated much and is terribly shy," Sidney said.

Then Katy sat down, butting her body up to Adolf as she placed his "sweet-hard" arm around her shoulders.

Ann's baby in utero kicked a good solid one into her sides. Ann's eyes bulged in a knee-jerk reaction. Her breathing altered into a pant. Confused by her body, Ann stared straight ahead. Katy was pleased Ann seemed calm. From what Katy saw from the back of Ann's head, she wasn't moving. Ann was sitting quietly. *Good, now Ann is trying to be a benevolent hostess and watching the television, or this vodka is calming my nerves.*

Despite Katy's beliefs, the blubbering on the talking black-and-white box was not where Ann was focused. Nope, above all else, the life somersaulting inside her belly stole Ann's attention. Playing mother hen, Katy rechecked on Ann during a commercial break and noticed Ann's awkward expression. Concerned, Katy squatted down in front of Ann, placed her hands on Ann's knees, and peered into her face.

"Hey, what's with you?"

Ann's eyes were distant in fear and confusion. Her breathing became louder and deliberate, as if she were in pain.

Katy repeated her unanswered question, "Hey, what's with you?"

"Katy, is she okay?" the men chimed in.

"Ann! We are all talking to you. Answer me!"

Ann was right. She knew this day was different from all others. The pregnant woman exhaled quickly and inhaled slowly. Looking Katy squarely in her eyes, Ann proudly announced the phrase she had been practicing: *"It's time!"*

10

SIDNEY SAID HE CRAVED EXCITEMENT, and his wish was granted on a most memorable first date with Ann. Only one scotch down after his "Hello, how do you do?" in his Flatbush, New York, accent, and he was driving Ann to the nearest emergency room. Ann may have experienced pain during birth, but the administration of "Twilight Sleep" erased any memories of discomfort. Strictly relying on the staff's word and hospital documentation, the birth of her child was recorded as:

Anna Clara Nagy was born: February 20, 1959, at 11:29 p.m. at Mt. Vernon Hospital.

Natural childbirth was not a consideration. Women in these times didn't know a thing about the birthing experience, compared to the hands-on approach chosen by the generation they bore. Fathers did as their fathers' legacies taught them. Men remained far from the birthing action, in a room down the hall. There, men puffed on obnoxious cigars, joked, and swore. They outspokenly hoped they fathered a son, all in the sake of preserving the family name and having someone to pass a ball with and maybe even hand over their business to. Seemingly, the male's job was done once their sperm was successfully donated and again when they responsibly "brought home the bacon" for their "little woman" and offspring.

Jewish people didn't touch bacon. Jewish men instead were raised to "bring home the *gelt*/money." Ann, a closet Jewess, loved her fatback, especially raw with raw onions. She liked bacon cooked, too, and congealed bacon grease and chicken fat with chicken liver chunks in it. That was a great common meal for the Hungarians, eaten with sour pickles and good bread.

There were no males, other than the doctors, in the delivery room. There were certainly no cameras allowed in the delivery room. The idea of it was vile. The whole birth issue was considered animalistic. The nation pretended not to know how women became pregnant. Women pretended to be the Virgin Mary with Child. Any occurrence between couples behind closed doors was not a topic of discussion; America was of high moral fiber and fortitude. Remember, it was a N I C E country!

A week after Valentine's Day, Ann was now the mother of an American-born child. Better yet, her child was legitimate. She was married, even if she wasn't living with her husband. Ann already had done better than Mutter. Clara's words sounded in Ann's head: "Life is like a staircase. If you can take a step up, fantastic. But if you can't, then at least hold the line. Good thing is I didn't go very far. I never made it past the bottom step, so the good news is your job is easy." Long-winded but encouraging because then Clara added with a chuckle, "Being on the bottom of a frog's ass like we are, it won't take much for you to step one up."

Ann sat up in her hospital bed on propped pillows. The nurse was handing Ann her baby to hold for the first time. Oh boy, oh boy, oh boy, Ann wanted a boy! In Hungarian, "*feu*" means boy, so when the staff smiled and said, "You did a good job. You gave birth to a nine pound ten ounce "*fe*" male, Ann understood she birthed a *male*. Ann was sure she'd scored! *Fe must be the Latin prefix for male,* she rationalized. *Finally, I got one thing in life I wanted. I will do the right thing and name my son after my husband."*

Ann never said why a boy was better to have than a girl. But if one had to guess, perhaps her preference for a boy had to do with her role models growing up. Men dictated women's lives. Women suffered the consequences. Ann's father took advantage of Clara, and Clara paid the price. Leo did as he wanted, while Regina's life was restricted and ruined with the burden of children. So having seen this, speculatively, Ann herself would have preferred being a male because of the societal freedoms and greater possibilities in the workforce that men had back in her day. And so, it follows, albeit subconsciously, that it may have been why Ann wished she had a boy. Societal pressures of passing down her husband's family name and a business didn't apply to her, but one also couldn't dismiss that there was a certain recognition of doing something right when one claimed she birthed a son.

Ultrasounds could have saved everyone a great deal of trouble. But the obstetric instrument invented in 1957 by Dr. Donald in England (along with others who contributed to the invention) was not a common practice yet. Women, naturally, carried the pressure of delivering the right sex; hormonal stress and body changes weren't enough to sacrifice. Men didn't know it was their own X and XY chromosomes from their sperm that held the indicative sex factor to their offspring.

Instead of Ann extending her arms to accept her newborn like other excited mothers, Ann motioned for the nurse to lay the baby beside her in the bed. Not wasting a second, Ann unraveled the newborn, like a spoiled child on Christmas expecting a particular present. After tearing off its blanket, Ann undid the safety pins of the cloth diaper to check its sex. You guessed it! No disposable diapers invented yet.

Leaving the baby exposed, Ann called the nurse. "Hey!" she yelled, pointing to the genitalia. Incorporating grunts into her sign language, the confused mother vehemently indicated she was brought the wrong baby. She pushed her child away as if she'd received a wrongly delivered deli sandwich. She was sure they had brought her the wrong baby. She'd ordered the one with the pickle in the middle!

It took the hospital staff a full day to locate a Hungarian-speaking doctor. Ann knew the Americans would tell her what they wanted, and she was disinterested. She wanted a boy. Needless to say, the words the doctor spoke weren't received well. Ann put on a scene that no one had ever witnessed before. The Hungarian doctor told Ann the long and short of it and shoved the baby into her hands, sternly directing her to "Deal with it!"

She felt like a monkey at the zoo. Apparently, the nurses were told to keep a watchful eye on the crazy Hungarian. Observation became mandatory for the well-being of the child. And then they really took double takes when they saw Ann breastfeed. At first confused by the staff's constant stares, Ann interpreted, *They never saw white women breastfeed; they think I am barbaric!* Money bought formula and bottles to take care of that issue; minorities breastfed. *What's that make me, a white minority?* Only sometime later in America would mothers breastfeed to bond with their babies.

This breastfeeding thing wasn't bonding to Ann; it was mere obligation. Teachings in the old country dictated that mother's milk contained the most nourishment to build a strong immunity. Besides, Ann wouldn't be able to afford baby formula once home even if she chose to bottle feed. After all, Mutter Clara breastfed Ann until she was four years old and not longer—only because Clara's lactation ducts dried up. It was the way impoverished Clara ensured her child was fed.

Too weak and lazy to enter the unknown awaiting her in the outside world, Ann planned on remaining in the hospital until they kicked her out. She wasn't lying when she motioned that she was too weak to stand on her own two feet. She just meant it monetarily, while the hospital staff concerned themselves with her physically. At least at the hospital, Ann received everything she needed for her and her baby. There, Ann was fed well and slept all day. *Why would I want to leave? I would have to be crazy!*

Ann slept while the nurses watched her in the daytime. Unsupervised at night and during the nurses' meal breaks, she slipped away to roam her surroundings. She found she was the only white woman on the ward. She concluded that white people weren't having babies in America anymore. The idea was not so outlandish. Hungary had a zero growth rate in 1950 and close to negative 5 percent growth rate in 1959.

Having grown up in wartime depression and the Holocaust, Ann did not entertain healthy recollections concerning babies. Before the war, she was the last-born burden—the baby in her family. Ann witnessed soldiers rid mothers of their babies by gunpoint at the edge of the Danube River. The blue river turned red from their blood. Ann saw people's bodies, including babies and children, float downstream face down. She stood and watched mothers with crying babies get shot first with a single bullet for both, before the mothers holding more obedient silent ones went next. She heard stories of babies being smothered by their mothers in the ghetto to keep their babies quiet when they began to cry as a Nazi passed by. She heard weeping mothers grieving those dead smothered babies. She also heard plenty of stories of cursed, unwanted children like herself, born burdening their families.

With this being her only experience with babies, she marveled at the ease with which these women in adjacent rooms displayed love for their newborns and their visiting children. The room she at first occupied alone was now filled with other mothers in her same situation. The hospital's placement of Ann in the indigent ward worked out best for her. She didn't feel like an isolated case. Like Ann, the other indigent women were not visited by their newborns' fathers either. Visiting hours in Ann's section didn't bring open-armed, grinning fathers or kissing grandfathers who presented well-deserved chocolates or flowers. Their society of dominant, strong women played roles of both mother and father to their children and was an education Ann honored receiving.

Ann watched in awe. The interaction between these mothers and their babies was magical. No matter how many children she had, the mother loved them all. When their visiting children came, there was always room for another in a group hug. Their entire bodies caressed. The exchange of energy between them was mutual, each giving the other what the other needed. Ann had never witnessed such beauty. She hoped she gained their soft, gentle ways through osmosis. "Come and give Mama a hug," were words she learned from its constant repetition.

They all cooed and giggled with their babies. Ann did *not* feel the same way. Her baby was a strange, foreign entity and not an extension of herself. She was colder than any thermometer could gauge. Ann wished she could display the same love to her child, but she didn't know where she was supposed to extrapolate this emotion. Ann was awkward at showing loving warmth. Her attempt at exuding the emotion was an imitation. The whole concept of love was out of her realm of reach. Coming from her, it was uncomfortable and, therefore, phony.

Ann reasoned: *Americans are so much more loving than the Hungarians.* She perceived love to be a positive byproduct of living a better life. People offered and displayed love from living in a free world. *Maybe humans are innately good. It's their twisted circumstances that change them.*

Wars damaged her people. Hunger, hate, and suffering altered a populace forever. Ann struggled to understand how mothers loved their babies. She equated babies with garbage, mistakes mothers should be wishing to throw away. In the same breath, it was understandable how Ann looked at her baby and thought, *How am I supposed to love this piece of garbage,* and pushed it away.

Ann was more rested nearing the second week of her hospital stay than she had ever felt in her life. Other mothers left in three to five days. She knew she had to leave. But before her release, she had to defy regulations and go to the fortunate ward, where she heard mothers received delivered flowers.

"F**k your mother!" Ann said under her breath, shocked at the difference a walk down the hall made. Eight women shared her room, while one or two white women occupied these other rooms. The eight of them didn't even have one plant. The other rooms had enough flowers to fill a funeral home for a week.

The special people around Ann had become her temporary family. Ann didn't know if she could practice the "love" they shared with their babies, but Ann wouldn't forget them. She thought about her whole family being killed off, well, the good ones, anyway, leaving her with with Flora and her Mutter. Clara was the only one Ann considered of any value. Oh, that reminded her—she had to mail her Mutter a postcard with the latest news.

Dearest Clara:

Congratulations are in order.

You are a grandmother.

Anna Clara Nagy

Born: February 20, 1959

Kisses,

Anci

Anna Maria Nagy was home with her daughter, Anna Clara Nagy, the longest baby born at the hospital at twenty-two inches, breaking the record by two full inches.

"See, Katy, you kept saying I would have twins. I was right. I told you I was giving birth to a horse. After all, only horses are born after ten months," Ann said, laughing. "No one knew how close Little Anna came to being named Steve Junior. Good thing I didn't understand the volunteer handing out birth certificate forms, asking me what I wanted to name my child, when I confused female with (feu) male."

Without Katy being there to interpret for Ann, Ann didn't understand what was being said or know how to read English, so she didn't know she was filling out a birth certificate form. Oddly, Ann thought the paper requested her name in the space provided for the child's first name. That's how both her and her daughter wound up with the same first name, Anna. Mother Ann thought the form was asking for her mother's first name in the space requesting the middle name. The result: her daughter's middle name became Clara. Baby Anna was lucky her mother didn't screw things up worse with her name, considering the half-ass way her mother did things. Had Mother Ann thought they were asking for the father's name instead of her name at the time of the name assignment, Baby Anna's name would have been Istvan or Steve. Now, that would have been a mess of confusion for the child to explain to her peers growing up in the 1960s.

Ann was so confused by the paperwork that she didn't know she'd named her child until checkout time at the hospital when Katy came to take her home. At that point, Ann and Katy looked at the birth certificate and noticed the hospital stamp was next to a large footprint.

"Katy! I really did give birth to a horse; look at the size of that hoof!"

Katy noticed the baby was claimed by both a mother and a father, her husband Steve.

"How the hell did Steve's name get on the birth certificate?" Ann asked. "I don't remember ever filling out forms for this birth certificate."

Katy pointed out that there was no religious affiliation, and Ann was quietly pleased. She didn't want Jewish written on the document, brandishing her or her child. The best part of the whole certificate was the words "United States of America." Her daughter wouldn't experience communism or a dictatorship. Anna Clara Nagy was born a United States citizen. No one could ever take that away from her.

11

ANN WAS OFF TO WORK WITHIN three months with her baby in
tow. She had lost the job where she worked with Katy. The architect firm used
Ann's absence as the perfect excuse to rid themselves of her dead weight. Firm
management was well aware that Katy had been doing both her and Ann's jobs.
Besides, Ann needed to take her child with her to work. She couldn't afford to
pay for a sitter. Fortunately, Ann found new employment in a bakery shop that
had advertised in the newspaper.

Ann ran the shop by herself, so she thought no one would know her baby
was on the premises when she placed Baby Anna in a weave basket on the floor
in the bathroom. As a desperate mother juggling childcare and needing to earn
money, she had no alternative. Every red cent counted for survival, and no one
except Ann ever used the bathroom. Customers entered the pastry shop, placed
their orders, and left.

Two months later, Ann, still stuck in the same low-paying job, anguished for
alternative options to accommodate her rapidly growing baby, who was jammed
into a shrinking weave basket. On a break, Ann picked up her baby to tend to
her without realizing her baby's pinky was tangled inside the basket weave. The
baby hadn't been crying before her mother clumsily yanked her out. But now,

the little one couldn't stop screaming in pain. Ann, short on nerves and unsavvy about how to care for a baby, left the bawling baby in the bathroom, thinking the crying would surely stop. Baby Anna couldn't stop and wouldn't stop crying for two days straight. Mother Ann hated this baby who was causing all kinds of problems. The customers came in and were markedly irritated by the sounds of endless distress cries coming from an unseen baby. Ann thought she would lose her mind. What she lost instead was her job.

Baby Anna's first memory was formulated from the excruciating pain of that broken pinky finger. The baby wept and bellowed for what seemed like an eternity, yet no one consoled her. At first, the little one didn't give up when no one came to help her. She cried louder and longer because of the physical hurt. Resting up from overexertion in between her best attempts at calling for someone to hold her, Anna noticed her surroundings for the first time. She noted the shifting shadows and their locations on the wall as the sun changed direction. The light from the windows came and went twice, with pure pitch-black darkness in between. Her cries to get someone to hold her continued endlessly during that time.

It took a few cycles of thrashing her body to call attention to her hurt before she realized that doing so only made the pain worse. At that point, Anna whimpered in grief—devastated that no one cared. Then she sniveled angrily because no one cared. And then Anna shed tears when she learned she had no one.

Lying on her back, Anna would forever remember the desolate, sinking feeling in the moment she realized no one was coming. Her voice was gone, her throat red and sore, and her body ached from her wasted efforts.

She mustered one last attempt by giving all she had. Suddenly, she felt a different bodily sensation whisking her outside of her body to hover over her physical body. She did not recognize the unclothed, sweaty body and flailing arms and legs sloshing in a pool of urine on a plastic mattress. The body she saw was breathing irregularly. Every labored, inhaled breath then exerted a bursting yelp for help with no sound trumpeting. Her boiling red, screaming face was drenched with tears that escaped her salt-crystalized, shut eyes. Her only sustenance was the cool, salty tears her feverish tongue caught.

"What's that mess of a blob?" she exclaimed with disgust to the intangible being she felt next to her.

"That's you," the soft voice told her, belonging to the intangible being.

"Me? That's me!" The shock drew her back into her body.

Somehow, this baby connected to something, to someone. Someone she was familiar with from previous interactions. Someone Baby Anna had received words of wisdom from, giving her knowledge prior to her earth life. Baby Anna mentally took note of what was transpiring because she knew it was important. She was amazed at the clear and concise messages that entered her mind, even though she knew she only babbled to an intangible ear.

The conversations transpired telepathically. She had exchanged thoughts with this familiar being before and enjoyed His soothing and wise answers. In time, Baby Anna would learn she could call upon Him as often as she remembered to do so.

Collected now, she was at peace, finally recognizing she was being heard. Baby Anna tuned in intently, accepting that this being was present to comfort her. She didn't have a name for this someone at the time. It wasn't the ordinary encounter: "Hello, how do you do? What's your name?" And besides, she didn't know of such a protocol. When recanting the happening to herself in order to etch it into memory, she did not refer to Him by name. Instead, He was the glowing picture image from when she first recognized Him. It wasn't until sometime later that she asked Him what He was, to which He replied, "Global." She understood Glow Ball.

Once she was older, she used that resonating term Glow Ball when she shared this particular occurrence with her closest friend. The purpose was to see if there were others with the same experience since no one she knew talked about such things casually or otherwise. As she matured, she referred to Glow Ball as All Knowing, since that seemed more acceptable and comprehensive instead of a being that may have been misconstrued as cartoonish. After all, All Knowing described Him correctly.

In this moment of great epiphany in the discovery of not having been alone, Baby Anna was so grateful and overjoyed to realize she had someone by her side, someone to talk to, and someone to feed her starved, isolated mind. The glow she felt and saw surrounding her in the moment of His recognition dissipated, but his presence lingered.

She immediately and repeatedly apologized to Him, and later to herself, for not listening to Him sooner. She would have been at peace earlier. Wanting her mother, Baby Anna had dismissed Him numerous times when He'd said, "I am here." The crying baby hadn't realized His significance. When Baby Anna finally accepted Him, she felt and saw a warm *glow* around and through her, and telepathically, Baby Anna asked Him the first of a series of questions.

"Thank you, thank you, thank you for coming!"

"I am here for you, at your asking," He whispered.

"You know everything. Why is it no one came? No one came when I cried."

"And you cried hard, and you cried long, and no one came."

"Right. You know. Why didn't anyone come?"

"The question is: Why did you think you need them?"

"I needed someone to make me feel all right."

"No one came, but you are all right now."

"Yes."

"Why is that?"

Time and thought transpired. Anna thought, *He wants me to figure out the answer myself.*

"Why is it that I am all right when no one came? Why am I all right when no one came? I'm all right? No one came. I am all right, yet no one came. I calmed myself?" Baby Anna repeated, pushing herself to get the answer.

"Did I not come?" He whispered.

"No, no, no. You always come. You are always here. I have to be at peace within myself in openly accepting and trusting You. You are here by my side."

"So, then someone came."

"Yes! You came." This time, Baby Anna shed a tear of joy. Then she asked, *"What about my mother? Why doesn't she come?"*

"Why do you need her to come?" He asked.

"To hold me in her arms and make things right. I don't want to be alone."

"You don't need anyone. You have yourself."

"Myself?"

"You are never alone if you have yourself," He said.

"Why is that?"

"You only have to listen to the voice within yourself, the voice that connects you to Me, and you will find you know everything you need to know. You have all the answers connected through Me."

"So, I have now learned I can be happy knowing I have all the answers I am looking for when I am connected to You. I am never alone. I am so happy." Baby Anna continued, *"Now, I want to ask you more questions."*

"Yes."

"There's a place I see in my mind. I am thinking of it. Is that the place I came from?"

No answer.

"I am picturing it now. It is a bright star after we pass many white lights [in a circular cluster] *against a blackish blue. I see it, and then I am pulled there before I say, 'Yippee! I am home.' You come to me in a whisper at night as I wait for Your words, 'Are you ready?' As soon as I reply, 'Ready,' we are off traveling through a tunnel. Exiting the tunnel, I see* [a circle cluster of] *bright lights, and my home is a star on the far-right side. I say, 'I am home,' and then I remember nothing else. I am picturing it all. I would like to know if this is where I am from?"*

"Yes."

"I have been hearing Your whispering voice from before I got here [on this planet]. *I remember telling You I was tired of being alone. Everyone that I saw as a shining, twinkling light had already gone. You would come around sporadically and ask me, 'Are you sure? You have a while before you are to go. I will give you more time to think about this.'*

"Every time You came back, I replied, 'I am suffering here all alone. Anything has got to be better than this loneliness.' After a few back-and-forths like this, You told me, 'It will not be easy where you are going. Since you were to spend more time alone here, you will be in a new place, spending time alone there.'

"'I am ready to go,' I remember saying then, certain of wanting to be out of there. The same way Your whispering voice disappeared, it returned and spoke, 'Did you think about it long and hard?' I said, 'There's been nothing to do here but to think about it. My mind is made up. I see no one, I hear no one except for when You come around, which seems like very, very long times in between.'"

There was a long silence. Baby Anna repeated herself numerous times before He responded. She had learned from their interactions that He didn't respond when she wanted. He responded when He wanted. Then she thought to ask Him, "That was You in the other place, wasn't it?"

"Yes," was all He said. But that one word was powerfully meaningful to Baby Anna.

Wow! He really was with me since I can remember! What else can I ask Him while He is answering questions right now?

"I have one last question. Why is it my mother and others don't understand me talking to them, while we can talk?"

"Babies are born to have to learn a language, so they have enough time to forget everything they know. Their knowledge would scare adults here."

"So, I have to forget everything?"

"Yes, forget everything," He replied.

"What if I can't, and I remember these things?"

"It will be different."

"Something tells me to be sure to remember them."

That encapsulated Baby Anna's first memory at five months old. Baby Anna went over and over the events that occurred that night, like she would continue to do with moments she found significant in her life to remember. Baby Anna slept most peacefully that night.

When she woke up the next day, the sun was hot, and she was no longer in the slippery-slop she had no control of producing. She was clean, diapered, and on her back. She remembered the crib was up against the furthest right wall, and her body faced the door further along the same right wall where the crib was positioned. This time, the door was open.

Some time had passed, and Katy entered the room in all smiles, asking, "You had a good cry? You've been crying for days, darling."

Baby Anna looked back at Katy, thinking, *You know I've been crying and didn't come? No one came.* Katy clapped her hands loudly and then louder and louder. Baby Anna lay there looking back at Katy without emotion. Katy clapped louder and added "Boo!" to get a response from the baby. Baby Anna didn't respond. *Why should I? They are not coming if I cry anyway.*

Katy shouted to Mother Ann, "Hey come here, your baby is deaf?!"

"Leave that piece of sh*t to drop dead already! It drives me crazy. Forget about her, Katy! Come here!"

Katy left.

They really don't care about me. But now is different than before. Baby Anna was at peace, knowing she was connected to All Knowing. Linked to All Knowing, she reminded herself, *I am not alone.* The tricky part was remembering not to ignore His whispers.

As for Baby Anna's pinky finger, it hurt, and it was in her way for a long time because of the pain it caused. Anna was five when she realized it didn't function right. She had to cup her hand to make her pinky meet the other fingers. At eleven, she told her mother about what transpired with Glow Ball when she was five months old, and Mother Ann remembered the two days she didn't come to her daughter's aid.

"Heeee! You remember that? How do you remember that?" Mother Ann asked with surprise, shaking her head. Mother Ann never said sorry. She said, "That whore Katy told me not to pick you up or else I was raising a spoiled child." Anna, doing her utmost to make the best out of the worst situation, loved her broken pinky. The way it positioned itself made her *look like a lady* when she drank from her teacup.

MOTHER ANN'S DARKNESS was the antithesis of light. She looked at her Baby Anna and only saw ugly garbage. She tied a white knit pom-pom hat over Anna's head, claiming it was "important to cover half the deformed head, concaved on one side due to forceps used during delivery."

Something was wrong, but not with the baby; it was the mother. No pictures supported the mother's fabricated claims of her child's malformation. There were plenty of pictures, first of Baby Anna as a tear-filled infant and then later as a tear-filled child. The framed pictures displayed on Mother Ann's dresser captured cruel reminders of how the child feared her mother. No loving mother would display a framed picture of their child with horror plastered on the child's face for all to see, especially not with the mother smiling.

A lack of attention Mother Ann gave Baby Anna was no longer the problem; there was plenty of attention, but it was negative attention. The snapshots were cruel, encapsulated reminders of Mother Ann's verbal and physical beatings prior to the camera clicking a captured moment of Baby Anna's horrified face. The images screamed despair. There were no visible bruises. Instead, the images reflected the open-mouthed face of painful surprise from just being beaten and slammed back into place, a knock to the back of her head and tears that came from that blow, as well as verbal slander filled with hate while the photographer stepped away. Mother Ann was all smiles when the photographer returned to snap the picture while the baby was a mental mess, wishing she were as far as possible from her crazy mother's vicious hands and words, worried when the next blow was coming.

"Aww, come on, kid, it's not that bad," the cameraman said, trying to get his job done.

"Just take the picture. She is an idiot child. She can't help it," Mother Ann said, posing.

Snap!

Every glance of Baby Anna's own image replayed unwanted memories of past hurts and rising dislike and fear of her dangerous, not-to-be-trusted, abusive mother.

"You rotten animal, good for nothing, the good Lord punished me with you. Do you know how you ruined my life? You are stupid like a hyena; you are as green as a frog and yellow like piss. You are a stupid piece of sh*t, a lousy whore. I hate you. You have a forehead like a horse and a nose like a pig. Who has a forehead like that? Only bad evil ones have a nose like you. You have a crooked mouth like someone kicked you stupid. Who wants you? No one wants you! You are a stupid piece of sh*t. You are a dog's dick; you will never amount to anything."

The woman wouldn't stop. The only difference between the pictures and the mother saying these slanders was Baby Anna's ability to scurry from the pictures. She couldn't pull away from Mother's grips, punches, and throws. Baby Anna didn't know Hungarian, other than the tone and these slanderous terms spewed at her at least once a day or whenever Mother set eyes on her. The second Mother Ann saw Baby Anna, she went at her like a troubled child beating her rag doll.

Baby Anna was in diapers and asleep when she remembered being thrown from her mother's bed into the wall and falling onto the floor, stunned. Not realizing her mother didn't want her, she crawled and climbed her way back to her mother to lie in the bed. Her mother repeated her violent actions, yelling, "Your chin sticks into me and hurts me! How many times do I have to tell you that!" After a few times, Baby Anna crawled away to her room for safety.

Baby Anna had a dismal realization: a river of fear flooded her valley where love was supposed to reside. Throughout Anna's infancy, toddlerhood, and childhood, she couldn't understand why no one but her read her anguish in these pictures that documented her doom. How long was she to be alone at the mercy of her abusive mother? One day, her mother slammed shut a drawer to the dresser, and the pictures toppled over. Her mother left them face down for a while. As Anna grew to reach the counter by climbing up the open dresser drawers, she'd say, "I hate those pictures!" under her breath as she quietly toppled them over on purpose.

As Baby Anna grew into being a toddler, her mother's hatred didn't subside. Anna's heart panged from the hatred she felt her mother held toward her. Each time Mother Ann laid eyes on her daughter, she unleashed the hate held within her. Mother Ann wrongly excused her outbursts as a reaction to living through the Holocaust, her hated life as a bastard child, being an incompetent employee, her self-loathing, and God knows what else. "You're going to pay for all the wrongs done to me!" she'd scream. The torture Mother Ann perpetrated was inexcusable.

Plenty of people suffered without the need to lash out against their own children. Mother Ann had witnessed plenty of abuse growing up, but she had never been a victim of physical abuse personally. Yet, Mother Ann tore her own daughter apart, limb by limb, self-esteem and all. Mother Ann was incapable of loving anyone.

Eight years before the Germans occupied Hungary, Mutter Clara took her two-year-old daughter, Anci, to the park to play with others in the sandbox. "Come, Anci, this nice girl will share her pail and shovel with you." Anci's response was to take the shovel and smack everyone in the sandbox in the head or face with it. Then, she placed a pail filled with sand over the nice girl's head, upon which she played the pail like a conga drum, all the while laughing, "I show you nice!"

After a few such incidences, Clara stopped taking Anci to the park. She had no choice. The other mothers saw her coming with Anci, and they cleared the premises. When Clara attempted to take Anci's hand while they walked together, Anci kicked her in the ass or the shin and ran away, only to return home at dusk. Being told what to do, as in, "Play with the nice girl," was an Asperger's trigger, just like being touched. All that might have been helpful to know.

Love-void, meaning Ann was empty where love should have been in her heart, she was the worst sort of mother. Hate filled her every corpuscle. Little Anna did her best not to cry. It didn't make a difference anyway. She had learned that lesson when her mother broke her pinky. But the beatings became so bad at one point that her cries of pain couldn't be suppressed. She did her best to cry quietly because her crying was an invitation for Mother Ann to beat her unconscious again.

From early on, Anna prudently learned to keep silent and out of sight. After *coming to* from being beaten, sometimes next to her own vomit, most likely due to a concussion, she struggled to gain knowledge of her whereabouts. If she was in her room, she felt safe and hoped the door was closed. If it was open, she shut it. Most times woozy, with the room spinning, she would call out telepathically to her "Glow" vision. Her favorite reply from Him was, *"Are you ready?"* At which she always answered, *"Ready!"* It meant the day was done and she was going to the bright star: *"HOME!"*

One time, while seeing circles of twinkling stars and weak from a beating, she asked All Knowing, *"Why is this happening to me? I am a good girl. I do what I am told, and Mother hates me. Why?"* She would have to repeat herself multiple times. She took this to mean *either He was busy helping someone else and she had to wait her turn, or she didn't ask the right question.* Or it could have been that the question she asked was one she had to ask herself to come to an answer. *"Am I supposed to become a bad girl? Maybe Mother will like me then?"*

"Could you become a bad girl?" He whispered after a long pause.

"Nah, I wouldn't like myself."

"Why not?" He asked.

"I like to do things right. Like Mother says, she doesn't know whose kid I am because of little things, like the way I place my slippers neatly by the bed. She says I didn't learn that from her."

"Interesting."

"Why interesting?" she wondered.

"You didn't learn that from her?" He asked.

"Yeah. I didn't learn that from her."

"But you knew how to do it," He said.

Anna had to think for a while.

"Are You saying I will know how to do things without her?"

"Exactly," He said in His comforting voice.

"How am I going to learn?"

He left that for Anna to ponder.

He did teach me that I am on my own. I should have stayed where I was before here. I was alone over there, though. This is very much worse.

IN ANNA'S TIMES OF NEED, He came at her calling, guiding her through her times of despair with great words of wisdom. She was fortunate to have the ability to connect with Him whenever she experienced perplexing pain. It would be many years before she understood how lucky she was to be able to call upon her greatest gift: All Knowing.

First memories are said to greatly influence and shape lives. Anna's early connection with All Knowing drove her to grasp Its significance. As she grew, she strived to become better and not bitter. With her growth, her words and ways of how to do that blossomed.

With much time, she embraced her life guided by Him, and this evolved to become her truth:

Those without struggle, those who do not experience great pain, extreme negligence, cruelty, hunger, and hatred, aren't pushed to know their greatest gifts: who they truly are, along with guidance and wisdom from an All Knowing. Those who complain of their suffering and do not work through their suffering miss their greatest opportunity to connect to their Highest of Selves. Our hardest moments lead us to ask for help and accept His guidance. The reason humankind is pushed into pain and suffering is to be pushed to learn a lesson by working through the pain, after which the reward of happiness and growth is obtained.

For Anna, finding All Knowing, All Loving, is what helped her survive. The name of the Guiding Light is not where the importance lies. He is *not* God Christ or Jesus or Mohammad or Buddha, if He is not the best and most loving, the most understanding, the most guiding of all. He preaches no hate. He preaches everything we must appreciate.

12

AFTER A YEAR OF LIVING IN WHITE PLAINS, New York, the two Hungarian women, Katy and Ann, decided to part ways. Katy's old boyfriend, Adolf, died—which meant her money train stopped rolling in.

"Good luck to Katy in finding a man with her face and that square body!" Ann boasted. "Katy looks like the typical peasant girl back in the woods where she came from. She is not a looker; she is nothing special, not like me."

Ann thought she was smarter and better than everyone, including God, if there was one. She often said, "God would be lucky to be as smart as me." Moreover, Ann had no filter and she spoke what she called "the truth." The woman was not known for finesse or a care. She had a razor blade for a tongue, another of her many Asperger's traits that would have been good to know.

Where Ann said whatever came to her mind, Katy possessed the uncanny ability to speak kind words through her lying teeth like a charming hissing snake with an extended forked tongue tickling its victim's ear, calculating the right time to strike. "That Katy has a way of convincing people to eat sh*t from her hands, thinking she is feeding them vitamins. This is a gift I wish I can do," Ann repeatedly told her daughter throughout the years.

Ambitiously in search of a new victim, Katy quickly zeroed in on her next target: a Hungarian fellow. Both peasant stocks understood each other better than anyone else, and the two "fell madly in love"—that was Pauli the barber's version of the story. Katy, on the other hand, claimed, "I moved into his tiny, one-room efficiency because of its location in New York City's Hungarian territory."

At five feet two inches, Pauli was too short by most standards but kept his brown hair and clothes meticulously well-groomed. His brown gypsy eyes twinkled, and his mustache umbrella accentuated his gold tooth smile, matching his gold necklaces. Pauli's demeanor was rough around the edges, but he was second to none in treating a client right in his barber chair. At home in his tiny apartment, the tiny man sat proudly on his large money chest, eating his meals and wearing his gold chains, wifebeater, slacks, and slippers. His treasure chest of money was a large wooden box he kept padlocked because, as he showed Little Anna once, it was filled to the rim with green bills. "Anna! Look how all those presidents smile and wink, welcoming me, Pauli, into this great America!"

When Pauli loved Katy, he beckoned her to share his throne. When Katy was no longer invited to sit alongside Pauli, she pulled a seat to the table from the one and only other room they shared.

"The meal turned out good, let us pray," one of them would say.

"I am not an unlucky ass-less dog; I am a proud gypsy peasant!" Pauli said. Their bellies both rolled with laughter.

"That's right, good daddy, you are the gypsy king at a table spread like this."

"My father's dick knows how good God gives it to us."

Both smiling with raised water glasses of head-foaming beer, they hailed in unison, "Praise God, amen, let's eat! Good God is with us."

There was a definite difference between city people from Pest and the country folk from the outer regions of the country, Buda. In America, the New World, Ann still considered herself city folk because of the way she dressed, ate, and read the daily paper—and not only the *Magyar Usag*, the Hungarian paper, but the *New York Post*. Ann understood she didn't understand everything, but she also knew she didn't want to be in a new country, stuck only knowing her old country's language.

Her ambitious goal was to "one day read *The New York Times*." Doing so would be her sign "to move away from the safety net of Hungarians and into the melting pot of America." She would add, "You will see, none of these Hungarians are going anywhere. It's enough for them to have made it to America. They are the peasants. They will die here. The city people, on the other hand, like me, will push onward and move on."

As far as food went, the country folk were known to swim their food in two-inch-thick fat, disgusting to anyone else. There was a large Hungarian population in NYC, and these new immigrants had moved into "German town," otherwise known as Yorktown, Yorkville, or the YUKON area, meaning the phone numbers began with YUK, or YU5, or 985. The Hungarians were so happy they discovered Second Avenue, where up and down 86th Street, Hungarian names hung on store signs, and Hungarians could obtain a Hungarian newspaper across the street from their favorite Hungarian butcher shop, "Hentes," on the corner of 82nd and Second Avenue. For a short while, standing on the corner of 82nd Street and Second Avenue, a Hungarian could pretend to be in their homeland, only better.

No Hungarian could imagine that amount of food stockpiled in the stores. Kielbasa dangled like nunchucks alongside the multitude of sausages, like stuffed liver sausages and blood sausages, next to an array of cold cuts tightly but neatly piled in meat display cases.

"The amounts of food goods are as snugly stockpiled as the Hungarians themselves packed in this store," was a sure bet comment to come out of at least one widely grinning, silver-toothed Hungarian waiting to place her order at the counter.

Hungarians, including Mother Ann, were so excited about their food that they made their sandwiches right there in the shop and ate them standing up before they left. The owner caught on and, before long, arranged tables for his patrons to have designated places to eat. There were no seats, but his intention was to save face for his own people, who looked like uncontrollable, raging Neanderthal savages around food.

Slices of fatback, chicken livers, tongue, and a couple of kielbasas were Ann's usual order. Bologna was a special purchase, bought on an occasion like a birthday when Ann shopped. Katy, on the other hand, purchased pig's feet, ox tails, cow knee joints, fatback, duck fat, chicken livers, and chicken fat. There were other stores selling the same items up and down 86th Street, but they were more expensive and German-owned. Small Hungarian restaurants, small-time grocers, and pastry shops popped up, sprinkled throughout the "German town" neighborhood, and the prospect of Hungarians employing their own fed their hopes in their promising new world, so they supported each other.

WITHIN A YEAR, KATY AND PAULI both received their licenses to tend to people's hair. Each departed for work, chasing the American dream with an attaché case in hand. In the morning, their attachés held their packed lunches. On their return home, their cases carried fists of earned American dollars to be counted and stored. Pauli's monies went stuffed into his money chest-dinner throne, while Katy's were deposited to earn interest in the bank the following morning. Both saved diligently to soon own their own business.

Ann moved to the Big Apple from Mount Vernon, New York, with her Grandma Regina's hand-embroidered money satchel in hand. She was not following Katy but rather another Hungarian friend of hers, Lili, who lived only four blocks from Katy and Pauli.

Sidney continued to assist Ann minimally. Mr. Flatbush, Sidney decided to file for his dissolution of marriage, discounting the years he invested with his wife in order to pursue Ann, who was thirty years younger. Sidney purposefully did not aid Ann any more than he did financially to keep Ann dependent on him. His words were straightforward and honest: "Ann, if ya want more doll, there's no problem. Just say I do, and I will."

Ann moved into 409 E. 84th Street. The downstairs buzzer to the building sounded more like an irritating bug zapper or someone frying in an electric chair when announcing the arrival of guests. As if that weren't deterring enough for company to enter Ann's lair, there were six arduous, nose-bleeding flights to conquer before arriving at her doorbell. The out-of-breath visitor, reaching the final summit, was usually passed out at the top of the stairs or found leaning against the door, hunched over. One hand clutched their heart while the other hand grappled with a stitch in their side.

Unfortunately, not even Boy Scouts were taught to carry a pair of earplugs in their preparedness kit, but entering Ann's domain with the small item would have saved many ears from deafness. Waving surrendering hankies wouldn't be enough here!

Games began when a visitor, albeit Lili, Katy, Sidney, and other male visitors, knocked on Ann's apartment 6A door. On these occasions, Little Anna was allowed out of her imprisoning room. Mother Ann waved her daughter to, "Come watch the show! You might learn something." Mother Ann began her silly slapstick shtick by counting to ten as Little Anna watched at the end of their long foyer, wondering *What's Mommy doing?* as her mother, like a character actress, transformed from depressed to cracking herself up in laughter.

The person at the door knocked again, pleading, "Is anyone home?"

Ann retorted, "Yeah, God curse you, I am coming! God beat you, you ass-less dog; I am coming!"

Heading down the long foyer, Ann stopped in the bathroom. She hoisted her breasts, adjusted her stockings, and checked her lipstick in the mirror. If the person was American, they only understood, "I am coming." The rest of her words sounded like mumbo jumbo. Hungarian visitors waiting outside the door felt right at home with Ann's colloquialism.

Ann didn't open the front door when she got there. Instead, she hollered, amusing herself, "Na, which kicked-in-the-mouth, mentally retarded, prostitution whore is here?" Ann already knew who it was. The visitor had called before coming and also announced him- or herself at the downstairs buzzing intercom, and lastly, was viewed through the apartment's *kooky-de-lookey*/peephole. But

Ann wanted the out-of-breath person to identify him- or herself again. Only then did she turn the same two locks to the door five times back and forth to make it sound like she was opening the Fort Knox vault. Ann laughed at this hysterically and more so while kicking the door with her feet and bumping it with her meaty ass. All the while, Ann never considered or cared that her half-dead guest panted for water on the other side.

Ann counted to ten again before she finally opened the door. No sweet grandma or mother holding a freshly baked apple pie welcome was to be had there! No hello, hi, or come on in. Ann's first words were, "Step back!" with a shove. "It's show time." If the person wasn't familiar with Ann's shenanigans and stepped over the threshold, they were pushed back harder the second time. This time, she'd push the person across the hallway with one shove.

"Don't ruin my fun. Step back and watch the show!"

"What do you want me to do?" the out-of-breath person would say, gasping, "I need water."

"Stand over there! Shut up and watch."

Hopefully, Ann's mood wouldn't be ruined. If it was, the person would be sent "to hell, to drop dead under the rock where your mother bore you, to think about how to learn to shut up and do better the next time you think of knocking on my door." If she was still in show mood, punishment was delayed.

"Okay, are you ready?"

The person looked wide-eyed and confused, afraid to answer.

"Okay, shut up, stupid, you're killing my act," Ann said as she shut the door in their face.

She then counted to another ten and reopened the door, pretending there were stage curtains to her performance. Ann stepped into the doorway sideways, striking her masterfully practiced Marlene Dietrich pose. Her hand positioned with her palm flipped upward, she held a rhinestone bejeweled cigarette holder with a freshly lit "ciggy" between her thumb and middle finger. Ann's head dropped back in synchronized motion with the flipping of her wrist to flick the cigarette ash. She held the pose for ten seconds before she leaned her back against the thin doorframe and held still again for another count of ten seconds. For dramatic purposes, she avoided eye contact with her guest.

For the next freeze frame, Ann raised one leg like an elegant flamingo on holiday to rest that foot against the thin doorframe behind her, thus allowing her robe to slide apart and expose her leg. The flow of thrilling movement effectively enticed her visitor to inspect the rest of her scantily clad body. Behold, Ann's sexy regalia comprised a black lace corset, matching black panties, black garter belt and stockings, and black patent leather stiletto heels. After another ten seconds, she puffed a long drag off her cigarette from her cigarette holder, looked at her audience, and asked, "If you like what you see, darling, smile *boobaluh*, God loves you, and next time bring the camera. Pictures last longer, and then I can charge double." With that, she burst out laughing and said, "Okay, you son of a bitch, show is over. Come in now!"

A first-time guest would ask, "Can I ask for a glass of water now?"

"Little Anna will show you where you can get it yourself," she'd say, then she'd turn to her small daughter and instruct her in Hungarian, "After that, you hurry to your room."

Little Anna, not yet two years old, would do just that and not come out until told. On her way to her room, she'd hear her mother's audience issue their accolades.

Katy, Lili, and Sidney all loved the show. "F**k, Ann, you should be an actress! You missed your calling, darling," Katy would say. "Great stuff, I come here to steal your material," Lili would say. "Wow, doll, you really are amazing!" Sidney would say.

Company stepping over their apartment's threshold meant it would soon be Little Anna's cue to disappear into her room. Times like these were welcomed by Little Anna. Mother was occupied, so the child felt safe. With nothing else to do in her room because she had no toys, she stared at the brick wall of the adjacent building and recanted the recent events in her mind, reviewing past occurrences frame by frame—click, click, click—to sear them into her memory. Her main reason was to make sense, at a later time, of whatever had occurred.

She wondered how other children learned to count to ten. Her hunch told her, *It wasn't the way I learned.*

Ann's raunchy attire depended on what she had planned. It came down to which high heels and color cigarette holder matched. She chose red for day, black for night. Ann wore no robe in steamy hot months and an open robe otherwise over her strapless bustier and panties.

Sometimes, Mother ordered Little Anna to stay by her side.

One male guest dared to comment on Mother's rules. "You dress like that with your baby daughter around?"

Ann projected her voice proudly, repeating her rehearsed line, "What, darling, I am air conditioning myself? Are you kidding? I have all the windows open. I still died a hundred times today in this cursed devil's pit! Good Lord, don't you feel how hot it is? Na, come on in. Water is dripping from my peach." That's what Little Anna understood her mother to say anyway.

Such men didn't know Ann wasn't interested in their opinion and were promptly ordered to "Get out!" in the next breath.

Little Anna didn't ask questions; she took mental notes. And that was a good thing because after that guest was gone, Mother Ann would ask her daughter what she thought about her replies to that man.

"Did you hear what I said when he asked me about how I dress?"

"Yes, Mommy."

"What did I say?"

"Mommy, you said it's so hot you had water dripping from your peaches."

Mother laughed out loud. "Good, you pay attention. And more importantly, I kicked him out. Don't take no sh*t from no man," Mother Ann added. "Big mouth ones are not allowed back," Mother laughed louder, saying, "I threw that bastard out just like this," as she demonstratively tossed the contents of her ashtray out the open window.

Little Anna learned: *I better laugh because I know what she wants. And it's a good thing I listen to every word she says because I don't want the sting from the back of Mommy's hand. And something's not right with my mommy.*

If first-time visitors said, "How the hell do you live here? These stairs are ridiculous!" Ann would answer, "Your mother's vagina, a dog's penis should eat you! You're complaining, and you still made it here anyway. Nothing keeps you away. Remember how tired you are now, for the next time you think of coming over. I am glad we understand each other, hello to you too!" She would slam the door in their face. Ann didn't have a problem speaking her mind. Her problem was curtailing her loose tongue.

For Sidney, she added in, "Don't complain. Shell out the money; I'll move. You old bastard, you come here to use my body. You're complaining because you used all your strength climbing the stairs. Come on, the breeze in the doorway feels good, but the door is getting heavy pushing on me. I am sure you would rather be the one pushing on me."

WITHIN THE NEXT FEW YEARS, Little Anna met three other men—one she would come to know as Cigar Stanley and two who were not permitted to enter. Ann considered marrying Cigar Stanley, but she couldn't get over his horseshoe-shaped head of hair and his perpetual five o'clock shadow. "Don't even mention he is a poor baker," Mother added more times than not when describing him to other Hungarians.

As old as Sidney was, he didn't exactly make Ann's life any easier. Granted, Ann was a hard, bitter pill to swallow. She yelled and threw tantrums worse than the worst two-year-old without any rational reason. Interestingly enough, Sidney was a father figure to Ann as much as he was to Little Anna. There was a sick sibling rivalry from Mother Ann toward her daughter when it came to Sidney. Because of Mother Ann's envy, she didn't appreciate any affection thrown her child's way. But that actually carried to everyone who liked Little Anna. It was as if Mother Ann didn't want anyone to like her daughter. Why else would she return to the store every present the child received either from Katy, Pauli, or Sidney?

"Look what so-and-so got you for a present. It's nice, isn't it?" she'd say, holding it up for Little Anna to see. The gifts were usually dolls. For years, Pauli always presented Little Anna with a beautiful Easter egg, which Mother returned to the German store on 86th Street for money. "Be sure to thank them when you see them. That's the only reason I am showing you. You have three dolls. That's enough. One you can only look at, one Chatty Cathy—you have to ask me to pull the string because you are not allowed to touch it—both are up there on the shelf where you can't reach them. You have only one you can do whatever the hell you want with. Now I am taking this sh*t back to the store and getting the money they pissed away on you." That controlling behavior of not allowing anyone to play with Anna or give Anna anything started as far back as Anna could recall and never stopped, no matter how old Anna became, even throughout her adulthood.

The first time Anna remembered this occurring was when she was introduced to Sidney when she was only a toddler. Anna was still in diapers, so she had to be less than two. Moments prior to Sidney's arrival, Mother slammed Baby Anna into the couch in the living room with a stern instruction, "Hey you! Stay! Sidney is coming over. He insists on meeting you."

When Sidney arrived, he bypassed Ann, who was holding the door open for him, and walked straight to meet wide-eyed Anna. With a grand smile, he whisked the toddler Anna up over his head and tossed her around like a toy airplane. Laughingly, in this fella's Flatbush, New York, accent, he said, "She gotta be played with like this here or else she'll grow up being afraid of people." Anna was petrified. She thought, *Oh no, another one like Mommy wanting to throw me into a wall.*

Ann exploded and knocked Sidney's shoulder. "What, your parents dropped you on your head as a baby? Your mother raised a stupid crazy? What do you think you are throwing, a pizza?"

Sidney didn't stop. "Next time," he whispered in the toddler's ear, "You'll see, you'll be laughing. You're learning to trust me." He kissed her cheek and hovered the toddler over his head again. "I call this here helicopter."

Flatbush Sidney's choice of interaction baffled and frightened the child. The only time Little Anna was lifted and released was not to be caught but to be thrown like a human missile. When Sidney lifted Little Anna, flashbacks of being shaken and then thrown into the wall flooded her recall. Suddenly, a previous experience of her mother holding her up, yelling in her face, and screaming came back to her. Her mother's words, "I think I shook you too hard once. You have not been acting right since," flooded Anna with fear. Then yet another memory of her mother shouting, "I am only going to throw you this time," and then her mother threw her fragile daughter from one side of the family room to the other, slamming her into the wall.

Little Anna hadn't been toyed with or tickled before she was introduced to Sidney. Panicked, anxiously expecting a beating, a shaking, or being thrown again, her fate was out of her hands. Little Anna learned early on that Mother was dangerous. Still, that didn't mean Little Anna didn't love Mother. Little Anna loved Mother very much, maybe because Mother was all she had.

Mother was now approaching with her monster face. Sidney put the child down. Baby Anna scampered to the corner like she had seen a roach do when its life was in jeopardy, and she watched Mother blow up at Sidney like a time bomb for paying attention to Baby Anna and not Mother. Sparks flew like fireworks. Like a crazed lunatic, Ann rattled swear words, one after another. Her outburst was anything but pretty. Unfortunately, a horse tranquilizer or a straitjacket wasn't on hand. And the handy dandy fire extinguisher in the communal hallway outside of their apartment was of no use! Sidney did not comprehend half the obscenities as Ann switched from metaphors in English of twirling pizza to more unsavory descriptions in Hungarian during her tantrum. Yet, he did not call the police. Perhaps Sidney knew that if he did, Baby Anna would wind up in custody of the state.

Having heard all these sayings before, Little Anna understood them and gained a first-rate Hungarian education. "I beat your sloppy, hanging, stinking, rotten ass and smelly, saggy, turkey-necked balls until you won't know where or how to sit. I kick your stupid head until it busts open like a cantaloupe. I find and dig up your God-fornicated, rotted, dropped dead mother with her stinking vagina, and I stick all of your beaten bodies back up into where you came from, that pitiful mother of yours whose life you ruined by birth. The both of you would have been better off if she died on the table giving birth to you. You two cursed souls would have saved everyone a great deal of trouble by not having to deal with you pieces of sh*t, lower than the garbage I throw out."

Hungarians, not all Hungarians, but Country Katy, Pauli, and some others all had this harsh, rough-around-the-edges way of speaking to each other. It seemed it was what Mother Ann was most comfortable with or the only type of people comfortable with Ann.

Sidney had never heard so much yelling out of a woman's mouth before. He was in shock. Ann finished her rant with, "Get out of here!" She grabbed the house garbage and shoved it into his chest, soiling his jacket, shirt, and tie. "And take this with you, you piece of garbage. You all go to the same place." Ann didn't stop until she had shoved Sidney out the door.

The phone rang just as she slammed the door shut and threw the locks. The phone rang again. Ann flipped her hair behind her ear and plopped her body onto the sofa. The phone rang again. She shook her head and inhaled an exaggerated breath. Her boiling point went from high to medium flame. The phone rang again. Ann looked at the phone and planned to place her hand on the receiver but realized she had plopped herself on the couch too far away from the phone to reach it. The phone rang again. Ann exclaimed aloud to no audience except her baby daughter, "Na, let's see which whore devil has the balls to call me from their mother's stinking ass!"

With the next few rings, she raised herself off the couch and sat back down again. This time, the woman situated herself next to the house phone. "The phone rang ten times. I'll pick up now." As easily as Ann ran her forefinger over her right eyebrow, the woman wiped away all evidence of her recent insanity.

"Hello, hello Lili. I was just thinking about you. How are you, darling? My interview with the famous Hungarian actress Zsa-Zsa Gabor's mama didn't go well. I went to meet her in person to get advice."

"What for, Ann? You want to be an actress?" Lili asked.

"Yeah, sure, anything. I want to know how I can earn big money to pay the rent and bills. I said, 'You advised your daughters so well, what can you advise me?' You know what genius answer she gave me?"

"What was her answer?" Lili asked.

"The old whore said, 'You have a vagina, don't you, my dear?'"

LITTLE ANNA WAS FOUR the next time Sidney visited Ann. "He is to let himself in. No show," Mother Ann instructed her daughter. She was behind schedule in getting ready. "Anna, listen, you play hostess, say hello, and take yourself to the park."

Ten minutes later, Sidney solemnly walked in the apartment, laid down his belongings in a big black bag, went to the kitchen, poured himself a glass of water, then quickly drank it. His face sported a genuinely happy smile when he saw Little Anna standing in the living room to greet him. He got down on his knees, disregarded creasing his shiny blue sharkskin tailored suit, and said, "Hey kid, look, we're eye level now. You remember me at all?" Indicating his desire for an embrace, he stretched his arms out, like the image Anna had seen of Jesus on Pauli's medallion hanging from his necklace.

Anna was nervous. *I don't want to be a helicopter. I have to get to the park before Mother sees me with Sidney. I said hello to Sidney, and now I gotta hurry out.* Those were the instructions. Anna didn't dare not do as she was told. She knew her mother's fury all too well.

Sidney, a father to grown children, had plenty of practice and knew what to do to cut the child's tension. "That's it, that's all I get? Come on, kid, I know I haven't seen you in a while, but where's my hug?"

Anna gladly obliged and ran into Sidney's arms, toppling him over. Quickly forgetting her mother's wrath, she was thrilled to have an adult show her love.

"That's more like it. Now that's how we do hello from now on. We gotta deal?"

Anna, not familiar with this term, just smiled and said, "I like you, Sidney!"

"We'll have to work on that!"

"Huh?"

"I am not stopping until I hear you say, 'I love you, Sidney!'"

Little Anna really liked Flatbush Sidney; she felt safe with him. *He brought me a Mr. Potato Head. I hope I get to keep it!* she thought as he handed her the gift.

"Wow, Sidney, I love you!"

Little Anna could count all the toys she could actually play with on two fingers. One was the one doll she "could do whatever the hell she wanted with" and this, Potato Head, was her second. She was so happy that she swelled with tears.

"Oh kid, you're the best, you really are." Sidney became emotional. He looked like he was about to sneeze; his face flushed. He pulled his neatly folded handkerchief square out of his jacket pocket and said, "Say hello to Mr. Handy Dandy Hanky." He lifted his glasses and wiped his wet eyes and blew his nose.

Little Anna giggled at the sound of Sidney blowing his big red nose.

Ann burst onto the scene. "Sure, you bring her something, you cheap bastard, and you come looking at me to work it off. Don't you have to be somewhere, Anna?" Mother said with her hand on her hip.

"Yes, Mommy, I go to the park now."

"Whose taking ya, kid?"

"I go by myself, like always."

13

MONTHS LATER WAS THE NEXT TIME Little Anna saw Flatbush Sidney. She would forever remember she was still four because she had been moved out of her crib and into a twin bed. At that young age, Little Anna presented her argument to her mother about why she should get a bed. Referring to another child they knew, she repeated the term she'd heard his mother and her mother call the boy. "Suni is a lot younger than me and has a real bed, and he is what you call retarded. You're not a mother to a stupid one, are you?"

"It's too expensive," Mother answered.

"Mommy, buy the mattress, and you will get longer use out of it," the child said, fighting for herself. "You have to buy it sooner or later."

"It's dangerous; you can fall out of bed."

"Mommy, that's not so bad. I climb in and out of the crib. I can fall on my head when I do that."

Little Anna stood at the end of the foyer, waving at Sidney when she saw him arrive. He had flowers and the intention of taking his girlfriend, Ann, for a non-melodramatic rendezvous.

"Let me get me a glass of water and one for these flowers too. Then I want my hug."

Sidney whisked Anna over his head and sat her on his shoulders. "Hey, how'd you get up there?"

He tickled and played with Anna, and along the way, kind Sidney decided to ask Little Anna if she wanted to tag along. "Hey kid, would ya like to join us?" Then he presented Little Anna with a gyroscope toy outside of her mother's view and asked, "Hey kid, go downstairs. I'm double parked, so sit in the car, and if ya see a copper, lay on the horn. Will ya do that for your Sidney? That's a good kid."

The child was thrilled to be included; she giggled all the way down the six flights of stairs and repeated this new word, "copper," with her new toy lodged in her armpit. She exited the tenement and sat behind the wheel of the double-parked car as instructed by Sidney. Little Anna turned around on occasion, watching out for the coppers, taking her responsibility seriously.

The glass-paned door separating her bedroom from her mother's was always open. This was great for Anna because it reflected the television programs Mother watched from her bedroom. James Cagney films and Edward G. Robinson were among Mother's favorites. She loved any storyline with gangsters and molls. Sitting in the car behind the wheel for the first time and having watched James Cagney films, Anna imagined she was in the car on the lookout for coppers as if she were one of Cagney's lookout guys.

"Are you a copper?" she tee-heed. She knew she didn't have the nerve to actually ask an approaching officer, "Are you a copper?" She giggled again, thinking, *Please, please, no copper come by. I wouldn't know what to say.* "No copper, I am here, see," she chuckled again, "because, blah blah blah blah, see," pretending to hold a fat cigar like the mob actors did.

Anna was used to passing the time with her active imagination, but what was taking so long? *I think I grew an inch since I've been sitting here.* She began to worry. Previous to Sidney's arrival, Mother had ordered her to go to the park, but somehow Little Anna got caught up with Sidney's arrival and followed his instructions. Since they were both adults, Little Anna hoped Sidney cleared it with Mother first.

Sidney and Mother finally exited the building, and Anna quickly slipped into the back seat before either adult entered the car. Mother didn't think of looking in the back seat. Ann took for granted her daughter was already at the park, since the child wasn't anywhere in the apartment.

Long before this day, Little Anna had been instructed: "Go to the park every day the sun shines, winter with the biggest snows, summer on the hottest days … what's the big sh*t? This is America, no war tanks on the streets. You're a kid. Get your kicked-in-sideways mouth to the park, or I will give you an education you will never forget!" Little Anna heard those hated words resounding in her head, even when she slept. The child worried she would oversleep and would be woken up again with the blade of a steak or butcher knife digging into her neck. But today, she was getting a treat! Anna was included.

This Sidney-man is great! Once the car started to travel down the first block, Little Anna popped up from her seat and stood on what she called the "camel's hump" to play as quietly as possible with the new toy Sidney had just brought her. It made a shhh … shhh … shhh sound.

"What is that noise? Is something wrong with this car, Sidney? Hush … listen!"

Little Anna stopped playing with the toy to listen. The adults lowered their respective car windows to listen to the car engine. With all the noise in New York City, that was a joke! Sidney stuck half his body out the window, listening intently. "I don't hear nothing, doll."

"Ya no, Sidney, I don't hear it now either."

Anna chuckled in the back. She thought the three of them were as silly as *The Three Stooges*. Sidney fiddled with the tunes in the car. His fingers snapped and snapped again. Adding in a jiggling neck, Sidney conducted with his non-driving arm in lily-white-man rhythm to the sounds of the Rat Pack.

"Heeeeeee … Jesus Christos! How you driving, you moron? Use both hands on the wheel!"

In excitement for the day, he shouted, "Let's get this mini-vacation rolling!"

Little Anna stood up from the back seat to help Sidney lift Mother's mood and yelped,

"Yippee!!!" Luckily for Little Anna, an ambulance drowned out her exclamation, and she went further undetected.

Bored with the toy Sidney had bought her, yet appreciative of his thoughtfulness, she deliberately displayed her gratitude to the man trying his best to cheer up her mother. At the red light, she stood on the camel hump of the car and interjected, "This toy you gave me, Sidney, is great. I love it!"

Ann's head whipped around like a long-necked bird catching its prey. Predator Ann seized a strong hold of Little Anna's arm. "What the hell are you doing here? Sidney, what is this diarrhea sh*t messing up my life again for? What happened to our plans? Sidney, to the park. We are dropping her off. I don't want her with me! Don't you understand? I don't want her with me!"

Sidney tried to calm down the hysterical woman. This was the first time that Little Anna remembered Mother ranting and raging like a lunatic in front of another person, expressing open hatred toward her, and Mother wasn't stopping.

"You know we are almost on the highway?" Sidney tried his best to keep calm.

"Do I care? Turn this damn car around and drive her to the park entrance, or so help me, God, I will open her door and dump her out the car right here."

"Do you know you sound crazy?"

"Crazy, you haven't seen me crazy yet! I'll kick your ass all around this town, too, you piece of sh*t, calling me crazy in front of my kid!"

Ann slammed her right hand on the dashboard and her passenger side window repeatedly with great force while her left hand repeatedly smacked Sidney upside his head and against his shoulder closest to her. Ann's head banged up and down like she was at a heavy metal concert, but that, too, wasn't invented yet. An observer could say Ann looked like a wound-up monkey toy with all its parts moving, hands drumming and knees knocking the cymbals. Or she looked like a mental patient badly in need of medication. The end result: a mutation named Ann created by a crazed scientist's experiment gone haywire. If Ann weren't dangerously angry, she would have been funny.

"All right, I was thinking the kid deserves a little bit better than how you treat her. I never done seen nothing like this here. I'm turning around. Now, get

your hands off of her and quiet down! I'm driving, for godsakes. You're dangerous. You got me so worked up that I can hardly drive. I seen the war and never
seen people act like this, not even vets dismissed for having gone AWOL. You
are going to kill us all."

Ann shifted her physical outburst to directly beating the child. All the way
to the park, the crazed woman threw her fists, landing them over and over on
Little Anna's head and body. Little Anna was emotionally crushed and physically pulverized. Moments ago, the child's heart was thrilled to be included with
Mother and Sidney on a fun car ride. Now, without rational reason, every good
feeling the child gleefully had was beaten out of her.

Mother Ann surpassed hating her daughter into despising her, openly stating, "I wish you were *dead and gone!*"

Neither Sidney nor anyone else could shield the child from Mother. The car
pulled in front of Carl Schurz Park on 84th and East End Avenue.

"Do ya want to apologize?" Sidney said.

Sobbing, trying to catch her breath, Little Anna uttered, "I am sorry."

Sidney looked squarely at Ann. "Are you kidding? You're the one who needs
to apologize here."

"Apologize? I show you apologize," Ann pulled up her door lock. "Get out!"
she screamed. With brute force, Ann kicked her car door open. "The bad scab
should rot you dead."

Tirelessly, Ann continued her slobber-flying yelling. She leaped to her feet
and flew around to Little Anna's window, giving her a preview of what was
coming. She smacked her fist on the window and spat at her daughter. With
saliva still streaming down the glass, Mother Ann hurled Little Anna's door
open with such strength it snapped back to hit her ass. With gritted teeth, Ann
reached in for the terrified child with both arms. The added momentum of
the retaliating door threw adult Ann on top of slight Anna. Mother grabbed a
clenching hold of the frightened child's leg and pulled the light child forward.
Brutally grasping hold of the child's hair and arm, Mother catapulted Little
Anna out of the car like a Frisbee. Flung, Anna twirled until greeted by the

park's stone wall and harsh rocky ground. Too much had happened too fast.

Woozily, Anna removed the embedded street pebbles from her sore, bloody hands while still on her belly. Little Anna managed to sit on her hindquarters to circumvent her surroundings and surmise her distance in relation to her perpetrator. Mother was back in the passenger seat of Sidney's car with the door shut. *I hope she is done now.* Mother locked eyes with Anna. Her display of despise was not yet over. Hastily, Mother hand-rolled down the window and yelled in her usual pitch at the top of her lungs. "*Drop dead* out here, you rotten piece of garbage; don't ever try to wedge between me and my Sidney again. This is my Sidney! Clara had Tibby. Sidney is mine, not yours. Do you understand?"

Little Anna thought she answered, remembering the rule, "Answer when spoken to," but apparently no sound formulated.

"Do you understand me, you little piece of sh*t? Sidney is mine. Find your own!"

Sidney removed himself from the car. He had tried to get the child's attention, but she purposefully did not pay him any mind to avoid another scene. Sidney's kind actions and Mother's mad words did not make Anna's life easy right now. Holding dollar bills in the air, kind Sidney approached the whimpering child. "Ya gonna be all right, kid? Ya need some money?"

Sorely, Little Anna stumbled up from the ground, dusting herself off, keeping constant eyes on her abuser. The smell of hot dogs added insult to injury. For goodness' sake, Anna was thrown onto the street right next to the hot dog stand. Nice, sweet moms were buying their kids delicious, mouth-watering hot dogs. One of the kids was throwing a fit and complaining, "I'm not hungry!" Anna wished she could tell that mother, *Don't worry; buy me whatever you want. I can't remember the last time I ate.*" Her mind never turned off her case of imminent danger. Her mother was still in her midst.

Little Anna was filled with anger, pain, and frustration. Again, her heart sank. Obviously, everyone in her vicinity witnessed the cruelty she had been subjected to. She deduced that *no one cared.* Anna yearned for a hot dog but knew better than to answer Sidney and take his money. Mother would have beaten her more. Little Anna shook her head no, knowing that accepting the money from Sidney would just create another scene.

"Sidney, don't you dare! Goddamn you to hell, Sidney, if you go against me!"

Sidney exclaimed, "In good conscience, Ann!" and stuck some bills in Little Anna's coat pocket.

Mother Ann darted from the car straight toward the distressed child in a blaze of anger and shoved Anna back to the ground. After administering a whack to the back of her daughter's head, Mother smashed the child's cheek into the graveled ground. Ann viciously kneed the succumbed child in the back and retrieved the couple of dollars Sidney had just placed in her pocket. When Mother Ann released her hold, Little Anna picked up her head to see what other madness was in store, at which time, Mother issued her concluding public declaration of hatred toward her daughter. Mother Ann aimed and hit her target, Anna's face, with venomous spit and a spray of spiteful words. *"Drop dead. Nobody wants you!"*

Anna's hunger pang added to her plight. Contending with her crazed Mother wasn't enough. Her brain screamed to devour one of those fantastic-smelling hot dogs with sweet red onions located a few feet away. Without fiscal means to quiet her stomach, the child punched her stomach as she always did to fight her hunger pains, thinking, *Leave me alone. Enough is enough!*

"Money," Ann held up her pirated booty. The couple of pillaged dollars clearly indicated Ann's act of savage inconsideration for her daughter's well-being. Nevertheless, this incident would not dent the goodness of Anna's soul. Anna watched her mother in her acts of lunacy, and she hated her with every trembling atom in her body. *I hate my mother. I will not be like this woman. I will learn to be the opposite of her. No one is changing me.*

"Sidney, you screw me, you give me the money. I earned it. What is wrong with you, you bastard? Now leave this nasty, good-for-nothing piece of sh*t here to die! You think I care about her? I never should have had the pitiful ugly duckling in the first place. Now go or I get behind the wheel and leave the two of you to drop dead!"

Sidney apologized. "I am so sorry, kid. I would never have told you to come if I had known this was going to happen. This is horrible, really."

He returned to the vehicle, and with his arm out the window waving, he tore off. Dumbfounded Little Anna didn't bother to stand up again until the car was out of sight. She did not have a clue what she had done wrong. Yet the pain in her heart was too familiar.

Every time I forgive that person *and believe she is nice and I must be wrong, like she's sorry for hurting me and won't hurt me again, she hurts me. No, she is not a mom! She turns on me every time, every, single, time. She is a mother only. She birthed me, but I have no mom.*

Dealing with agony when Anna didn't know what her next move should be, the child had a habit of asking herself, like a punch-drunk prize fighter not knowing what round it was, "What time is it or what day is it?" Anna didn't know what day it was, but she did know she was four years old. She purposefully took a mental picture of herself. She took snapshot frames of the day's incident into memory. She squeezed her eyes tight, placed her hands on her temples, and clicked her tongue, making the sounds of her imaginary camera shutter while snapping black-and-white pictures. Anna, concentrating with all her gumption, clicked what she wore into her personal album: a pair of pants, a shirt, a jacket, and a thin cotton kerchief she obediently wore, tied around her head to keep her ears warm, even though she felt her mother made her wear it to make her look like a stupid halfwit. *How am I supposed to not look like a halfwit when my mother forces me to look like a dumb idiot?*

"*This bad thing that happened just now doesn't happen without a reason. To make all the pain I feel all right, I will give this pain a reason. Now, what reason can You give me?*"

One who knows Anna at all knows she called upon the All Knowing to offer a reason for her anguish. Anna asked for guidance, and the answer came, *"Books."*

"*What books? What do you want, with me, with books?*" She was still too worked up to home in on His answer. She pushed on, *"Books?"*

"*Right.*"

"*Books, right. What does this mean? Books, right, books, right, books ...*" she repeated, and then she got, "Write books!"

"*Write books, yes,*" All Knowing whispered.

Little Anna paced the street back and forth. The distracting aroma of the hot dogs caused her stomach to growl. *Okay, stop it! Think of what is being said here! Just stand still. You can put this behind you. If you can make sense of this, you can go to the park!* She applied deep focus.

"*You will make it, all right, when you write books,*" He whispered.

"*I am four years old, and I know I will write books one day. I will talk about the bad things done to me. Mother won't be able to get away with this! The whole world will know this story and others. The books will make all I went through all right.*"

The pain rose off her. Once again, Anna felt a sense of belonging to something greater than she could explain. Importantly, she felt she was no longer alone in her life without purpose.

I have given a reason for the pain. All Knowing explained what I need to do. I have a reason to live. I am not a big nothing like Mother says. Time will have to pass before I can write, but I will wait, collecting stories along the way.

Fulfilled with a sense of justice to prevail in the long run, Little Anna turned around in search of the stone-arched entrance to the park.

Every exit is an entrance ...

14

As far back as Anna could remember, her mother had a bad habit of beating her. Mother was triggered by the mere sight or sound of her. Sadly, daily beatings would not end for Anna until she was thirteen, and coincidentally, that was when she no longer lived with her mother.

Sidney never talked to Ann about anything in front of Anna; Anna would have remembered since she was secretly hoping an advocate would come along. But outside of Anna's earshot, Sidney must have had a considerable talk with his girlfriend because Ann started a new habit of dropping off her daughter at Katy and Pauli's in the evenings. Mother used the excuse she was a cocktail waitress working evening shifts. Ann dropped off her daughter when the sun was still up and retrieved her the following morning. Little Anna couldn't recall when she began staying overnight, but somehow, the occurrence seemed to repeat from one day to the next.

Truth is, Ann escorted her daughter up the two flights of stairs to Katy and Pauli's apartment door only once. After that, Little Anna had to remember how to find the apartment building and Pauli's apartment herself. Once at the building, she told herself, *It's the first door to the right on the second landing.* The door was easily discernible by Pauli's obliging, polished, hardy brown leather slipper that held the door ajar. Pauli was proud of his handmade slippers. He'd worn them since he was a young man back in his homeland where his beloved mother lived.

Anna recalled her mother saying, "You know his mother wears all black with the kerchief on her head and everything. That's how the gypsy women do when their husbands die. Pauli's a good son, loves his mother and makes sure she is well taken care of." Perhaps that right there might have been why Ann wanted a son. She wanted to have someone to provide for her.

As soon as Little Anna announced herself with a *szerbusz*/hello, Pauli threw the locks to the apartment door to ensure their safety and clasped Little Anna's hand in his. Together, they walked to the refrigerator. Pauli asked in his autonomous, smiling way in which he served his customers, "So, what's it going to be today?" Except he replaced his usual words, "Gentleman, shave or cut or both?" with the more appropriate, "Little girl, soda, beer, or water?"

After a while, Pauli just asked, "The usual?" followed by, "And what does that mean?"

Anna smiled back, "Soda, beer, or water?"

"And what do you want today, a big or a small glass?"

Little Anna didn't know how long, but quite a number of visits passed before she noticed her reply was inconsequential. Pauli always poured her a water glass of beer. Before she knew what had happened, night had fallen and gone and the sun was out, with Pauli and his Jesus-on-the-cross necklace resurrecting her from the dead. "Anna, get ready. Your good mother will be here in five minutes."

When Mother was later than Pauli expected, he paced back and forth in front of the windows, peered out every so often, and said, "The good Lord should let your mother live long enough to come pick you up, then I don't care what happens."

"Pauli, what do you mean?"

"Your mother says she will be here at eight in the morning and gets here at ten. I am worried sick that something happened to her and she is lying dead one hundred times before she gets here. Once she picks you up, you are no longer my concern. She is *always* late!"

"Oh Pauli, that. Mommy says she is *sometimes* late, and I should tell you not to worry."

"Good God Holy Mother! Your mother is a piece of work."

On the few occasions the couple had Little Anna join them for dinner in the kitchen, jovial Pauli, attired in his at-home uniform of a white wifebeater tucked into his pressed belted slacks, sat himself at the table first. Handsomely sitting high and proud, with a straight back and his hands on his knees, like a gypsy king on his throne atop his money chest, Pauli ordained everyone to sit. Dinner only began when the gypsy king deemed the food ready and the table perfectly set, and a prayer of thanks was given to the Lord.

Pauli's bowed head signaled his desire for those in attendance to say grace. "With the good Lord with us, dinner will begin." The ceremony concluded with Pauli kissing his Jesus-hanging-on-the-cross medallion. Little Anna, finding this to be one big game, learned to stand by the dinner table and wait for Pauli to tap the spot next to him before she took a seat.

"Again," Pauli would say if the procession of events didn't go just how the gypsy king approved. He raised his water glass filled with beer, saying, "How good and blessed we are to have you with us tonight. Big Little Girl, we will eat. The Good Lord is with us, and you are too. We are blessed," Pauli added and sanctimoniously kissed his religious medallion.

"One on your ass," Little Anna said, intentionally mispronouncing the expression "to your health" with her empty hand held high. In the past, stories of her mother's Grandfather Leo doing what she just did had received rewarding chuckles, and Anna wanted to add to this harmless fun.

"Go get your glass, Big Little Girl," Pauli urged on. "Now, again, with our glasses in the air, we clink them together."

"Bless us all, Good Lord!" they said in harmony.

Anna noticed Pauli consistently kissed his medallion each time he mentioned the Lord. He said, "I can never kiss the Good Father enough when He is so good to me!"

"Wait, Pauli, what the child said?" Katy inquired with a giggling belly jiggle.

"One on your ass, to your health," Little Anna replied cutely, smiling.

Then everyone all together said, "One on your ass, to your health!"

United with beer glasses in hand and laughter filling the room, the joy Little Anna felt extended outward from the walls of the confining apartment as the smell of food filled the corpuscles of her nostrils and up into her brain. The child liked contagious laughing. "I could get used to this!"

"Right, tell the truth? Have you ever seen so much food, Big Little Girl?" Pauli smiled, sporting his gold tooth and silver fillings.

"This is America!" Katy said indiscernibly, jamming another hunk of raw onion and uncooked fatback into her already past humanly possible stretched strudel hole, making Katy's cheeks look ridiculously like Dizzy Gillespie blowing his horn.

Pauli asked the child, who was mesmerized by the Houdini routine Katy performed with food, a second time before Anna heard him ask once, "Big Little Girl, do you know what we are sitting on?"

The child got up to look.

"Sit down, eat, child; don't let him exercise you when you are eating. He does that enough with me," Katy said.

"See, she takes what I say seriously. Bless this child," Pauli squeezed her cheeks. "Now come on, let us get some meat on these cheeks. So, what do you think you are sitting on? Katy, you reminded me—stand up, get me another beer. The cold one, so help you God if you question me. Mine is in the refrigerator."

"Pauli, you cursed little crippled man; you sure snap your fingers a lot for a cheap little dog dick."

"I don't know, toilet paper?" Little Anna guessed, driving the adults back on track.

Katy laughed. "As far as I am concerned, you're right. He always tells me to kiss his ass when I tell him I need some."

"This is a chest filled with money," Pauli said. "Don't pay any attention to the talking hippopotamus. One day, I am going to leave it all to you. But that depends on how much you love me."

"Don't hold your breath on that one, little girl! God knows, he doesn't spend any on me or on himself. So, I don't think he's going to give it away either. You can't take it to the grave with you, my daddy!"

Sitting at the dinner table, Anna watched two people interact with each other and with her. Anna felt alive. The child preferred being out of darkness, void of stimulation, and in a world full of color. Table contents spread across every square inch of the round dinner table. There were large slices of bread with a whole slab of butter alongside a dish of pickles, pickled peppers, pickled green tomatoes, and then their dinner entrée: a large bowl of hardened chicken livers and congealed recycled bacon drippings heavenly sprinkled with salt.

"A slice of bread is spread with these livers sitting in jelled drippings and then salted; then take a sour—a pickle, a green tomato, or what have you—onto your plate or hold it in your hand like this. Now, with every bite of bread, a bite of sour is taken. This is how the Hungarians eat. All the flavors on the plate marry together as one," Pauli proudly instructed his young guest on their culture's customs.

"The flavors are the only ones getting married at this table. Anyway, my little girl," Katy continued, "we don't eat like Americans—first the potato, then the meat, then the salad. No, a little of everything on the fork, all the flavors combine as one. Everything adds flavor to the other. This, we Hungarians call healthy eating."

"My mother says the other maids move to another table when she eats this stuff in front of them."

"How much do you love me?" they both asked at the same time.

Little Anna grinned from ear to ear; her feet danced a *czardas*/native Hungarian dance of happiness under the table. Her body demonstrated her heart's joy at positive attention.

Katy explained with outstretched arms the different degrees of measured love. "If just a little, then you show like this, and if you have a lot of love, you love like this."

"I love you both like this, like flying bird wings."

Again, Pauli flashed his shiny toothed smile. "Let's drink to that! What time is it? Is it time? Can I have another beer?"

"Only if you finished the last one, Gypsy King," Little Anna said with a smile.

"Great, not only do I have Gypsy King here flexing me now, but he has a helper like he is St. Nick! That's your third beer. Get your own, you cursed father's dick, which f**ked your mother creating you!" Katy said in good spirits.

Little Anna never understood what happened to the time between drinking her water glass of beer and being woken up in the morning. But when she was old enough to have a sneaking suspicion that beer was not meant for a child, Anna alerted her mother. And with the notice, Mother Ann searched for a new place for Little Anna to stay overnight. If Little Anna had known the consequences she faced, the honest child probably would have kept her tongue silent. After all, Big Little Girl enjoyed her time with those two fun-loving, country-style Hungarian bumpkins.

In the meantime, Ann—unable to place her daughter just anywhere due to financial constrictions—managed her growing frustrations with her complicated life by electing her daughter her personal human punching bag. Like a mosquito attacked a host for blood, each day, Mother Ann assaulted her daughter for the taste of her blood the second she laid eyes on her.

As Little Anna grew older, she became increasingly cognizant of her vulnerability and dealt with her hazardous situation by remaining in her room unheard and unseen, at least on rainy days. Unless the child's body forced her to utilize the toilet, she held back her body's natural function as long as painfully possible, not daring to leave her safe haven. The result she faced was a beating. Paralleled with self-imprisonment, young Anna dreaded the streets but dutifully adhered to the mandatory house decree, "Get out of the house at sunrise," on days when no rain was forecasted.

Prudently, Little Anna opened the door to her room to see if Mother's adjoining bedroom doors were open to the living room. This was important because Little Anna had to pass through the living room to get to the bathroom and then the kitchen and finally, the exit door from the apartment.

The problem was that Anna's curiosity was stronger than reason. *One day, Mother will tell me she loves me.* Sadly, but truthfully, Mother Ann did not allow her daughter to experience love from her. In fact, the only time "this person," mandatorily referred to as Mommy, touched her was during a physical or verbal reprimand.

As she stepped out of her dungeon, Anna checked to the left to see if the coast was clear. The precarious position Mother slept in intrigued Little Anna for a closer look. *That's Mother. What does she look like? I only see her when she's yelling. How does she look when she's quiet?* Unable to anatomically identify her mother's features, the child freaked! *My mother is a monster!* Mother Ann's naked body lay uncovered on her back. There was an upside-down head with the top of her head touching the carpet and her torso draped over the side of the bed. The alarming head looked like another monster had chopped it off and laid it there to eat later. Her eyes were shut and her mouth was wide open. Arms dangled over the sides of the bed past the head. The child's overruling inquisitiveness and need to understand what body part was attached to what limb walked her around the bed for a closer look. *This looks like Magilla Gorilla from the cartoon Mommy tossed like a rag doll across the room and left the way it fell. Hmm ... kinda like what Mother does with me!*

Without warning, this monster snorted and opened her eyes. Little Anna stood still, not exhaling; she was in absolute fright. By now, Anna knew better than to dare wake her mother. But nature had called. The glance in her mother's direction had sidetracked her, and now Anna's urges were battling wills. At times like this, Little Anna wished "this person" dead. The child stood frozen like a carved ice statue, not even daring to breathe. She asked herself, *What time is it? What day is it?* Then rephrased her thought to, *What do I do? This is really bad. I gotta think of something to say.*

The monster spoke first. "What do you think you're doing?"

"Yes, Mommy, I know. I just want to look at you. You're very pretty," Anna lied. She needed the commode, but she also had to be careful of her words. Dealing with Mother was like sucking on a charred glass Popsicle. One slip of the tongue and painful regret was certain.

"I am sleeping, and you know the rule."

"The rule?" Anna gulped, remembering.

The sleeping rule originated from Ann's childhood experience when Nazis occupied Hungary. Her cousin Irene was good for not a darn thing except aggravation. Aunt Teresa didn't realize her own daughter, Irene, was a product of the "monkey love" showered upon her. "Monkey love" is spoiling a child to the point of crippling.

Aunt Teresa, aged eighty-plus, was rightfully tired from "monkey loving" her "good-for-nothing woman-child Irene" that she'd created. In planning her own passing, Aunt Teresa spent her last year busily preparing for the inevitable day she would perish. First, she sold her gold and her other worldly possessions to then finance a fully stocked food cabinet she planned to fill with Mason jars of food. She worked night and day to prepare this legacy to sustain her daughter, Irene, for a considerable duration after her death. When Aunt Teresa considered her job done, with every Mason jar filled and every shelf packed tight in the pantry she kept locked, she plumped her chair pillow and sat her exhausted body down for her calculated last time. Her head fell back, and her body went limp.

"Wake up, Aunt Teresa! Wake up! Wake up, Aunt Teresa! Wake up!" eleven-year-old Anci yelled as she shook the lifeless body vigorously.

"Anci! You better make it good! You brought me back from the dead!"

The angered woman grabbed Anci by the ear and scolded her, according to Anci, "until the next day." Anci learned on that day to, "Never wake a sleeping person."

The next time Aunt Teresa sat in her comfortable chair to go to sleep, the woman glared and gnarled at Anci long and hard, sternly demonstrating without words, "Stay clear!" The lesson was well remembered. So well, in fact, the message was passed down to her child, Little Anna. And Anna understood its implications.

In addition to not waking a sleeping person, Little Anna recalled other rules like: "Don't talk to Mother unless answering Mother's question." Talk was unwanted noise as far as Mother was concerned. And Anna was never ever to answer a question saying, "No." Mother would slap Anna to the ground, saying, "That word is not in our dictionary!"

Little Anna, still four, remembered all that. Pressured to say something, she muttered, "That's good, Mommy, you sleep." The urge to use the bathroom became intolerable, as if someone had kicked her innards. In side-splitting anguish, Anna hastily removed herself from Mother's sight to get to the bathroom. She hurried to be done, hearing sounds outside the door. *The monster's up!*

The frightened child creaked open the bathroom door and scurried to exit the apartment, fumbling with her shoes, socks, sweater, and jacket that she secured between her chin and her tiny arms. She managed to close the door just in time to escape a second shoe Mother threw at Anna's head.

The last words she heard were, "And don't come back, you piece of sh*t, until the sunsets. No one is interested in you!"

15

Wow, today is gonna be a good day! Little Anna thought after she heard
a thump against the door. Anna had her usual headache, but she happily rubbed
the back of her head as she la-la-la'd down the tenement steps, grateful to have
escaped the usual morning whooping. *I've been doing these stairs since I was in
diapers. I remember Mother putting me down at the bottom of the stairs on the
ground floor. She said, "You're heavy. You recently started to walk," and as Mommy
went ahead, she added, "That should keep you piece of sh*t busy for a while." I
climbed the mountain of stairs while yodeling my way to the top. I tried all different
ways of scooting up. I finally figured out that crawling forward on all fours worked
best. I couldn't reach the doorknob to the apartment and was glad to find the door
chain kept it open so I could scoot through.*

Forced to take to the streets each morning was perhaps the best way Little
Anna's mother kept her child away from her reach since she lacked self-control from
beating her child unconscious. Cold weather or hot weather was of no significance.
Little Anna had to stay outside except for the days God decided to have "a good
cry," as she thought of rain, in order to show Little Anna some mercy.

Darting out of the apartment with an empty belly was a common everyday
occurrence too. It was better than getting her ass beat by someone who didn't

love her before being discarded to the streets. Ironically, Little Anna didn't consciously or subconsciously accept that Mother hated her. How was she to know most mothers in the world were capable of love and not just on television? What the child did know was that the cold brutality was easier to tolerate from the outside world than from her very own flesh and blood. Without question, she learned that not stopping to fuss and eat breakfast was the better way to go.

Little Anna's daily grind to do everything on her own consisted of waking, dressing, and making her bed before she ventured to the kitchen to prepare herself breakfast. Attempting to function in an optimal rhythm, the young child utilized the bathroom on her way to the kitchen because backtracking proved perilous. However, on days when she'd missed eating a few consecutive meals, she had no choice but to grab something. The only problem was her nerves. Little Anna was so scared of her mother coming to beat her that she couldn't eat!

Trying to force down food kicked her gag reflex into overdrive. Frightened, she repeated not only her food but also her circling thoughts. *The monster is walking in at any moment. The longer time I spend in this roach-infested apartment, the more likely I am to get my hurting head banged in.*

Unbeknownst to Little Anna, her fury worked against her whenever she tried to hurry. Slamming the icebox closed, banging open cabinets shut, dragging the squeaking metal chair across the hard linoleum floor, smacking dishes against the porcelain sink, and running water to wash the dropped silverware were sounds of discord, angrily stirring Mother Ann from slumber.

On one such morning, her mother yelled out, "Does that little whore know how lucky she is? All that cursed piece of sh*t has to do is go to the kitchen to find food!"

Somehow, Little Anna continued and prepared herself a half-assed meal: a banana, a cup of milk, and a bowl of stale, roach-stomped cereal. She chewed and chewed, watching the rushing hands of the wall-mounted clock run circles above her head. The ticking of the clock's inner workings increased in loudness and frequency. The mounting pressure, her head ready to burst from being beaten like a piñata every day, and her hunger made her mind scream: *The monster's coming!*

Little Anna must have been in the kitchen for an hour without making a dent in her food. Panicked, she knew Mother Ann was up now. On her way over to the kitchen, Mother cursed the daughter she was raring to beat the crap out of.

"That good-for-nothing little crap! There is no one to do crap about it! Sh*t! The little sh*t should have been out already! What the hell has the piece of sh*t been doing? That little sh*t drives me crazy! She does this sh*t to me on purpose!"

The monster was closing in, slithering her way toward the kitchen, wearing what she did to sleep—either nothing or attire reputable women would not own, let alone wear. Specifically, Ann widened her wardrobe to peacock her scandalous lingerie: black garter belts obediently keeping her stockings in line, black bustier firmly holding her breasts high and her waist cinched, and nothing more below the waist other than black panties and dominatrix stiletto heels. Little Anna flinched when she heard her mother's lighter spark its flame and again when her mother dropped the lighter onto the coffee table in the living room down the long hallway.

The cloudy exhalation off Ann's smoldering cigarette lingered in the air and whisked Ann's attention away into a flashback to 1944, when Anci's twelve-year-old eyes were affixed on the ghetto gates with her ill-gotten gains: some hardened bread she'd scavenged from underneath the rubble of a bombed grocery store.

*Her tempo altered slightly when she noticed something amiss. A thick haze of smoke ahead was not dissipating but lingering. Everything slowed down to a strange, warped speed. Anci hoped to run for cover. "Better safe than sorry." But too late, Anci caught the eye of a lethal Nazi ghetto guard gateman who snidely remarked, "Hey, you looking like skin and bones! You're something only dogs could howl at," to which the other mongoloid Nazi henchman added barking noises. Anci sped up and walked past the guards while holding her breath, hoping the brutes were done with her. Just as her heart jumped out of her chest, she caught sight of a congregation of Nazi bastards further ahead, demanding, "Everyone out of your sh*t holes! Move it, now! "Schnell, Rausz!!"*

The Nazis were making a dangerous power display of their dominant authority. People's faces and cries of distress forewarned Anci: "Danger! Beware!" Her pace lessened. I passed the first set of executioners, and now I must hide from the second. *She stopped and successfully fell into a crevice created by an earlier bomb explosion on the side of the nearest building. Scampering like a rat on extermination day, the twelve-year-old collected her wits about her as easily as she tucked her coattail in from behind her to sit on to buffer herself from the cold winter ground. She sat, and she did not look away. No, Anci observed what was occurring through an undetectable peek hole. While squatting, she found an even better place to hide, so she moved while taking full advantage of a short stretch before readjusting herself.*

The Nyilas, meaning "Arrow Cross," who were the Hungarian Nazis in command, were such hardened killers they made German Nazis seem like grade school sissies. Peering out from her rattrap, Ann watched the drunker-than-usual Jew haters play their favorite evil game, "Jew Round Up!"

The Nyilas separated mothers from their children of all ages, including very young babies. The men, already drafted at another time, left no men to fight and protect the women and children. Those remaining were an easy bunch to round up. Mad men ran the world while the meek stood helpless. The Nyilas were mandating orders: "Schnell!/Go!" They waved their rifles in the direction they wanted Anci's crying, desperate people to go. Among them, Anci recognized three of her friends. Two she knew for sure; the third she squinted at and wasn't 100 percent positive about their identity. A Nyilas demonstrated his authority, shooting a whimpering child who was scurrying around in a hissy fit. Then, as the mother rang out a bloodcurdling scream, the Nyilas pumped a bullet into her head at close range to silence her out of her misery. Another cried out for God's intervention. "Good God, help me!"

The Nyilas answered, "As you wish," coldheartedly issuing the woman a rifle butt to her head.

All other prayers went silent, although they were all on the same page of the Talmud. Everyone prayed for their Good Lord to save them.

The Nyilas shoved and grunted at the children to begin their procession toward their designated killing square. Children of varied ages aligned, touching hands and forming their last circle before meeting their grave fate. Worried eyes wondered,

What cruel, sick game have the Nyilas planned? Keeping momentum steady, Nyilas moved the remaining mothers to form an outer circumference around the youngsters. In this way, the Nyilas organized spectators for their sport. Fear mounted, and it seemed everyone was marched into a calculated position. Are they going to harm the girls? *the mothers thought,* while we are forced to watch? *The suspense of the unknowing was unnerving.*

Then, the brutes escalated in exhilaration. The power they gained from feeding on instilling fears into the Jews caused them to thirst for more bloodshed. In a mad bursting shout, as loud as a spray of bullets, the Nyilas howled and opened fire on the children. The young bodies went straight down like dropped utensils. Anci held her breath. She wasn't sure if she shrieked. If she had, luckily, her squeal was lost in the mothers' shrills of horror, witnessing their children's deaths. She knew she better shut up! Mothers who ran to protect their children in the mayhem were caught in the crossfire. The executioners were too trigger-happy to stop.

One Nyilas commanded, "Halt!" *Dead silence resumed. Perversely, just like the premeditation of consuming cake is just as good as masticating the sweet treat, the Nyilas savored the tension of their dispirited victims staring death in the face to be just as lick-smacking delicious as committing murder.*

A few mothers and three older male children were still alive. Their eyes squinted as they prayed through trembling lips. First, for thanks—their first set of prayers were fulfilled—and then for another act of mercy. But the Nyilas had a method to their barbaric madness. They didn't want to pile the dead out of sight themselves. Instead, they cunningly ordered the three remaining children to the gruesome detail as the one mother forcibly watched.

"Where are you, God?" an outcry rang out.

The Nyilas answered, "You will find out soon enough, you swine."

The weak, frantic, shaking bodies pushed and tugged on the corpses until the dead were piled one on top of another. One of the boys became overwrought when he grabbed hold of his dead sister. Jarred by his sister's blown-away eye suddenly thrust in his face, he released a horrific shriek.

"Why don't you join her if you love her so much?" the boorish fiend gnarled.

Another shot echoed through the air. The remaining two children grappled at the bodies to finish their dreadful assignment. They pulled and pushed the dead by the arm, by the hair, and by whatever means possible to move the bodies like over-sized ragdolls into the designated site. Then, ending the cat-and-mouse game, the Nyilas sprayed their bullets, shooting the last two children and the remaining mothers down, except for one. One lone mother was left to do as she had helplessly observed the children do. Finished with her ghastly detail, she fell to her knees, trembling.

"God take me, Good Father, I am ready!"

Her kerchief-covered head looked to the heavens, and with no more strength left, not even for prayer, she dropped her wet, sobbing face into her hands.

"You pathetic woman, you have fallen to your knees, and you will meet your God on earth before you depart!"

When the last of the three Nyilas was done pulling his vile member from within her, the self-declared God but truly disgusting devil of darkness unjustly called the tortured woman "dirty swine." He spit in his hand, made a mark with his spit in the middle of her forehead, pointed his pistol at the marked spot, and blew her brains out. Anci stayed in the rat hole, not daring to move.

An ambulance siren with loud NYC attitude six floors below rattled Ann back to her present. Her cigarette was almost a butt, now smoldering in her skull-faced ashtray. Sunlight hauntingly illuminated its bright, ruby-red eyes while smoke escaped like a dancing serpent through its open jaw. Almost foretelling, the scene was eerie but not half as scary as what was about to transpire. Ann slithered her way to silently stand in the alcove of the kitchen. She stood undetected just as she planned, loving the idea of employing another surprise attack. Excited, she rubbed her hands together and even let out a little pee.

The struggling child was doing her best to work food into her system. She desperately shoved the banana as far down her throat as she could to rush the eating process along. But, as anyone else knows, gag reflexes worsen with such forceful action. Ann saw the torment, but her motherly instincts of concern and caring did not kick in. In contrast, Mother's sick, uncontrollable reaction was to harm the child in a growing rage of hatred.

Little Anna was familiar with the spot where Mother lurked like a looming electric eel hiding undetected between coral cover, waiting for its opportune time to attack. The child glanced at the particular spot in the alcove, as she obsessively did every few minutes. *Am I still safe?* Not this time! Her eyes locked with trouble, and she froze in fear. *Oh no!* She knew she was getting beaten again, and she was petrified. Anna flinched to duck the blow coming from the monster's customary cruel salutation. Little Anna's move was premature; Mother did not make her move yet. Mother licked her lips anxiously, tasting her strike of blood. Mother was a professional; she tossed mental and verbal cutting knives as skillfully as she pitched physical forks.

"How in God's cunt are you eating?"

Mother Ann stepped into full view. The monster stood with one hand on her hip. Her hands were empty. Anna took notice; the monster was planning to attack with her hands and fists. Before the child could account for anything else, her nastily clad mother unloaded a mouthful of slander like an AWOL army officer riddling his victim with machine gun rounds. Next, Ann seized the child by her two braids with the same elation as the Nyilas possessed as they intimidated Jews in the ghetto, and she yanked the child out of her seat. Mother Ann then turned Anna upside down and ripped the clothes off of her, never, by the way, stopping her tirade of vulgar, verbal slander. She was yelling at the top of her lungs.

Mother Ann had no one to account to. She had no father, mother, husband, sister, aunt, or brother. No one gave a damn what happened to her child, least of all her. And Mother made sure Little Anna knew how alone she was in the world. "No one gives a sh*t if you live or die."

Mother proceeded to take the now-naked child whose body she had already beat and, holding her upside down by one leg, twirled her right-side up like a hollow baton. Then Mother Ann gripped her human discus and hurled her around the kitchen by her braids. Ann was not satisfied with this hold. "Goddamn you to hell. I don't want to look you in the ugly face! You are not even good for throwing around, you piece of sh*t." She dropped Anna on the ground and seized the child's ankles to spin her upside down. Anna's head hit the stove, next the kitchen chair, and after that, the kitchen table then the sink.

Little Anna, not one to talk back and afraid of repercussions of further backlash, dared to speak up to this monster who had no intention of stopping anytime soon. Little Anna was being revolved for a third time.

"Here comes the stove. You are hitting my head into the stove."

Mother kept swinging the child.

"The stove's coming again," Anna desperately pleaded. "Please drop me, the stove is coming at my head, now the chair, now the table, now the sink, enough, enough, you don't want to do this!"

"Good, I don't care if you drop dead! Take what you got coming to you!"

Who knows how long the rage lasted. Little Anna woke up, like countless times before and so many times after, with her twisted body against a wall, her legs folded over her pounding, aching head. Sometimes she could recall some of the preceding events. Sometimes Anna didn't know how long she lay there like an unwanted, torn, and discarded plaything. What she did know was that her jaw was out of place, and she didn't know how to hold her mouth properly other than not to say a peep.

Through an X-ray as an adult, her jaw showed "evidence of being," as the dentist stated, "in a car accident," and the only way to realign and fix the displaced jaw was through corrective surgery. Doctors in Anna's adult life said the same thing when she was diagnosed with thoracic stenosis/a crooked neck and spinal stenosis/a crooked spine. Little Anna didn't know all that for now. What she knew for the moment was that she better recollect her bearings and get out of sight, back into her dungeon, quickly and *quietly*.

If the monster hears a peep out of me, I am getting another beating.

"What's your problem?" Monster shouted.

Little Anna was aware she was in harm's way. The monster was returning, but Anna was unable to obtain her bearings. The combination of the room spinning and her head swimming made it impossible for her to clear out of the room. Arising from unconsciousness, trying to think through her unbearable pounding head and body pain and not understanding why her legs were not below her but over her head, didn't help. Neither did her body's involuntary unstoppable trembling and her sobbing help. *Why does my body have to fight me too? I have to get out of here!*

Mother walked in and cracked Little Anna a hard, swift backhand smack across her mouth as if it were a lobbing tennis ball. "Goddamn it, it was quiet in here for a while. What's it going to take for you to learn to shut up, you ugly retard? You know the story of the ugly duckling? Well you should! You're the ugly duckling."

Her mother yelled such a long string of degradations that the heated mess seemed like a never-ending noisy train pulling into the station. A kiss upside her head by her mother's fist trailed. Falling in and out of consciousness, Anna blinked her eyes more slowly. The child tried her best to stay tuned to her demise. Anna couldn't believe the bottomless pit of anguish this monster she was stuck living with and forced to call Mommy delivered to her without a care. Unless one considered that Mother showing her care meant a good laugh with a shove. A shove so incredibly hard that Little Anna's limp body slid across the room. The nice wall courteously stopped her from traveling further.

The side of her head was beyond pounding. It was as if a jackhammer were at work or a relentless wrecking ball was crashing into her skull. Her body shook as if she were naked in the snow. Her face, an inch off the floor, was a slobbery mess. Her eyes were open, but her mind succumbed to sleep. Calmness came over her. In slow motion, her body slumped over until her cheek was on the filthy, black-and-white checkered linoleum floor. The girl was no longer crying; she was falling unconscious again. Either way, her mother had not declared being done with her, so Mother Ann picked up her daughter by the tufts of the back of her hair and smacked her another one.

"What you crying for, you piece of sh*t! Are you still crying? I will give you something to cry about. Looks like you want more. There's plenty where this came from!"

No area of the child's body was off limits, including her already-beaten head. Then, like nothing had transpired, Mother opened the refrigerator door.

"I worked myself up a thirst."

Teetering in and out of unconsciousness, the child's body still whimpered. Her subconscious ruled. That, too, could not deal with the travesty it was forced to endure.

"Shut up, shut up, and shut up! I can't stand to look at you, you disgusting piece of unwanted sh*t. Okay, now that I am here, take this goddamned cod liver oil!"

Again gripping the child by a clump of hair, Mother yanked the child's head back and poured a drowning amount of the stinky fluid down her throat.

"It's good for you, shut up!"

ANNA'S DAILY THRASHINGS continued behind closed doors where there were no witnesses and no possible intervention. The watchful eye of the public altered Mother's demeanor toward her daughter. On those occasions, Mother played her maternal role like an Academy Award-winning actress. Mommy Dearest comes to mind, but Anna would have been so lucky to have Joan Crawford for a mother, and that film wouldn't come out until 1981.

Little Anna hadn't yet put together what triggered her mother to turn against her. The longer Mother Ann pretended to be the sweet, jovial person she wasn't, the graver the backlash would be that she let loose on her daughter.

Little Anna did understand she had to stay out of sight. Anna retreated behind the safety of her room, no differently than she hid behind the locked public bathroom stall when escaping park bullies. It seems Anna's life was filled with constant hiding.

Age four is not an appropriate age for any child to go unsupervised in New York City from sunup till sundown, let alone a little girl. Especially not every day of the week for months on end. Anna wished she had a safe haven instead of being constantly trapped with her back up against a door, literally. *Will there ever be a day I won't be afraid? Will there ever be a day I have a place where I am safe?*

"*It will be a while,*" He whispered.

"*You're here.*" The feeling of not being alone brought Anna some consolation. She wiped her eyes and snotty nose from the long, hard cries she was too familiar with.

"*I am always with you,*" All Knowing's voice whispered into Anna's right ear.

"*Good, good, you remind me I am not alone. How long do I have to get beat? It feels like forever.*"

"*It is not forever. The day will come when it will have all ended.*"

"*I remember I am on my own, but thank you for the nice words.*"

Even though He wasn't physically able to do anything for her, at least she had a comforting whisper in her ear promising her that suffering wouldn't be forever.

Perhaps Anna's pleas were heard with Godly intervention. Even Mother Ann subconsciously uttered, "Let us pray for the good lord to help me." Ann knew she had to find a safe place to send her daughter out of harm's way, as far away from her as possible. Perhaps Ann knew that sending Anna to the streets was the way she curtailed herself from attacking her young daughter even more. The mere mention of her daughter's name rang Ann's box-fighter bell. Ding, ding, ding! Ann's jaw clenched so tightly she chipped a tooth. Finding a place to deposit Anna safely, and quicker than the next second, wouldn't be soon enough!

16

AS GOOD A PLACE AS ANY, some brass-knuckle truth needs to be injected here before continuing with Little Anna's story. Big Steve, Anna Clara's father on her birth certificate, may have been correct in trying to persuade Mother Ann to get an abortion. The conception of the child—the mistake—affected not only Ann's life but, just as importantly, her unborn.

Later in Anna's adult life, she met Kornelius, Flora's grown son. Flora was Mother Ann's aunt, Clara's sister. Kornelius shared with Anna something she didn't know, but when she learned about it, the information forever altered Anna's perception of her Mother Ann.

Anna respected Kornelius's words since he was a medical doctor and a spiritually guided man. Anna trusted his caring, finding that Kornelius had nothing to benefit from what he shared.

"I have letters in my possession that your mother wrote to Flora and Clara back when you were very young. Your mother, Ann, expressed that she didn't really think her husband was your father. She was a promiscuous woman with extramarital affairs, including during the time of her pregnancy with you." He took a sip of water and then added, "In the letter, your mother wrote that she also dabbled with heroin."

Such words cannot be retracted. First, the information stole Anna's breath away, then the words perforated her heart. Sometimes, the truth is better not known. Once the painful sting settled, these secrets became answers, needed puzzle pieces that offered clarity about Anna's life.

Mother Ann's heroin habit lasted many years before she was finally scared straight. Ann wrote in a letter that she had been very much in love with a man who she felt was the father to her baby. This man was also her co-drug user and dealer. Ann never mentioned his name. Mother Ann wrote, "He boasted, 'this sh*t will take you out of this world.'" He wasn't lying. He died from an overdose in front of her eyes using the stuff first. The sight startled Ann but not enough to turn her life around at that point.

Anna recalled a time when she was roughly eleven. Mother Ann was invited to party with new friends. Mother looked forward to the event, speaking about it for weeks, glad to be invited at long last into the inner sanctum of the *cool clique* she wanted to hang with. On the night of the party, a car came to pick up Ann. To her chagrin, they rudely excluded her, claiming their car was packed beyond capacity. Feeling ostracized, discounted, and humiliated, Ann became even angrier when none of the members of the clique called her again. A couple of months later, Ann called to confront them, as Ann did to people, saying, "I want to give them a piece of my mind. I have nothing to lose anyway!"

"Everyone in the car died from a horrific car accident on their way to a party," the person on the other end of the receiver cried. It happened on the way to the same party Ann had been disappointed not to attend since they left her behind.

Stone white, Ann hung up the phone and turned to her daughter. "There are no accidents. It was not my time to go. Someone gave me a second chance," she said. That incident scared Mother straight and was the start of Mother Ann's mantra, "I have a second chance."

It's sad to consider that Ann wasn't scared straight until her daughter was eleven. For now, Little Anna was still only four. At four, Little Anna wished with all her might: *Some kind of somebody, come help me. This monster is very hard to be with by myself. Please! Help!*

A small miracle did occur soon thereafter, at least for a short time.

"Listen, my little girl, it's too late to reverse your birth; God knows I would if I could, but it looks like your mother found you a nice old Irish woman, a Mrs. Koss, to watch you. Thank God," Mother said, walking her fast city pace as Anna ran beside her to keep up.

"Come on, Little Anna, Mrs. Koss is highly regarded and lives within close walking distance. I am taking you there now. So pay attention." Mother then added, "I am only showing you how to get there this once."

The timing couldn't have been better. Mrs. Koss's lucky Irish green clover had recently wilted. She was retired and in need of stipends. Now the dismay of Mrs. Koss's new circumstances and Mother Ann's need to watch her problematic child would fuse their lives together.

Ann escorted and deposited her daughter at Mama Koss's apartment door and left without so much as a kiss or a pat on the head. Instead, Ann said, "From now on, you find your way, little girl. If you paid attention, you will have no problem. Go! Fat, money-grubbing Koss is waiting for you."

Little Anna's memorized travel consisted of successfully scooting and climbing down six mountain-steep flights with her short, four-year-old legs to then walk an endless hallway lobby before first exiting her tenement. Prior to stepping down to street level, Anna ingested as deep a breath as possible. Interestingly, she knew she had done this before, and although she had traveled these stairs numerous times alone, she continuously remembered when her mother set her down the first time, saying, "You're too heavy." She was still in diapers. Since that time, she'd monitored her own progress in all the different ways she experimented and traversed those stairs to figure out which worked best. Backward wasn't easy, while using all fours worked well enough, but now she was a big little girl and discovered that sideways let her use two hands on the rail. That felt like a great accomplishment.

With one last long breath, not exhaling until she walked the long hallway and stepped down the last big step out of the tenement, she sharply turned her small body to the direction of her right arm toward First Avenue as she attempted to calm the idea of the overwhelming world she was about to face alone.

Anna had to face one of the most difficult parts of the first day of her new journey to Mama Koss because the direction she needed to take was different. All the way downstairs, she'd worried about having to walk past the boys playing ball. Once Anna was out of the building, she always turned left to the park and avoided the boys. Today, Anna had to make a right to get to Mama Koss's. She was scared to walk alongside the red brick wall of her building to reach the public receptacle on the corner. Here, unruly neighborhood street boys played handball or stickball against the wall. She preferred the boys playing stickball to handball.

Handball meant she would walk in the direct line of fire of multiple balls that she would have to dodge, along with the degrading comments to duck because she was in the players' way. She didn't understand their animal calls. Anna just knew she felt uncomfortably less than human. *It is enough that Mother tells me I am unwanted garbage.* Either way, pretending to wear invisible earmuffs, Little Anna practiced the art of pretending to be deaf, ignoring rude comments in the same way the ruffians blindly ignored the "No Ball Playing Allowed" sign posted along the red brick wall.

Somehow, that placard was only adhered to when the A&P delivery truck drivers unloaded their cargo of dead carcasses into the store's side delivery entrance located in the middle of that long red brick wall. These tough street kids didn't respect authority or give a lick about proper politeness. So Anna was happy to see the hard-bodied meat packers' abilities to intimidate the smart-ass kids without the use of a single word. As far as Anna was concerned, the grocery store needed to sell lots of meat to keep a steady flow of deliveries, so Anna had easy access to and from her tenement.

Once Anna braved her way to the corner where the metal mesh receptacle filled with garbage stood, she gladly didn't cross the large, imposing Second Avenue intersection. Instead, she thankfully turned another right to pass by the entrance of the A&P grocery. Having been to the grocery store plenty of times before with Mother on what she considered special days, Anna would see a dog or two loyally waiting for their masters, safely tied to the red-painted fire hydrant. Anna was surprised that not even the street hoodlums stole these prized possessions. On those special days, Little Anna petted every furry friend she introduced herself to while her mother stood in line and paid at the register. There was only one entrance/exit, and the dogs faced that door, so Anna felt she would safely not miss her mother leaving the grocery store. Since Mother had no problem leaving her daughter behind, Anna had to keep on her toes. Anna didn't need another reason for a beating.

As she passed by the A&P on her way to Mama Koss's, one larger dog was fastened to the fire hydrant. Anna didn't think twice and mounted it like she'd watched John Wayne straddle a saddled horse in the bang, bang shoot 'em up cowboy movies. "Aw, look how cute you are, what a good little horsey. Giddy up, horsey, giddy up."

Just past the A&P was a pedigree store for dogs. Bewilderedly, the child marveled at the bedazzling dog collars, fancy coats, and specialty-crafted beds available for man's best friend. "Better to be born an animal in America than a human where I come from," Anna's mother said, even though her mother wasn't with her. "Mommy, these dogs are so lucky they get beds like this to sleep in, wow!" she answered back in her mind.

Moving on to the end of 85th Street, Anna turned her last right, passing a row of brownstones. She kept a watchful eye for Mama Koss's building, which was the second from the end of the last on the block. It was the one with two sets of five steps with main double doors. Having learned to count to ten came in handy now. Anna took a deep breath, nervous about having to soon walk through the next and most challenging part of her journey. She remembered there was a part of the hallway she had to walk through that was dark and spooky. She was appeased at the time because she had her mother by her side, but she'd worried ever since she was told she had to make the trip on her own, all because of a door that disappeared into the darkness of the hallway.

For now, Anna first had to master the steep brownstone steps to get inside. Using both the strength of her arms and legs to climb the steps like a dog, since the railing was too high to utilize, she then walked into a small entranceway. Mailboxes were stationed on the left, next to which she found the buzzer she referred to as "Wizard Oz" because the magical box spoke and granted entrance.

Buzzed in, the ominous, long hallway waited. Anna focused on the little white floor tiles with sporadic black ones sprinkled among them in no particular pattern or purpose except to secretly point Anna in the right direction to Mama Koss's door. Once Little Anna bypassed the ascending stairs to her left, the scariest part of her journey was now immediately approaching. Things didn't feel right in this area. Behind one particular door was where she felt something *spooky bad* going on. The light above the door was out and would always be out for all the times she would ever have to pass it.

Danger, she thought but didn't know why. She just heard the word *danger* whispered in her right ear, which made her stomach drop and the peach fuzz on her face and the back of her neck stand weirdly electrified, followed by a full body set of goose pimples. *Yikes!* Anna counted to ten like she saw her mother do, working her courage to face stepping into that dimly lit area where that spooky door was. Without fail, the hallway seemed longer than she remembered when she walked with her mother. Her heart pounded as much as her head, hastening her feet to pitter-patter her to her destination.

Finally, in front of what she hoped was Mama Koss's door, anxious Anna filled her cheeks with oxygen, as if she were ready to extinguish birthday candles, before knocking. Her body was prepared to flee in case a witch like the one in the *Hansel and Gretel* story answered the door. She heard Mother's voice, although she didn't understand how that was possible when she was standing alone. "Don't worry, even if it is the witch. She won't want you. Once she checks your fingers and sees you have no meat on your bones, she'll send you away." Anna calmed herself with the reassuring thought of safety. *Mother's right. If the witch checks my fingers, she won't want me. I'm too skinny.*

"Anyone home, hello?" Anna knocked.

Mrs. Koss opened the door. Fully relieved that she had found the right place on her own, Anna expressed a cheery, "Hiya there, Mrs. Koss!"

Immediately, the sweet-tempered woman with a wee bit of an Irish accent smiled and issued her first instruction. "You best be calling this poor old lass Mama Koss. Dearie, I be insisting."

"Yes, Mama Koss."

"Aye dear, you been here ten minutes already. Where's your mother?" She then called out, "Ann?"

"She's not here, Mama Koss."

"I will leave the door unlocked. You ran ahead. Your mother will catch up."

Little Anna knew Mother wasn't coming. Mama Koss checked outside her door in five-minute intervals.

"Your mother, did she get lost?"

"No, she's not coming."

"How did you get here then?"

"My legs; I put one foot in front of the other, and I try not to step on the cracks."

"Well, child, we can't be having none of this. This is preposterous! A young child such as yourself let loose to fend for herself in busy city streets is unheard of. I wouldn't allow a dog to run outside in fear it be run over. This here's New York City; cars running crazy like they do. God knows what can happen. No mistaking, child, I will have a word or two with your mother. "

After about fifteen minutes, Mama Koss told the child, "I guess your mother really is not coming. Come in then."

Turning right past Mama Koss's black, dark, dank hallway, the child was welcomed by an unexpected, sudden, blinding, reverential illumination. *Gasp!* Anna was breathless. She took a deep breath to absorb the radiant sunlight beaming into the humble apartment windows. An irreverent sense of goodness melted the child's anguish and filled her with blessed healing in a Godlike experience. The wondrous sight never lessened in its marvel during the time Anna stayed at Mama Koss's, and the desire to be in the room's bright light became somewhat of an addiction for the child. Without understanding, without questioning, Anna accepted the beautiful rays of incoming light as warm arms that enveloped her in safety and goodness.

The despair of the outside world did not enter this wonderful space, as if the old woman's angelic goodness was divinely recognized and in turn powers blessed her "worthy of a saintly safe haven." The wall of windows situated on the right of the apartment did more than permeate the glow of angels; it was, in reality, also a portal to "the parish of three cats."

Somehow, Little Anna transformed when she sat on Mama Koss's white cloud of a couch, feeling divinely free of fear. Little Anna didn't care that Mama Koss rarely sat next to her to talk. She didn't care if Mrs. Koss sat with her at all. Anna was outside of the confines of her dungeon bedroom, cozily sheltered from the outside world and the harshness of the city streets. Anna contently sat on the cloud of the couch and watched television all day, playing with Mrs. Koss's three cats, Felix, Alex, and Pinky, Anna's first three best friends.

Little Anna enjoyed her stays with Mama Koss, but Mama Koss frequently expressed that, "Business means money need be paid for services rendered."

Anna didn't understand what Mama Koss was saying. Nonetheless, the child replied as instructed by Mother, who foretold, "The Irish woman will complain I've fallen short on payments."

"Mama Koss," Anna repeated, "you gotta talk that stuff with my mom. I'm just a kid."

After a couple of months, Mother Ann was one week behind in her payments to Mama Koss. Mother told Anna, "There's no more Mama Koss. I can't afford her, so take yourself to the park," but Anna went to Mama Koss's instead to see if she could just carry on as usual. *It's worth trying. Mama Koss likes me. Maybe Mother is lying and I can go.*

Mama Koss complained every day, first thing, last thing, and in between. "I like ya, dear child, but me needs money for bills. Do tell your mother."

Maybe Mother's right. But Mama Koss always lets me stay. "See you tomorrow, Mama Koss."

"Not without a check, you don't."

After two weeks, Mama Koss answered the door and said, "I like ya, kid, but unless your mother be having a check for me, you're not coming in."

That day, Anna took herself to the park, and that evening when she returned home after dusk, as house rules dictated, she told her mother, "Mommy, Mama Koss needs a check."

"How do you know? You been going there? I don't know what's wrong with this f**king world! Every penny I earn waitressing goes to Mama Koss, and then my rent don't get paid."

Ingenuity, and plenty of it, was needed to earn money in the 1960s for a single woman absent an extended family to help tend to her child before kindergarten. Free daycare places like preschool hadn't been invented yet. Women stayed home with their children. A mother without a man to lean on was highly irregular. Mother Ann's biggest "catch-22" was how to earn money or catch a man when ball and chained with her dilemma: Little Anna. There were no resources at hand for Mother or the likes of her. Alone, indigent, and desperate with a child, Mother felt hopelessly screwed, without direction, like a broken needle on a compass. That is until fate reintroduced Lili to Ann for companionship.

17

ANN REFERRED TO LILI AS "always the wild and crazy one." Lili was not the best influence on Ann's life. Apparently, the two met as young schoolgirls in Hungary. Ann, not feeling well, was on her way home before her school day ended. Lili was on her way home too. Only Lili's "street walking" was prostitution. Strangely, Lili's bad-girl ways did not correlate with being raised on the right side of town. Lili came from a decent background, with good, solid Christian parents and ample money.

According to Lili, "prostitution happened by chance." The story goes that some man spotted her walking in the rain and offered her a car ride. Lili accepted, not thinking the cost of kindness required more than a generous display of appreciation, meaning an ear-to-ear grin and a "thank you." To the young schoolgirl's surprise, the man rigged the door locks, preventing her escape, until he stole her virginity, after which the rapist threw her out of the car with a fist full of bills and sped away.

Nice, decent girls didn't have the Hungarian *forint*/ currency for new clothes, and they certainly didn't frequent dance halls and nightclubs and do the rest of the things these girls enjoyed. While Country Katy was busy building her empire and City Katy moved on to higher society, Ann and Lili reminisced their old times in their new world, with lit cigarettes and raised foamed beer glasses, and cheered their proverbial motto:

"Nice girls get married; bad girls go to Paris!"

Lili was a piece of work and undoubtedly alluringly attractive. "She looks ten years younger than her age on a bad day and fifteen years younger on a good one. Her natural jet-black hair and coal-black eyes complemented her small, heart-shaped face," was how Mother described her. Little Anna, on the other hand, found Lili *catlike,* with her petite body and her *cat-shaped eyes.* Time, the great revealer, would soon show that as cute and innocent as Lili seemed to be on the exterior, displaying her chiclet-sized teeth, she was equally rotten on the interior, like Little Anna's own mother. Even worse, Lili was an open alcoholic who drank all hours of the day, starting with breakfast.

On occasion, the two women met for the cheapest item on the menu at the local soda shop down the street: a cup of coffee. Ann always arrived no less than thirty minutes early. First thing she did was put her pack of Winston's on the table. Lili consistently showed up late. She'd sit down and rudely rush Ann to finish her coffee. Ann, preoccupied by her own worries, did as she damn well pleased. "I hear you yapping, but all I see is your mouth moving. I don't pay attention. No different than I care about the fly on my food I shoo away."

Lili, with her own agenda, snapped, "Ann, finish with your f**king cup already!"

Ann was oblivious to Lili's current condition, shaking like a leaf, trying to survive a hurricane.

"Are you finished already, Jesus?" Lili snapped louder. "Put the f**king cup down. It's not your father's dick you never had."

Ann put the cup down. "What the hell did you do now, Lili? Do we have to leave?"

Lili, without permission, poured booze from her flask into Ann's coffee cup. Holding the cup with both hands, Lili closed her eyes as she drank like a child delightfully savoring hot cocoa. Lili drank an entire cup of hot firewater faster than most guzzle tepid water.

Lili would call Ann the following day like nothing happened. Ann, desperate to keep her companion, appreciated Lili's cavalier attitude and pretended not to care. Lili couldn't remember what happened from one day to the next. As Ann put it, "Drunk bastard, drank her brains away."

To Lili, Tom Jones was all that mattered. Lili was happiest when she woke up and saw her Tom Jones record ready to rock her world. The Welsh-born pop sensation was the big hit in 1960s America. It's a toss-up as to which gyrated more—Tom Jones while performing or the superstar's black vinyl in Lili's apartment in 1964.

Since Mother couldn't afford to send her daughter to Mama Koss and Pauli fed Anna beer, Mother Ann knew she had to keep the girl out of her sight. Her neighbor and friend Lili had a son close to Anna's age, and somehow, putting the two children together for hours at a time seemed ideal for both mothers. As a result, Little Anna was sent to Lili's apartment. "Anna, you're going to walk yourself two floors down right under us. Go to the second, not the first, door you see right under ours." Anna did just that and knocked. Music was blaring, so Anna turned the knob and announced herself. "Hi, *Szerbusz*/hello, it's me, Anna, my mother sent me?!"

"Come in, come in, go sit next to Suni on the couch!" Lili's voice instructed.

Lili's apartment was the flipped version of Anna's. Anna walked the long corridor leading into the family room, looking for Lili, but instead spotted Lili's son, Suni. She didn't know what to expect since she was meeting him for the first time. He was younger than her by a year or two. Looking around the room to see where she was to situate herself, she noticed that the blasting music was coming from a record player in the one connecting bedroom off the family room. Suni sat parked in neutral, not turning his head to say hello, staring straight ahead in front of the skipping horizontal lines on the television that was on mute. *He must have just gotten beat, and that's why he sits there like that,* Anna thought as she sat down in the only available spot on the black leather couch. The record player was on her left and Suni on her right. *This loud noise is hurting my head.*

"Tom Jones! Don't you love him? Hi, I am Lili!" A small-framed woman jumped out of nowhere into the middle of the room, performing "hot potato" dance moves right in front of the TV. She had a cigarette dangling from her mouth with another cigarette burning in the ashtray on the table next to where Suni sat. The surgeon general's warning, "Smoking is hazardous to your health," wasn't yet established.

After her first introduction, Lili's bony ass and hips swayed and spun through the apartment at the onset of every Tom Jones song. From wherever she was, Lili ran to the record player to swoon the words "Tom Jones." She'd sing the first few words, horribly off-key and out of sync, wearing not much more than her asinine smile. When Lili messed up the words, she winked at her toddler boy and twisted her way to the ashtray next to him to drag off the cigarette, lighting one off the one she had put out into the ashtray and then another one. In other words, she had two cigarettes going at the same time, one in her hand and one in the ashtray. Lili exhaled the smoke into Suni's face, and he turned shades of yellow and green.

"You like that cigarette smoke I blow in your face?" his mother asked him with a stupid grin. Anna was in disbelief as she watched Lili place the cigarette back into the ashtray, positioning the streaming toxic chemicals to wiggle their way into Suni's brain via his nostrils.

Even when Suni's mother danced in front of the TV, facing her son and Anna, Suni's attention remained glued to the black-and-white picture box. After Anna witnessed Lili's unmotherly behavior, she couldn't blame her new buddy's attempts to block out Lili's stupidity, and she tried to follow suit. Unfortunately, she was lured back into Lili's unwanted, awkward show.

How alike and different the two mothers were. Lili danced, parading around her apartment as scantily clad as Mother Ann sported her dress code. Lili's breasts, unlike Ann's, were small. Lili was tiny around her waist and did not benefit from wearing a corset like Ann did. Lili's figure was more boyish. Ann had defined Lili as "young schoolgirlish." She had a flat tummy and a tiny backside. Ann wore the corset "to help keep my middle in line," she explained, because when she removed the waste hugger, her brain demanded, "Eat more."

Anna understood how the two mothers were friends. *Both these mommies are wrong and bad mothers!*

"Suni, where are your books or crayons or toys?" Anna asked.

"The what?" he replied, never flinching.

"Okay, don't feel bad, Suni. I don't have any either."

So, there Anna sat, occupying space on the sticky, sweaty, black leather couch next to a human mannequin, Suni.

Anna wondered, *Does his head hurt like mine? My brain hurts because it wants to learn, but not this stuff!*

"Tom *Jones*!" Lili blurted, but this time she slurred.

Lili shook every body part her dead mother birthed her with, starting the record a third consecutive time and dancing sloppier each time the record played. This time, Lili stumbled to her makeup mirror a few feet away. She briefly stopped to apply makeup and to swig a bottle.

"You like that, Suni?" Lili taunted Suni after she swigged from another bottle and extended her hand with the bottle to him.

Suni grabbed for the bottle. Lili pulled it away from his reach.

"You would like that, huh, Suni?" Lili taunted.

Standing coquettishly in panty and bra, Lili retracted her arm and placed the bottle under her pit to free her hands to wave her forefingers at him. Teasing him, she dumbly smirked, "Not yet. You have to be older to have the good stuff!"

Little Anna wished Lili would *go walk a tightrope without a net or a parachute* like she'd seen on television cartoons. More realistically, Lili should walk the clothesline outside her kitchen window. But Anna settled for Lili swerving into her zip dress. At least Lili was another step closer to being out the door. After one last primp, Lili applied her last coat of hair spray. "You like that? Smells good, right?" Lili asked with a drunkard's twinkling smirk and sprayed some more.

Anna wondered if she was the only one wanting to hurl. The cigarette's stream of serpent smoke from the ashtray penetrating both their nostrils, Lili deliberately exhaling her cigarette smoke into their faces, the aerosol can of hairspray, the non-ending horizontal lines of the too-close television set all on a hot, hot night was too much. Add in the music and shouts of *Tom Jones!* and Anna was wondering, *Maybe I am better off on the streets. At least I can go lock the door to the bathroom stall in the park. This is too much. My head hurts bad.*

Just then, Anna noticed Lili doing something very strange and dared to position herself behind Lili in her bedroom, remaining crouched down and hidden so she could take a better look. Anna began taking mental pictures, keeping her clicking sounds quiet this time. *This is important. I am taking pictures to understand this later.* Lili removed some metal objects from an oddly shaped zipped black bag. Lili then used her lighter under a spoon that she had put something into. Then Lili wrapped a flimsy, long plastic thing around one arm, put the needle into the spoon, and then put the needle into her arm. Lili turned three-quarters around, catching Little Anna's eyes on her. The woman didn't say anything when their eyes met. Instead, Lili's face morphed with a devilish grin. Click ... *definitely don't forget that.* Anna forgot to breathe in that moment, afraid she was going to be yelled at or worse. But luckily for Little Anna, euphoria swallowed Lili away. Years later, Anna would figure out she had watched her mother's friend shoot up heroin.

Little Anna darted back to the sofa. She peered sideways to see Suni still sitting like a suited mannequin. Suni appeared piqued. *Maybe he saw what I saw. What did I see? I want to ask him.* Anna called his name. He didn't answer. Anna called Suni's name again, and this time, she elbowed him in the side to get his attention. In reply, Suni gagged. His gag made her unable to contain her nausea. They both looked at each other, wanting to race to the bathroom bowl. The two children prayed they could refrain from vomiting until after Lili left. Anna recalled her mother saying, "Lili will be up here in an hour," before she left to walk down to Suni's apartment. With that, Anna thought she would remind Lili out loud.

"My mother is waiting for you upstairs, Lili. Was I supposed to tell you that?"

"I am getting ready," Lili slurred, missing the chair she aimed to sit in in front of her makeup mirror, not once but twice, and all the while moving in strange slow motion.

Anna wondered, *What's going on? I never saw my mother do that.*

"Lili, should I go get my mommy to come help?" Anna asked.

Sometime after two prayer hands on the clock indicated noon and a few drinks intermingled with Lili's blood system, she was straight and raring to go. The conclusion to Lili's one-woman show finally ended with her rhetorical question, "Suni, you like your mommy pretty?"

Suni could do no more than sit without saying a word as he turned chameleon colors of nausea. Anna was feeling even worse now. Her head felt like it was exploding. She looked over at Suni and felt bad for his suffering. After all, he was a lot younger than she was, and his mother was not a good mommy. She felt for him in a way she hadn't known before. Anna looked at Lili with the same blank stare Suni did and couldn't help but notice *how stupid Lili's clown makeup looks.* There was a correlation between how badly painted Lili was and how intoxicated she was.

Lili was as poor of an excuse of a mother as Little Anna's own mother. Neither thought twice about leaving Anna to be a freebie babysitter. Anna clutched her friend Suni, for whom she felt sympathetic compassion. She adopted him into her good graces as if she were his big sister, treating Suni with great importance. The two toddlers were being abandoned and unsupervised for a full day. As soon as Lili locked the apartment door, Suni leaped off the couch to begin his treasure hunt and shouted, "I show her ... me no baby!"

His goal was to find his mother's favorite liquor bottle that she'd recently waved in his face from one of her many hiding places. His body trembled as he waited for his mother to leave. Anna thought Suni was sick from the cigarette smoke, hair spray, and loud music—like she was. Anna, a child herself, had no clue that Suni was a suffering alcoholic. Suni was addicted.

While Suni conducted his search as the greatest kid detective, he intermittently rewarded himself, drinking whatever he found to stop his tremors. He climbed kitchen chairs, tabletops, and countertops to scavenge closed cabinets until he uncovered the particular alcoholic flavor he craved. Suni preferred the flavor of dark tea-colored water to plain drinking water.

"Come, you take. Yum good!" Suni said, elbowing Anna.

"No, I don't want," Anna said.

"Come on or I say you hit me. You want to get beat?" Suni said repeatedly.

Anna had enough trouble! So she took a sip. Other than it tasted like firewater in her mouth, down her throat, and in her gut, she became ill. The girl suffered all day on the couch from hot sweats, spinning nausea, and a pounding headache more painful than usual. During which time, Little Anna promised herself to not be bamboozled "by that sweet little Suni-turned-devil to drink firewater again!"

Suni's full nickname was Suni Muni. His real name was Alan. His mother was in a slurring stupor when she nicknamed him. Suni Muni meant Lili's love for Alan was as wide as "from the sun to the moon." His father was a bona fide Swedish diplomat at the United Nations, but most unfortunately, he died in a tragic car accident when the boy was less than a year old. By that time, Suni was bottle-fed a unique baby formula—namely, beer—whenever Lili fell short of milk.

As the hours passed, Anna wasn't sure if she liked Suni so much anymore. She did know she was too little to help Suni stop drinking firewater, and she needed to be her own best friend. Of course, wishing Suni would behave well didn't make it so. Suni's addiction to firewater only worsened his behavior. He became more violent and out of control as the day progressed. Acting crazy, he pushed Anna down on the couch, pounced on her, and thrashed his body on top of hers. He yelled in her ears and continually hit her. None of his behavior felt right. Anna's only refuge was to lock herself in his bathroom. She stayed there until she heard Lili announce that she was home. It seemed like an eternity— many, many hours had passed.

Anna decided she would tattletale on Suni's bad behavior. Anna knew she might face grave consequences for telling on him, but she decided she was more important than the rest of the sickos around her. Without knowing who else to turn to, Anna told on Suni to her mother.

"Mommy, Suni Muni is very sick. He drinks firewater, and that's not normal."

Her mother replied, "I remember Lili saying to me, 'Hey, it's good enough for me,' jokingly while squirting beer from the baby bottle nipple she removed from Suni's mouth into her own mouth, 'so, it's good enough for my baby.'"

Ann and everyone else thought Suni's almond-shaped eyes were from the Mongolian race running through Hungarian blood. No one had heard the term alcohol syndrome yet.

SUNI GOT BEAT. Lili finally knew what had happened to her missing liquor bottles. Lili was furious; she and her fiancé had had plenty of altercations regarding the subject. Each accused the other of taking the stuff. Suni being abused by his mother was nothing new, but Lili's fiancé, Latzi, was now also beating Suni for causing the couple problems. Latzi is Leslie in Hungarian and a very popular name, usually abbreviated to Les. The name Les suited this child abuser and wife beater well because he was *less* than a man and definitely not a *blessing*. Lili's name was also fitting since she was as pretty as a flower, and the stems of her and the lily flower are poisonous.

Lili's newly learned information that Suni consumed their alcohol fueled her aggression toward him. Suni's physical and mental abuse was as much daily news as it was for Little Anna. There wasn't a time the boy didn't have a bump on his forehead or the back of his head. Black-and-blue bruises didn't even count. Morbidly, the engaged couple proudly accepted merit for their handiwork perpetrated on Suni and competed nightly for who did one better than the other. Their favorite sick nightly pastime was to push against a black-and-blue bump on Suni's head with a cold spoon or knife kept in the icebox for the purpose of minimizing its swelled size.

The first time Anna witnessed Suni yelping like a hurt puppy while Les pressed that spoon into his head, Anna pleaded on her friend's behalf. "Mommy does that to me too. That hurts, Mr. Les, you know that."

"I see you've got a big mouth. You want some of this?" Les said, waving a fist in Anna's face.

"Not at all."

"Then shut up, kid!" Les and Lili both yelled at frightened Anna.

Contrary to the use of common sense, after Little Anna divulged that Suni's changing dark moods were due to his consumption of firewater, she wasn't removed from her bad situation. Neither mother cared, perhaps because there were no free options since they hadn't found the tree money grew on. Consequently, Anna was sent to Lili's apartment, where brutalized Suni was dumped into her lap. Anna, filled with anger and frustration on behalf of the two of them, consoled her younger counterpart the best she could. Most times, cradling Suni soothed him best. Anna, no stranger to pitted hell, sympathized with Suni and found her attempts to aid him helped heal her too. The two toddlers fell asleep hugging their arms around each other, bawling in a slobbery, drenched mess. The release of their grievances to the only other person who understood was a good cleansing and bonding cry.

"When we grow up, we can never be parents like them!" Little Anna told Suni, petting his sweat-drenched hair.

How sick life was to allow the injustice of a sweet child to be maliciously victimized by the hands of his own sick mother, while publicly, Lili declared, "I love my Suni Muni so much!"

When the tears subsided, Anna asked All Knowing, *"Why do I have to see Suni suffer?"*

"If not for your friend, would you recognize the misuse of power as clearly? Are you not glad you don't have to go this alone? You have someone who understands. He needs you as much as you need him."

"Thank you, All Knowing. I understand."

"Just remember your promise as an adult."

Anna's promise to not perpetuate harm to future generations would not be forgotten. In fact, Anna had, for a while now, maintained a strong constitution: *I will never allow Mother to change who I am: good, nice, and sweet.*

18

FOR FOUR, SIX, or eight hours a day, the two youngsters, Anna and Suni, both under school age, were left unsupervised, sitting and vegetating on a couch day after day without cerebral stimulation or food to eat. Suni became increasingly difficult to tolerate. Anna's sick alcoholic buddy acted stranger and more aggressive as days meshed into weeks, then months. Anna, the normal one, was left to handle her situation without losing her mind. Anna's brain felt like it was turning into boiled potatoes, receiving a non-ending mashing. Her headaches were continuous due to the television noise, her misbehaving friend, her hollering mother, and hunger. All compounding elements stirred into a big stewing desire to be back with Mama Koss in a state of normalcy and safe adult contact.

On the rare days when the weather intervened with Lili's plan to leave her apartment and Lili wanted the living room for herself, she dismissed the children to Suni's room. Anna took full advantage and made believe they were like Simon Templar in the TV series *The Saint*, robbing the rich and giving to the poor. Anna rummaged through Suni's toy box and found that not one of Suni's toys was complete. If there was a drumstick, there wasn't a pair and there was no drum. Suni owned a paddleball, but the paddle had no ball. Suni's toy chest was as out of sorts with a bunch of junk as Anna's collection of a Mr. Potato Head, gyroscope, and one doll she could touch.

But that's where Anna's active imagination came in handy. The paddle became an oar to their designated getaway rowboat—the bed—while the drumstick became their other oar. In seconds, the bedroom floor transformed into whitewater riptides with the magical wave of her arm and the declaration, "Row faster before the bad guys catch up to kill us both."

Suni lacked imagination, but on some occasions, he was sober enough to play along. When he did, the two created happy moments for each other, making the sadder moments to come and the sadder ones already past a little easier to bear. One thing was certain in those precious moments: Anna felt sibling closeness with her little buddy Suni because they shared a life of unspeakable *secrets*.

On those sparse occasions when Lili cooked a meal, Anna noticed Suni's reactions were the same as hers. He gagged and struggled to keep the foodstuff down. Both mothers' cooking was detrimental to their health, so the two joined forces and helped each other eat what was less likely to make them gag. In the beginning, the idea worked fine until a new set of circumstances made their chore of eating their meals deadly. Suni accidentally knocked the box of laundry detergent on top of his food since it was sitting next to his dinner, cooling on the windowsill. Problem was, drunken Lili was determined to have Suni consume the poisoned food anyway.

"That will teach you," Lili said, smacking Suni on the back of his head as she continued, "not to do things like this on purpose."

The same sort of thing had recently happened to Anna. Opening a can of sardines for dinner, Anna shrieked when the headless fish were marinating with a dead fly. Anna's disgust went disregarded. Mother Ann forced her to consume the entire contents of the can anyway.

"Don't screw around with me. I'm not stupid! I know you put the fly in the sardines! You're going to eat that sh*t anyway. You're lucky I don't make you eat the fly!" *Gag!*

Remembering her plight from the other day, Anna didn't want Suni to get sick. Suni was freaking out. He was afraid of his mother's beatings and was ready to put a spoonful of his dinner laced with laundry detergent into his mouth. With no time for suggestions, Anna waited until Lili wasn't looking, and then she took swift action and dumped the contents of his bowl out the window. Anna had capitalized on the same solution countless times in her own kitchen when Mother left her unsupervised with unpalatable food.

"Done, now remember Suni, you ate all of it, pinky swear."

The food landed on the A&P grocery store roof attached to their tenement. The plan was a success, and they continued taking that course of action to beat their mealtime challenges. Out the kitchen window from Anna's apartment meant she slop-dropped to hidden bushes below. Anna modeled the maneuver from Mother, who tossed ashes and ciggy butts from full ashtrays out the window. Everything sailed smoothly for a while until the building super knocked on Lili's door one day.

The superintendent had a rat problem on his hands, and he couldn't blame one particular apartment for discarding their garbage. The evidence he waited for finally came when a pair of little boy's underwear with fecal matter was found thrown on top of a food pile. He knew Lili was the mother of the only male child in the building, and their apartment aligned with the placement of the food droppings. By chance, the super killed two cats, so to speak, with one slingshot.

The super immediately understood why this strange activity occurred on opposing sides of the building when he laid eyes on Little Anna, who answered the door with the door chain on. He also figured out the two toddlers were left home alone all day because he knocked on Lili's door a few times on different days of the week over a course of months, and no adult was home. Talking through the door, Anna told him so, and he figured out the children's survival tactic.

Perhaps this would end an era of these two toddlers left alone, mentally idle month after month. Indeed, the boy's discarded briefs turned out to be the hailing white flag, innocently discovered by an unsung hero shining a bright light into a dark situation.

"Now that I know what's going on, I'm getting new tenants if this continues."

Both mothers using Anna to attend to Suni as a cost-efficient fix finally came to an end. Little Anna hoped Mother remembered the firewater story and added in what she witnessed Lili doing with a needle in her arm. Anna hoped to be sent back to visit Mama Koss, but Mother had something else in mind. First, Mother marched downstairs and yelled at Lili.

"I know what you did with the missing stuff I am accountable for. Are you crazy? First, you leave me alone with those men for hours while they demanded their merchandise was short, only to find out you were shooting it into your arm. That's not for us to use! I will deal with you later if they don't kill me first!" Little Anna didn't understand all that, but she knew enough to click and store photos for future adult analysis.

Within a week, Mother Ann, in total desperation, wrote her Mutter Clara in Hungary and her Aunt Flora in Germany regarding her battles with heroin. She stuffed the envelope with pictures of her dilemma, Anna, whom she struggled with.

Anna would *never* forget what Mother Ann said to her about this letter she wrote to Clara and Flora. Mother invited her under her bed covers and laughingly said, "Oh boy, I wrote things that are unforgettable. If you ever hear about it, remember it is *not* true. I just said what I said to get help from Clara."

When Anna, as an adult, heard about the letter from Kornelius, Flora's son, Anna didn't know what she wanted to believe or what she believed. Mother was a master manipulator and capable of twisting the truth to obtain what she wanted. On the other hand, Mother Ann on heroin made more sense because of her inexcusable actions. As an adult, Anna, believing that Mother was reprehensible due to her heroin use somehow fed Anna's hope that maybe there was a nice mommy trapped somewhere within the monster.

In the present situation, needing to work without assistance from friends or family, Ann felt thrown into a river. Mob-style, specifically, to drown with a cement block tied around her ankles. Treading water to survive, Ann swam full circle, placing Anna into Mama Koss's good graces. Mama Koss had one stipulation: "I be paid the same pretty penny as any day caregiver."

At least Ann knew, "The old Irish biddy was tested and true."

In return, Ann demanded her daughter be provided one square meal during the child's stay. The two, Mother Ann and Mama Koss, volleyed words back and forth on the issue. In the end, Ann's crazy determination won, making Little Anna a very happy camper. Mama Koss would teach Anna about delicious spaghetti and meatballs and what a sliced tomato looked like, along with the scrumptiousness of chicken with rice. To the child, Mama Koss was a great cook; Anna never had it so good!

Anna could hardly wait to be in the safe confines of Mama Koss, but Mother threw a tantrum every morning. Her latest excuse: "How am I to afford Mama Koss? I work all day kissing asses as a waitress to turn around and pay all my hard-earned money to that big old whore. Be not afraid, I will meet up with that old whore in the devil's house. I curse her. She won't know what leg to stand on. I will snatch the life from underneath her."

On Anna's return to Mama Koss, the digressed child, trained to sit lifeless, sat in fear on the edge of the couch. Mama Koss sensed something was wrong; the child was distant, motionless, uptight, and frightened, expecting the worst. Somewhere along the line, Anna had figured out: "Children are to be seen and not heard." Now, at Mama Koss's, Anna idly stared at the mentally impeding black-and-white television box like she did in Lili's place. The kindly old Irish woman, with a few more deep wrinkles than Anna recalled, sat next to her.

"Let's see what happens," the old Irish woman said in an engaging, loving voice, patting the white cotton sheet protecting the full length of her couch next to the wall of windows.

Little Anna's eyes filled with tears of joy as Felix, Alex, and Pinky pranced in to ingratiate her with their presence and sat next to her. The cats broke the barrier of the lonely world the child had succumbed to. Little Anna, void of siblings and normal interactions with others, petted her long-lost pals appreciatively. "You are all my very best friends! I love you."

Different from before, Mama Koss joined Anna to watch television, chit-chat, and even work on her crossword puzzles next to her on the couch. Little Anna loved being in her company—she hadn't been in an adult's company for any considerable amount of time and pleasantly found that the chubby old lady held a wonderful, even-keeled, soothing temperament. *Ah ... peace and quiet.*

Not meaning to make the little one laugh and merely carrying on as if alone, Mama Koss sat down on the couch to comb her head of thin, greasy, gray hair. The child giggled at the old lady, looking and acting like "Cousin Itt" from *The Addams Family*, talking through her bangs that covered her face. Finding Mama Koss comical, Anna wanted to participate in the fun and placed the woman's glasses gently on Mama Koss's hair-covered face. At first, the old lady misunderstood and quickly parted her hair in anger. Just as she was about to wave her finger and demand, "Stop it," Mama Koss noticed the child chuckling in good nature for the first time. In that moment, Mama Koss wisely recognized they both could use the healing playtime. In fact, Mama Koss played along and cackled so hard that she pissed herself, which, in turn, doubled over the old and the young in even more laughter.

"Well, I do declare, my child. I don't remember when I laughed so hard. You are a dear."

The shared moment of laughter led Anna to take an even better look at this funny, enjoyable lady. Anna didn't understand her mother's humor. The child had forced her laughter as a means of survival, whereas she genuinely participated in this slapstick humor of Mama Koss's. When not looking like Cousin Itt, Mama Koss wore her limp, lackluster hair with a cheap bobby pin. The old lady's wardrobe was that of a church lady, hand-me-down look. Other than a white cotton neck collar framing her face, her plastic buttons clearly indicated how the old lady aggravated her arthritic fingers with every dress she owned in varied muted solid shades of gray. The epitome of plain Jane, Mama Koss accessorized with beige opaque stockings and solemn, nun-like, black lace-up shoes.

If Mama Koss wasn't concerned with her hair, she was concerned with her stockings. Mama Koss should have contacted Jack LaLanne with all her exerted bending, tugging, pulling, and twisting. They could have collaborated on a new exercise routine. Mama Koss adjusted her constantly slipping stockings with numerous apologies accompanying her uneasiness.

"Sorry, young lass, all this exercise," Mama Koss huffed. "Makes me hands and forehead sweaty." The way Mama Koss puffed at a tuft of her fallen bangs covering her face made the child giggle, and Mama Koss would join in with lifted spirits.

During warmer days, Koss rolled her stockings up and down all day long. Her stockings were rolled up to mid-thigh once she stepped outside her city stoop. What that woman did with stockings, resembling the travels of a yo-yo, was cartoonish slapstick and hilarious to the child.

In the end, it was Mama Koss's Buddha belly that didn't allow her to reach her outgrown toenails, which caused her true dismay. However, Anna wasn't one to tell an adult the obvious reason why a new hole constantly popped up.

"Why you think I be struggling with this here so much? God, you think, is punishing me?"

"No, Mama Koss, God wants you to see how funny you are!"

Mother Ann, on the other hand, couldn't disagree more. "I thought I would kill that stupid idiot. What she does with those stockings is inhuman! I threw the donkey-eared one the money and left before I kicked her teeth to the back of her brain."

For different reasons, Anna wanted to tell both women, "Don't bother." Naturally, to Mother, "Don't bother nice Mama Koss." And as for Mama Koss, "Don't bother wasting your energy. There's no avoiding the inevitable elephant leg."

"We have to leave quickly, child!" Mama Koss instructed. Whether they were in the grocery store, on Mama Koss's stoop, in the subway, or in the middle of a department store, Little Anna knew what that meant. Not by the words but by the urgency in Mama Koss's voice and the beads of perspiration on her forehead and her sweaty hands as she dragged Anna away. The mortified woman's face turned pasty white when her stockings plummeted straight to her ankles. Little Anna, too young to explain to Mama Koss, who was too old to understand, wished she could yell God's truth to Mama Koss. *What you do with those stockings don't make a world of difference. Sorry, but you are way too ugly and old for anyone to care what your legs look like anymore. Thank God, I have a good enough mind to bite my tongue. See, I am not my mother!*

Anna loved Mama Koss so much that the mere mention of her name accompanied a smile and a gleam in her eye. Oreo cookies with a big cold glass of milk were the other reasons Anna loved Mama Koss. On the best of occasions, a big bag of Oreos was placed in front of her after finishing her Jiffy peanut butter and Flintstones jelly sandwich. Anna couldn't care less for the sandwich, but she sure was intent on polishing away the whole bag of whipped fat solids with sugar in the middle of the cookies.

Sadly, Little Anna was the worst eater. She easily spent three hours masticating a meal the size of a tea saucer, during which time she memorized everything there was in Mama Koss's kitchen. However, Anna became unrecognizable when a bag of Oreos was torn open. The two textures—sugary soft with a hard crunch in one bite—tantalized Anna to devour the whole bag in one sitting. *The trick is to dunk the cookie as long as possible without losing it to the milk pool of death!* Although her taste buds savored the cookies mushy or crunchy, Anna perceived the first way as a form of mastery, while the latter was a way of dealing with defeat. *No worries, I'll save you; milk spoon to the rescue!* In the end, the spoils were all hers. Her victory: confection!

Mama Koss was a dear heart; she didn't reprimand Little Anna for eating the large bag of cookies. Instead, she jiggled her round middle and said, "I'm going to ask for a raise if you keep eating me out of my cookies."

Mama Koss's place was the opposite of home. Anna abhorred the thoughts of her mother's caca concoctions called cooking. At home, Mother slammed down the food she'd prepared with resentment, demanding, "*Eat!*" Mother then paced like a gnarling hyena ready to pounce. *Boom!* Anna was given one grave smack to the back of her already aching head, accompanied by a punch to her back if she wasn't swallowing within seconds. Then came the broom placed horizontally across her back, held in place by her arms around it to keep her from hunching over.

This happened so often that the scene, embedded in Anna's memory, played in milliseconds of seeing her food, even when Mother wasn't present. The frightful thought of Mother approaching screamed in her brain: "*Eat before I tear your eyes out and feed it to you! Eat before I kick your f**king head in. Eat if you know what's good for you. You have ten minutes! I'm tired of your sh*t. When I come back, you better have made it all gone or so help me, ugh, God, I will tear you limb from limb.*"

Indeed, this was very different from Mama Koss's sentiments of "good appetite" or "simply enjoy." And Mother Ann's words were not empty promises. She was more dependable than the milkman, newspaper boy, or postman with her deliveries.

Flashback scenes of previous mornings ran the gamut in Anna's endless collection of her life thus far: *Mother grabbing Anna by the back of her head to fling her head back to then drown Anna in a concoction of two raw eggs stirred into a hot glass of soured milk that caused the scared child to gag. If the contents went down for a minute, Anna's stomach rebelled against Mother's cruelty and unwillingly exorcised the vomit like a Pollock painting, all over the kitchen floor, table, and walls. And Mother Ann kept true to her word.*

"*I am wiping this mess up with you, you ingrate piece of unwanted stupid brainless sh*t! I'm not making this a total waste!*"

Again, Anna was thrown unconscious. She woke up as if she were a twisted doll tossed through a dryer's spin cycle. Not knowing what finally knocked her out, Anna awoke uttering, "What time is it?"

Not surprisingly, Anna's nerves around Mother made her gag, the smell of food made her gag, the way the food looked made her gag, and the taste made her gag. Technically, food would not go down when Anna swallowed. Her throat was strangulated by nerves in fear of what events followed the sight of food.

But that's at home, Anna reminded herself as she snapped back to the merciful serenity at Mama Koss's kitchen table. In both places, she sat alone, but at Mama Koss's, she was steadily learning that Mama Koss would do her no bodily or verbal harm.

"You been in here for hours, dearie. Should I be worrying about what be happening to you, dear child? I best be sure to give you more milk for them cookies. Why didn't you say something, sweetie? Aye, the last time I checked, I wasn't a mind reader, you know?"

Mama Koss was the one person Anna trusted. At Mama Koss's humble apartment, Anna knew where to find the Hershey's syrup. The chocolaty thick substance stood obediently next to the puke-colored pink bottle of Pepto-Bismol, sharing space in the refrigerator door; Anna could find both items blindfolded. There was a reason for that.

On the evenings Anna slept the night at Mama Koss's, she waited to hear the moaning, ailing lady shuffle her heavy elephant legs to the refrigerator. Anna slipped out of bed and crept beside her, adjoining their shadows, knowing Mama Koss was going to need help finding the pink bottle of medicine.

"Go back to bed, dear."

Anna ran ahead and opened the icebox for the woman. "You gonna need me to reach the pink stuff for ya?"

Mama Koss wanted to be in and out of the icebox in seconds, like every smart, frugal person. This was back in the day when there were iceboxes—before refrigerators—when the ice man delivered a huge block of ice once a month. Mama Koss's eyes scanned the contents in her icebox, getting frustrated.

"Oh, dearie me, where did I put that stuff?"

"Told ya, Mama Koss, you need me." Small Anna interlaced her arm with Mama Koss's. "Come on, Mama Koss, lean on me."

"Aren't you a sweet child?"

"I love you, too, Mama Koss! You need the pink bottle?"

"Aye, I bought a new one the other day. I know I did."

"Can I have some too?"

"It's not candy, child."

The kindly woman didn't want to share her bottle. Since it was an added expense, she did her best to deter the child from its consumption.

"Well, I will show you where it is if you let me have some."

Anna wanted to interact with Mama Koss and convinced the woman to share. "The pink stuff makes my tummy boo-boo go away, and that's a good thing." The child didn't know why she wanted Mama Koss to share her Pepto-Bismol with her other than there was a human closeness *thingy* going on. The child hungered for human touch, as much as Anna felt the old lady longed for someone to listen compassionately to her pains.

Can the child be blamed for wanting human caring? The lonely child was basically left to herself most of the time. The cats didn't even stay with her; they had their own life to tend to in the streets. Everyone seemed to have something better to do than be with her. If Mother was around, she bypassed Anna's presence and reached for the phone or shoved her out of sight. And so, to Anna, the mental movie of Mama Koss extending her a spoonful of chalky pink liquid into her mouth was a fond memory of an adult showing her loving care. For this reason, Anna continually hid the Pepto-Bismol next to the Hershey's syrup one day and behind another condiment the next day. In her way, Anna's reinforced behavior was the loving thanks she received for her young genius.

The child didn't know she was lonely; she just knew she liked company. Mama Koss was an old woman and slept as much as Anna's mother did. The only difference: one was a monster, the other a saint.

19

SPEAKING OF MONSTERS AND SAINTS, Anna asked All Knowing about Suni facing his crucible. *"What's going to happen to Suni?"*

"He has a hard life," All Knowing whispered.

"Hard life like me? Yes, you said I see mine by seeing his."

"Harder," He answered.

"What? How?"

"He won't know one day of happiness, and he will die young."

"That's very sad," Little Anna cried. Wiping her tears, she hoped, *I really, really wish the best for Suni. I think about him a lot, but I won't ask my mother about him. I never want to go back there. I don't want to give Mother any ideas. So, I am not asking Mother how Suni's doing.*

NOT HAVING A PLACE TO DROP OFF Anna on weekends, Mother decided to take her four-year-old child with her to run errands. Mother wore her best red tweed suit with white fox fur cuffs. On this special day, Mother gave Anna a new hooded rabbit jacket that fit her like a coat down to her knees.

"It was nothing for Sidney to give that to you. He is a furrier. It costs him nothing. That's his business," Mother said.

"I love it, and I love Sidney, and I love you most, Mommy!"

Anna was excited for her new coat and to be with her pretty Mommy out of that stinking apartment. Her legs skipped as happily as her little heart fluttered with joy to keep pace with her mother's stride.

"Mommy, I am so happy to be with you today. You look so pretty. I can't wait to be with you more often!"

Anna grabbed her mother's hand to hold it, both in affection and to keep up.

Mother Ann retorted, "And I can't wait until you're out of the house, you piece of sh*t," and smacked Little Anna so hard in the back of the head that she was knocked to the ground. Little Anna was devastated. *I said nice things. She hates me. She really, really hates me. I am taking a picture and remembering this.* Click.

Mother yelled at Anna as she struggled to keep pace all the way to their final destination: a tailor shop. Mother counted to ten with her hand on the door and transformed her monster face into one that was totally composed and smiling. Large salutations were exchanged, as if Mother Ann had not sworn at her child all the way there. The proprietor spoke Hungarian with Mother Ann, and in English, he explained to Anna that his name was "Szabo, which also means tailor." Mother had been delivering food to him that he couldn't buy at the grocery store because he ran his shop by himself and didn't want to miss a customer. Mother then delivered tailored clothes to his customers for a fee. Anna quickly noticed Mr. Szabo had a German Shepherd, and the two wore matching bandannas. Anna loved dogs and got a chuckle out of that.

After a short while, Mother and Anna left. They returned a week later. Upon their return, Mother told Anna, "Shut up and sit in the corner of the place while I speak to Szabo." After their talk, Mother left to run an errand without Anna.

Szabo sat with his back to the wall and faced out the storefront window on his left. The window ledge held his elbow, and his palm held his heavy head. No dog was in the shop that day. Without Mother around, Little Anna asked him from the back of the room where she'd been ordered to sit, "Where's your dog, Mr. Szabo?"

In a glum, slow voice without oomph, Szabo said, "I don't know where my dog is. I let her out, and she hasn't come back."

"What's it take to get one of those fancy things around the neck to match the dog?"

"You mean the neck scarves?"

"Yeah, yeah, those scarves. How do I get one, Mr. Szabo?"

"I make those for us. My dog is like my kid."

"That's nice. You love your doggy, don't you, Mr. Szabo?"

"That dog is going to get run over by a car, and then Mr. Szabo will die a month after," Anna heard All Knowing say into her right ear.

Oh no, poor Mr. Szabo. The child's heart sank. *How do I let him know what I know?*

"Mr. Szabo, you know you can't let your doggy just run around. It will get hit by a car, and then what will you do?" Anna asked, concerned.

"I would die," Szabo said.

OOOH! All Knowing said so! Anna's heart dropped, and she said, "Exactly!"

"Wait a second, how old are you?"

"I am told I am this many," she answered, holding up four fingers. "Four."

"You're a very unusual child."

"You're a very nice man, Mr. Szabo. You take care of your dog. Don't let her out."

Mother swung open the door, making the bells hanging on it clang loudly.

Startled, Mr. Szabo said, "Jesus Maria! Ann, you walk in like a truck driver!"

"Okay, you piece of sh*t," Mother said, directing her comment to Anna, "let's go! As for you, Mr. Szabo, thank you for giving me ten minutes to run and do that for you, leaving her here."

"You have a very special daughter. Keep doing whatever you're doing."

Ugh! My mother has nothing to do with me being nice. Szabo knows nothing.

Mother Ann exited the tailor shop with Anna jogging alongside.

"I don't see what everybody finds so special about you. Everybody likes you but me."

"Mommy, it's very important or else I wouldn't talk. I know you want me to stay shut up. This is very, very, very important."

"Hurry up, you piece of sh*t, we have to hurry."

Anna told her mother what All Knowing told her without naming her source. "Szabo will die within one month after the dog gets hit by the car."

"Okay, I don't know where you get your stupid talk from, but shut up now. I am not interested in this sh*t."

Mother didn't take Anna to run errands for Szabo anymore. But each Tuesday, Anna remembered to ask Mother how Mr. Szabo was since she remembered that was Mother's assigned day for the man. For a while, all was fine—Szabo actually walked the dog instead of letting her out.

A few weeks later, Mother took Anna with her to the thrift store. On the way there, Mother told her, "Now listen, you're to sit in the same hidden spot. Don't move until I come back. It will be a long time, like three hours, but stay here. I can't have you pulling me back. Just sit!"

"Ask about Szabo," All Knowing urged Anna.

"Okay, Mommy, I will do that. How is Szabo?"

"Strange thing, I went there yesterday because it was Tuesday, and he had a sign on the door to come back tomorrow. I went there today, and the same sign was on the door. I don't have time for this sh*t!"

"Mommy! The dog died!"

"What the hell is wrong with you? I don't know why I bother with an imbecile child!"

"Mommy, find out when the doggy died because Szabo is dying a month after."

They arrived at the thrift shop on 84th and Second Avenue. "Remember what I told you?"

"Yes, Mommy."

"What did I tell you?"

"I am to sit here and not move. Just sit."

Mother left without a kiss or any display of affection. From where she was sitting, Anna could see the small traffic of people that trickled in. Anna noticed she was sitting in the storefront window, hidden behind a display placed on her right and a black curtain to her left, which kept her from the store clerk's sight behind the register. She sat for what seemed like a *long, long, long time.* The child became antsy, and she thought, *Something happened to Mother. She forgot me, and I have to walk home.* Anna climbed down from where she was and walked through the thrift store, searching for her mother. She found the bathroom instead and used it before she left and headed to the street. She waited for the light to turn green on the avenue so she could cross over. A policeman noticed Little Anna.

"What are you doing? Did you get lost? Where's your Mommy? How old are you?"

"I am looking for my Mommy. I am this many," she answered, indicating four with her fingers.

He placed her on top of the hood of his police car, and while he talked, all she remembered thinking was, *This copper is a nice man.*

A half-hour later, Mother ran over, and being the actress she was, she said, "*Ay yi,* officer, I am so sorry. My daughter pulled her hand away from mine and ran. Thank God you found her!"

"Oh! You look familiar. We've had this conversation before, Mrs."

Huh, this happened before? I don't remember, Anna thought.

Then he turned to Little Anna and said, "You have to hold your mother's hand and not let go. Now listen to your mother. She knows what's best for you."

If he only knew my mother is the bad one, not me!

"Yes, Mr. Officer man," Anna said, as she thought to herself, *Oh no, that's not right. She needs to apologize, not me. She blamed me for being bad. That hurts. She is bad, not me.*

"Thank you, officer. Thank you, bye," Mother said, tugging on Anna's hand yet smiling at the officer. As soon as Mother turned her back on the officer, so did her fake smile turn into hateful speech through gritted teeth. "Why is it you always find the policemen?"

I guess this has *happened before,* Anna realized, *even if I don't remember.*

"Coppers help people. I was worried about you."

"Don't ever go up to a policeman again!"

"I didn't, Mommy. He came up to me."

"I curse you like a bad dog. I am going to beat your ass so bad when we get home, you're going to wish you were dead!"

In between Mother Ann's delivery of threats, she fed Anna snippets of a previous occurrence when Mother got in trouble for leaving her daughter unattended.

"You're always getting me in trouble. I left you in the baby buggy for fifteen minutes at the bottom of the Ferris wheel in Atlantic City. How was I supposed to know that ride would get stuck with me at the furthest point and I would be up there for two hours? By the time I got down, there were all kinds of cops around your buggy. What an earful I got from them for that! Leave the police out of my life! You hear me, little sh*t?"

"Yes, Mommy, I hear no police. Sorry, Mommy. Sorry."

"I will show you sorry," Mother announced as she shot her hurtful daggers.

Mother pushed and beat Anna all the way home, up the stairs, and into the wall, where she was flown the second the front door was opened. Lights out.

ANNA WOKE UP from Mother's Sony radio blasting "She Loves You" by the Beatles. It was 1964. Apparently, Mother hadn't learned how to use her present from Sidney yet, or she blasted the device on purpose. Either way, Anna knew she better jump out of bed and get ready to be out of the apartment because her mother wasn't about to sing "She Loves You." Instead, she'd belt out, *I will beat the sh*t out of you very shortly.*

Rushing, Anna didn't want to forget a reoccurring dream she was startled out of. She made mental notes as she got dressed. This dream wasn't like her other dreams. She would learn as an adult that it was a flashback to another lifetime.

In it, she had tan skin and not the white she had now. She had short, straight black hair that went to just above her shoulders. She saw herself standing in a long procession. She was the last one in line, and it was because she was half the size of everyone else. She wasn't sure if she was fully grown or a child or perhaps even a fully grown little person. She wasn't sure if she was a boy or a girl. She remembered she had nothing on above the waist and just a brown animal skin or cloth skirt that went to mid-thigh. Each time she woke from this recollection, she said the same thing:

"I am so tired. I don't want to work hard in this life. I been worked so hard. None of us in this line has our own thoughts. We have been zapped of thoughts, and our bodies are made to do very hard physical work. In this life, I don't care what I do; I need to rest. I am so tired. I don't care what it takes. I promise myself that. And the other thing, All Knowing, I don't want to be short again. Never ever again."

It's important to note that Anna at age four was not read to. Mother Ann tried to read a book to Anna about an elephant once, and Anna kept correcting her mother's pronunciation. "Okay, you remember, this is the first and last time I read to you."

Only years later, on a third-grade field trip to the Natural History Museum in Manhattan, did Anna first see a display of Native American Indians, and then later, in fifth grade, Anna learned about Egyptian history when her class went to the same museum. From what Anna saw, she felt she could have lived during either time period because of how she recalled herself in her past life experiences without knowing anything about either of those cultures.

THE NEXT OUTING when Anna accompanied her mother was on a weekend day to Mrs. Kellamin's apartment, which was directly one floor below them.

The two women had met under peculiar circumstances. Anna was with Mother, getting the mail at the wall of mailboxes in their building's long foyer. Mother shoved Mrs. Kellamin to the ground because, as Mother put it in Hungarian, "You're too slow, you old bitch, get out of my way!"

Anna walked over to the elderly, gray-haired woman sprawled like a starfish on the ground and extended her arm as if she could lift her up, but what she was really doing was leaning over to whisper, "I am sorry for my Mommy," into the woman's ear. Mother cursed the elder woman further in Hungarian.

The woman replied to Mother in English, "Hungary is a small country, but one would do well to not underestimate how many of us speak Hungarian. My good woman, I am not what you called me. I understand every word you say, my dear. I am Mrs. Kellamin. You can learn a few manners from your child. She is a dear."

This lady got it right. Tell her, lady. Tell my mother, Anna thought.

Mother replied to the woman in improper terms.

That's a nice lady. How do I get Mother to leave her alone? Then Anna remembered and said, "Mommy, your TV show *The Edge of Night* is starting. You don't want to miss it. Let's go."

Mother took note of the woman's name and somehow figured out where she lived in the building. For some crazy reason, Mother thought it was a good idea to give this woman a knock on her door, accompanied by Anna.

"Why, Mommy? I don't think she likes you," Anna asked as they descended the stairs.

"Who cares? I got to see where I can pawn you off. Maybe she is the answer, or she will know someone."

"Mommy, what's with Szabo?" *It's been a while since I asked.* "The doggy died, right? Is he dead too?"

"How did you know that? The dog got run over by a car, and Szabo's heart was broken or something like that, and he died."

"Mommy, a month later, right?"

"Yes, a month later."

See, I knew. All Knowing told me. He was right.

"Okay, little girl, we are here. Straighten up and smile. Look sweet. I'm going to knock on Kellamin's door; I will be on the side of the *kooky-de-lookey/* peephole so she doesn't see me until it's time to go in.

Mother knocked. Little Anna said, "Hi, Mrs. Kellamin, it's me, the sweet girl from one flight above you."

Mrs. Kellamin didn't want to let anyone in. "Does your mother know where you are? Listen, little girl, I am tired. I don't want trouble," she said, with the protective guard chain still on the cracked door.

Mother spoke their way in. Nice Mrs. Kellamin instructed Mother to "cut up some watermelon for the child if we are going to talk" as she walked the long foyer to sit in the family room.

Anna had never seen watermelon before. She ate all of what was in the bowl placed in front of her, including the seeds. The two women spoke in their common native tongues in the family room while Anna sat in the one chair at a square table next to a window, which was where her mother's bed was upstairs. *I was hoping for a different view than being stuck watching those noisy boys play stickball like I see upstairs. Kellamin and us have the same apartment.* Anna observed Kellamin sitting in the one big chair in that room, leaving Mother standing the whole time they talked. *There's only the one place for Kellamin to sit, so no one ever comes to see her.* When Mother and Anna said their goodbyes, Anna held Kellamin's hand for a prolonged moment during their handshake. In that moment, Anna heard All Knowing tell her what she soon told her mother when Mother asked Anna's opinion about the old woman.

"Kellamin is tired and wants to just sit in her big chair and die. She won't live six months."

"Yeah? I have known someone like that ... Aunt Teresa. Hmmm ... Kellamin said no one comes to see her, not even the one son she has. She also said she was very tired and it was okay if she joined her dead husband's side. I don't know about you, Anna. Some things you say are like from an eighty-year-old woman. I am going to watch this in you. You may be a good judge of character."

That's the nicest thing Mother ever said to me. She can be nice! I love my Mommy!

"Mrs. Kellamin liked you too. Funny thing is she recommended you stay with Mama Koss. You already know and like her. Seems like you will keep going there for now."

Six months after Anna had returned to Mama Koss, Mrs. Kellamin died.

"All Knowing, why do I have to know these things?"

"The information helps you. So you are not in shock. You also gain trust in Me."

WEEKDAYS ROLLED AROUND, and Anna spent winter safely with Mama Koss. It was worth every penny Mother paid and was golden to Little Anna. Suddenly, summer was upon New York City, and life was good. Hot summer air transplanted Anna from Mama Koss's apartment to the stoops of the brownstone building. Nobody had an air conditioner yet—not Mother, Mrs. Koss, Lili, Pauli and Katy, Szabo, or Kellamin—and since Anna knew no one else, that meant the whole world.

At first, the hustle of the neighborhood made Anna uneasy, so Mama Koss sat beside her in her stockings. Not knowing what else to do when sitting on a stoop, Anna wondered why all the stooped buildings were called brownstones when they were different shades of gray. She quickly appreciated sitting on the outdoor stairs as a great way to do nothing more than play the part of a spectator.

With a whole new world open to her, the wide-eyed child loved trying to make sense of the inventive gizmos the Irish street kids wheeled around. Most popular were the makeshift scooter cars made of wooden crate boxes and outgrown or stolen roller skate wheels. In fact, one day, a rough street kid lifted Anna's skates off her stoop while she quickly ran into Mama Koss's apartment for a potty break. She came out just as the skinny thug snatched them. With Anna's skates dangling in the hoodlum's hand, Anna yelled out, "Hey, you can have those."

"Ha, ya sure, kid?"

"Yea, go 'head, I ain't wantin' 'em."

"Nah, I can't take 'em. You're just a baby."

"Yea, go 'head, I don't play in the gutter like you."

"Ya ain't gonna get in trouble?"

"Na, I'll get in trouble, but I didn't ask for them things anyway. Take 'em."

"All right kid. Only 'cause ya tol' me to!"

Anna was glad to give those stupid skates away; she hated falling on her bony butt all the time. *What do I want with them things when I got good legs?*

When Mother found out Anna had lost her skates, Mother chewed her up and spit her out. "That's it! I don't buy you anything else ever again! What the hell for? You are an idiot, and I'm a bigger idiot for throwing away money on you! You stupid sh*t!"

"He was a big street kid. What can I do against a big boy?"

"What's the difference? I'm going to tear you apart limb from limb for being a pushover! Stand up for yourself!"

Mother gave me those so I'll fall down and hurt myself when she's not around hurting me. Glad they're gone!

Some of us can learn no matter where we are placed in life. The desire to learn is a hunger burning from within. Anna discovered that sitting out on the stoop was educational. So far, Anna had learned that getting taken by strangers wasn't half as painful as being mistreated by her own blood. Moreover, the stoop was better than her confining room and even TV. Stoops became even better when Anna befriended a new girl who moved into Mama Koss's brownstone.

"Great, what's this pipsqueak want?" Anna asked Mama Koss when she first noticed the girl.

"Now, child, hush that tongue. What's with you?"

"Well, look at short stuff. What's that?"

"That lass be the same age as you."

This was the first little girl Anna had ever seen outside. Anna's inquisitiveness pushed her to walk down to the lower steps to the yellow-haired girl and introduce herself.

"You look like me. I'm Anna. What time is it?" Anna sat down next to her. "I don't have a watch." *I must be nervous. I'm asking what time it is when I don't care. I always do that!*

After a few awkward moments, they engaged each other in conversation of no importance. All went fine until Yellow Hair opened a pink vinyl case half her size that she lugged around, and Barbie dolls spilled out.

"Anna, change the clothes on the Barbie doll!" she directed.

Anna obliged her new companion, struggling with the zippers and buttons and all the ambidextrous hand-eye coordination needed.

"I finished dressing the doll," Anna said, glad to be done.

"Okay, good, now undress her and put this stuff on her."

With the miniature beauty queen not worth Anna's expended effort, Anna threw the half-dressed doll into the girl's case, zipped the case, and declared, "Nope, I'm done."

Yellow Hair was adamant about altering Anna's perception of the doll, but there was no convincing Anna to be enthusiastic about what she saw as a waste of time.

"Barbie's a stupid doll! There, I said it!"

"How can you say such a thing?"

"You're right, I take that back. Barbie stuff, all of it, is dumb!"

Yellow Hair began to cry as she reopened the vinyl case and organized her stuff to fit into the pink frilly box. Anna gladly helped her get the froufrou junk gathered and out of sight.

"I am never going to bring my beautiful Barbie out to play with you again! You hurt her feelings!"

"That's a great idea. Go and put her away!"

Yellow Hair was still sniveling as she walked away. Her mouth kept making comments that fell on deaf ears. Anna felt bad, but she didn't know what the little squirt wanted with all that pink-and-purple lacy stuff. She just knew the girl didn't come up for air, talking incoherent nonsense. Not once did she ask Anna a question that made sense. Neither did Anna know what to make out of not being able to relate to this tiny person who was her gender and size. *No one dresses like that! What's so great about doll hair or matching shoes to its outfit? Dressing a doll to redress a doll to redress it again, again, again is stupid!*

Yellow Hair's presence in Anna's life did not go without purpose. Reviewing her encounter, Anna was proud she spoke up for herself. Anna took a huge leap after that. Literally, right off the stoops! She set out to play with the big kids on street level. She joined those celebrating their childhood freedom, howling in wild laughter. She immediately learned she liked boys, but not to primp and pose for but to play with, race against, and throw a ball with.

In particular, she noticed this one boy named Timothy. She observed him for a couple of weeks from the stoop and noticed he was equally nice with everyone. Actually, he was the one who deserves the credit for being the first kid to invite Anna to play. They met when they were the only ones outside one morning.

He asked her, "Why do you always stay on the stoop and watch and never ask to play."

"I'm not allowed off the stoops."

"Who's watching?"

Well, that was all Anna had to hear. "I'm not sitting on those stupid steps anymore!"

The two of them hit it off with a great friendship. Anna loved the way he followed her suggestions with great eagerness.

One day, someone pointed out, "Timothy don't walk right. He walks like a *retard.* "

"What's wrong with Timothy that you make fun of him like that?" Anna asked.

"Timothy's one leg drags behind the other. You see anybody else walk like that?"

"No, but why does that make a difference? He's so nice. Ain't that what counts?" Anna responded, using words to try and fit in with the other street kids.

Timothy was Anna's first human friend out in the big world. He knew all the children on the block and included Anna in their races. The kids lined up straight across from the wall of a building to the end of the street.

"No one standing in the gutter can run! Huddle in. Everyone squeeze in tight, shoulder to shoulder," Timothy said.

"Tell us when to go, Timothy."

"Go!"

Anna, too young to understand the concept of competition, was glad to simply be included and didn't realize she came in last every time. Timothy, happy not to be the last when Anna raced, made certain she felt like a million dollars to keep her around.

"Don't worry about these hoodlums. You really beat them all."

Anna's expression spoke louder than words. *What, do you think I'm stupid?*

Timothy pulled her arm back. "You really did win." Other times, he added, "You really run fast for your age."

Anna shrugged her shoulders; she couldn't care less. She delighted in running in the streets, freely howling with the pack of neighborhood children.

Later, back in the apartment, Anna asked Mama Koss, "Why are the street kids so mean to Timothy?"

"Their fathers be too busy playing policemen to mind what their own kids are doing, and their mothers be too busy hitting the hooch, so they all be blind or not caring," was Mama Koss's keen Irish perception.

That sounded too smart to forget. Busy remembering that, Anna noticed how all the mean kids had freckles and Irish names. On a regular day, out of nowhere, a ruffian Irish street gang scooted onto the block, rushing in from all directions in an overwhelming, menacing way. The gang was particularly "looking for Timothy, the one in a shackled iron leg brace."

In no time, the leader spotted his target. "Hey Timothy, how is you running today, huh?"

The other kids laughed and pointed at Timothy.

"Stay there and watch. I win every time!" Timothy then walked over to Anna and crouched down to look her straight in the eyes. "Anna, you just do like you been doing all this time, okay? For me?"

"Just say go!"

The kids laughed. "That's who you're racing against? You're kidding; she's half your size!"

"Go!" Tim said emphatically.

Anna swung her arms, using greater upper body movements than lower. She grimaced her face as if exerting strain but didn't engage her legs as needed, not yet understanding racing. Still, Timothy barely won.

"See, guys, I won. I've got it!" He hobbled over to the leader, hoping to get his approval. "See, I'm still good enough for you guys. Please, please," he begged, "let me play with you guys!"

Anna looked on in disbelief; she didn't understand why Timothy would want to subject himself to further ridicule.

"He is in trouble if he goes," All Knowing whispered in Anna's ear.

She felt sick with worry in the pit of her stomach. *These bad boys are going to hurt him if he goes. Look around at the other kids. Look at their faces; they don't care about Timothy. What time is it? Oh boy! I'm really nervous! It's time I do something!*

Every picosecond counted right then. Timothy was hobbling away with the boys who had come for him.

"Don't!" Anna yelled out to Timothy, who was now a good distance away.

Timothy swung around for a second. His joy-lit face showed that he had misconstrued the gang's vicious intentions. He was sweet, easy prey to these hood rats with itchy whiskers anxious to tear him apart. *Quickly!* Anna had to think fast. How does she harbor him from danger, save him face, and still keep him in his happy place in one timely move?

I have to make him stop! Anna gathered a deep breath, filled her lungs, and yelled after him with all her might, "Don't forget to have a good time!"

Timothy pivoted his body around, poorly hobbling with his leg backward, and called back, wincing, "Say what?"

Anna managed to capture his attention. Now she needed to change her words. She yelled back, "Race me one more time?!" She hoped Timothy could not refuse her offer. Anna had to remove the blindfold covering his eyes. Anna had watched a lot of television movies and found Timothy was no different than an innocent victim facing a lawless firing squad. Maybe Timothy was blind to see what was clearly evident to her. Anna would do what she could to stop this execution!

Yes! Timothy turned around and walked back to Anna, lining up next to her; Anna brazenly called out to the gang leader, "Hey, Chief, say go when you feel like it."

Anna whispered into Timothy's ear, "Watch how easily your friends laugh at you."

Somewhere between the last race and this one, Anna figured out why Timothy always waited for her to race along with the kids. He had to beat somebody; his inner pride wasn't the issue, but his inner fear was. Anna knew he allowed her to win at particular times in order for Anna to feel good, but that was only when it was the two of them, and she paid him back for those times in spades. But now, Anna felt she had to be cruel to be kind and expose the gang kids for what he blindly did not recognize as foes. *I can't let them kill Timothy.*

"Go!" Chief bellowed.

"Hi-yo, Silver!" Anna burst forth with intent. She allowed Timothy a running head start, yet she was determined to beat him at all costs this time. Halfway done with the race, Chief became distracted and ordered to recall the race in the sake of "fairness." Anna joined the line, waiting to redo the mad dash, but not without first expressing her sentiments. "Fairness! In fairness, pay attention!"

"Go!"

The race was on again, and Anna looked back after crossing the finish line. Timothy was painfully hobbling along; his leg gave way, and he fell to the street, grimacing in pain. Grabbing his leg, he rolled side to side, his face contorted in excruciation.

"My legs, they don't do what I want them to anymore!"

His crying had the street kids snickering. The more he expressed his suffering, the more comical the street rats found his actions. Anna's heart went out for this great kid. *These gutter rats will never be half the person Timothy is.* Anna crouched down next to him, prepared to be shoed away. She knew people had their pride. "Help me up," his eyes appeared to say. With her strong shoulder for him to lean on, Anna gladly became his crutch, gingerly assisting him over to the fire hydrant to sit on a short distance away from the others.

"I will stay with you, Timothy, until you ask me to go," Anna said as she turned her head and wiped away a stubborn tear. He never asked her to go. Being a sensitive child, one familiar with emotional and physical defeat, Anna's heart felt for Timothy's suffering, and she did the best she could to comfort her friend whose heart voiced the despair his lips did not utter.

Anna remembered her pinky. She hadn't known it was broken when her mother picked her up out of a weave basket and the finger got stuck inside one of the weaves. She just knew it wasn't like her other fingers. Then one day, when she was older, Mother cruelly reprimanded her for her odd behavior, shaking the tightness from her right hand. When Anna showed Mother the deformed pinky, Mother Ann figured out what had happened by correlating the event to Anna's nonstop crying for two solid days.

Recently, Anna had prepared a few compassionate words for her friend Timothy in one of her many moments alone. She fused the two—Timothy and her pinky—together. She would make good use of her pinky, if for no other reason than to form premeditated comforting words for her Timothy.

Now, in Anna's attempt to soothe Timothy, she pet her friend's back, leaned into his face, smiled at him, and recalled her rehearsed words of encouragement to share with him. "This pinky has been crooked since I can remember. See how it can't stand with the other ones, not because it doesn't want to, it just can't? Go ahead, push it, and see if it will go with the other ones."

"So! *Who cares* about your pinky?" Timothy cried out. "What's that got to do with me?"

"Timothy, you remind me of my pinky. I love it very much because it is different and because it does such a great job trying so hard to keep up with the others."

Timothy threw his arms around Anna joyfully, exclaiming, "I love you too!"

Her face swelled in happy tears. "I've hardly heard those words before. Wow! Really? I love you too!"

Anna didn't know it, but she saved him that day.

The next time Timothy went outside to play, he was wearing a pair of crutches along with his one leg iron. He participated in a street race he orga-nized; naturally, the crutches made his running awkward and hindered his speed.

Anna asked Timothy, "Is it okay for you to run with those things?"

"Don't worry about me. I'm gonna get better. The doctors don't think so, but I know so."

Later that day, after a lengthy rest, he tried again using just one crutch, and later in the day when the Irish bully gang popped up, he laid down even his single crutch. Timothy called, "Everyone, line up," and ran on all fours like a dog to race. Everyone but Anna stood there roaring in laughter. Chief was laughing so hard he had to hold his stomach so it wouldn't shake so much.

"Go!"

The race was on. Anna knew to slow down. Her friend's dignity was at stake … Anna let Timothy win.

The next time Anna saw Timothy, he was wearing iron braces on both legs. Anna's heart fell to the pit of her stomach. "What's on both your legs now? Are you sure you're getting better?"

"Let's run!" he greeted her with lifting high spirits. "Let's run!" His grin was contagiously catchy, and together, they went off, with Timothy hobbling and Anna running. She let him win every race; she was happy to see him smiling. He just wanted to be like the rest. He openly pleaded for his legs to obey his commands. Somehow, he believed his strong will would refuse his body's own determination to fail him. *I know what that feels like after an ass-whooping from Mother! I wanna run, and my body doesn't listen!*

"I'll get better, you watch. I showed those doctors once; I'll show them for good."

There were times when Anna removed herself from witnessing Timothy's loud cries. She couldn't stand to watch the other children bark like a pack of wolves at his demise. She thought that if she left, Timothy might stop. *How did he manage to be blind to their meanness?* Somehow, the cost of playing would never be too high for Timothy.

Suddenly, one day, Timothy just vanished. He hadn't come around. Walking to or from her home, she never bumped into her best friend, Timothy. Anna waited on the stoops for Timothy, day in and day out, for what seemed an eternity, in the meantime avoiding the street rats who asked her to race. After a while, she realized that something was wrong. Anna finally worked up the nerve to stop the smallest one in the rat pack.

"I haven't seen Timothy for a long time. You know anything?"

"Pipsqueak, you ain't heard?"

I'm not Pipsqueak, that's Yellow Hair. But let's hear what this rat says.

"I ain't heard nothing," Anna replied in the way street rats spoke.

"Timothy, he got this thing called polio, you know that, right?"

"Polly-who, what?" Anna didn't understand.

"He's in a wheelchair."

"Will he come out to the street?" Anna asked.

"Boy, are you stupid. Timothy is in a special home for unwanted kids."

"I want him. Where do I go?"

"You're not getting it. You don't matter. His parents sent him far away. He's left to rot and die there, wherever he is."

God, this kid is mean, Anna thought before she asked, "Are we talking about the same Timothy? He told me he was gonna be better."

"He was in a home before; he did get better but now he's real bad off."

"I don't understand. What happened?"

"On a day you weren't here, he went off to play with those tough kids. You know Timothy's dad is a police captain, and the gang picked on Timothy cuz his dad put all their dads in prison. Timothy's dad was too embarrassed by his half-okay son in the first place. Them boys beat Timothy up real, real bad to teach his dad a lesson. So, his dad put Timothy in a home. His dad don't wanna deal with him no more."

"What about his mom; she don't love him?"

"She's a drunk."

Now Anna had learned a few things. First, Mama Koss was right with what she said. "Their fathers be too busy playing policemen to mind what their own kids are doing, and their mothers be too busy hitting the hooch, so they all be blind or not caring."

Second, Anna now understood why Timothy tried so hard to be like the other kids. He didn't want to be sent away again. He was in remission, and he wanted to stay with his parents. He relished better than anyone what being a kid meant, at all costs.

Third, *Timothy taught me a lesson. You can be the nicest person, but mean people will be mean anyway.*

Last, and most of all, *All Knowing was right about those bad boys. They were gonna do bad things to Timothy. I saved him when I was there. It's all I could do.*

Tears poured from Little Anna's eyes. She went in search of him, hoping the neighborhood street rats were playing a mean prank on her. She woke up early in the mornings and went downstairs, looking everywhere she had found him in the past. She couldn't find him. She prayed for him.

God bless you, Timothy, wherever you are. I hope you know you're special and how special you made me feel. I wish I could visit you and make you all better. I love you, Timothy. I know you know that.

Timothy's presence in Anna's life was God-sent, a young saint in the making. He was the perfect example of how everyone could live every day. He taught her to remember that we don't know what tomorrow will bring. Overall, friendship carried a sweet bitterness—sweet when all is well and bitterness when feeling the pain of someone she loves. Also, Timothy's strength was Herculean, strength that Little Anna admired; she wished she could dull her sensitivities the way Timothy had mastered his. At times, Anna felt more for Timothy's suffering than Timothy felt for his own. Anna's mother made her feel that being "too sensitive" was a bad thing. Indeed, Anna would have traded this for some piss and vinegar in her blood. But we are who we are, and Little Anna wasn't going to change—just like Mother was never going to turn into a sweet Mommy.

"God bless you! I will never forget you, Timothy!"

20

ANNA WAS GLOOMY and non-responsive to Mama Koss's silly antics since Timothy was gone.

"What be wrong with you, child?"

Anna shared her grief over Timothy with Mama Koss.

"Would your mother be allowing you to wear a locket, child?" Mama Koss inquired in her wee bit Irish way. She had to repeat herself a couple of times, not because the child was hard of hearing but because Anna had no clue what she meant by "locket." Mama Koss was blabbering to herself about a special piece her daughter didn't wear.

"Anna dear, you might take a shining to it. Why, it does no good just sitting in a drawer. It's meant to be worn."

Mama Koss removed an item from her dresser in the adjacent bedroom then returned and sat next to Anna. "Turn around, dear," she instructed as she clasped the chain around her neck. "Now, let's see how you be looking ... aye, like a young lassie."

"I love Lassie! You like Lassie, but you're a cat lady?"

Anna then sat there. Mama Koss was preoccupied with thought. Anna had learned to silence herself at such times, in fear of a beating from Mother. She wasn't allowed to disrupt Mother's concentration. So she sat waiting for her next instruction; she didn't know what was going on.

"Go on, girl, go on, take a look at yourself."

The girl spun around a few times.

"The mirror is in my bedroom. Go take a gander."

Anna glanced at the necklace around her neck, not understanding why she had to look in the mirror when all she had to do was look down and see it around her neck.

"It's great, it's very nice, it'll make whoever gets it happy," she said, turning her back to Mama Koss.

"What are you standing like that for, child? I thought you would be happy for it!"

"I am waiting for you to take it off. I don't want to like it. It's not mine."

"Would you like it if it were yours?"

"Oh yes, Mama Koss, it's very nice, but now you're being mean."

"Mean, how? I am trying to give you the necklace."

Anna finally caught on. "This is for me?" She jumped up and down for joy. Mama Koss took the child's hand and guided her to stand in front of the mirror to see herself. Anna didn't want to look at herself in the mirror, so she looked away. The only times she saw herself in a mirror were when Mother forced Anna to look at herself as she brutally beat Anna's head like a ping pong ball, paddling the child with the brush's bristles. Anna's face, at such times, matched the framed picture Mother displayed on the dresser for all to see.

Mama Koss, unable to pass her fingers through the child's hair, picked up a brush to remedy the situation. Anna flinched in fright.

"You know, child, you have become very close to me." Mama Koss gently continued, "I would trade you in for one of my real daughters."

"I am not saying anything, Mrs. Koss, but I have a feeling I know which one."

Mama Koss laughed. "Oh do you now?"

Anna turned around with her hair combed without a tug or a swing to her head and gave Mama Koss a big hug with a smile in thanks. Mama Koss made her feel special and loved that day; she wore her necklace like a badge of special-ness—a proud declaration that someone loved her.

Anna made certain all the street rats knew that "Mama Koss, she loves me. She gave me this!"

ONE DAY, ANNA WENT OUT to the street to play, but none of the rats were around. Instead of going back inside, she decided to explore her area with a new set of eyes. Just two brownstones over, she spotted a coffee shop. *How come I have never seen this before?* She was hesitant about stepping inside. The door to the place opened, and a big Irish kid walked out.

"Hi ya! What they got in there?" Anna worked up her nerve to ask.

"Yeah squirt, soda and candy in the back."

"I got five cents. They got pretzels?"

"Don't know, get yourself a free burger."

Anna ventured in despite her knees knocking from nerves. The place was packed with people shouting at each other, even the ones occupying the same table. Anna forged forward and got stuck in a spot, unable to move due to the density of the crowd. She stood next to customers who were seated at a table and noticed they were still bigger than her. They caught her gawking. Anna heard Mother yell at her like she did when her mouth fell open and stared for any length of time: *Little clitoris, close your legs, you're attracting flies.* So, catching herself, she asked the people who seemed to disapprove of her stare, "Are there pretzels? It's all I need."

"In the back," one person said and pointed, *as if they are cowboys hitching a ride cuz their horse skedaddled ... like I've seen in cowboy movies with what's-his-cigarette-smoking-face, John Wayne.*"

Anna wanted to get out of there. All the people and all the noise made her second-guess her desire for salty pretzel sticks. Then her stomach growled, so she forged on.

Lost in a sea of buttocks, she nudged her way in further. *I'll be like Elmer Fudd hunting rabbits, but I'm hunting for pretzels. I'm keeping going. I hope they have penny pretzels in here!* The ordeal of being so short made her promise herself, *I'm praying extra hard to become tall tonight. I'm tired of being little.* She weaved in and around people who were standing and waiting to place their orders at the long counter.

"*Someone here is up to no good,*" All Knowing said.

Oh! Anna immediately froze. Suddenly, a shudder of goose-pimpled skin from head to toe traveled the gamut of her small body. The hairs on the nape of Anna's neck and the hairs on the side of her face all stood static electricity straight. An ominous feeling of danger flushed through her. Wide-eyed, Anna checked her immediate area. Her creep radar that NYC dwellers obtain and her warning from All Knowing placed her on high alert.

In a glance, there's not much difference between a bat and a rat. A rat has eyes. A bat is a tailless rat that flies blindly. Sonar is the bat's gift, compensating for its blindness. Just like a blind tailless winged rat, a bat is guided away from impending obstruction. Similarly, Little Anna was given keen sensory percep-tiveness attached to her oversensitivity, which dealt with more than emotions. If a bat flies into a wall, it probably meets its death. Little Anna was soon going to learn that trusting her strong sensitivity was a great advantage in detouring doom. So yes, Anna sensed things others were not able to. She was akin to the blind bat that had to learn to use another sense: a sense of hearing. When Anna listened to her inner voice, her connection to a higher vibration—All Knowing—she saved herself much harm. And as far as Anna was concerned, she likened the oblivious people in this establishment to dumb rats for not sensing an obvious dangerous person among them.

"*Who is he?*" She concentrated.

"*You'll know,*" All Knowing said.

No doubt, Anna sensed a predator within. Her keen perception zoomed in on one grotesque old man devouring her and scheming as he watched. Unluckily for her, the creep strategically placed himself where Anna had to pass by him to find out if this store carried pretzels.

"I want pretzels, and I've got to watch out for that man. I don't like him,"

Anna said out loud. Doing so might have been labeled as awkward, but with her luck, the place was anything but quiet.

"I want pretzels. I gotta find out if they have pretzels." Her mantra helped her focus on her mission. All the while, she kept an eye on the grotesque old man. His presence grew more imposing as Anna walked her way closer toward the back. *He's a grotesque, old, fat, spotted thing, not a man but a yucky monster.*

Anna controlled her impulse to jump onto the countertops to yell: *"Danger! The devil's here!"*

Obviously, *no one saw* what Anna *saw*; otherwise, the police would have been on the scene and the restaurant patrons cleared out. Anna was sure this old man definitely had skeletons in his closet; for that matter, they were in his walls too.

Evil cries of victory escaped from within this demonic-ruled entity posing as human but slithering as a beast in and out from the depths of his dank, dirty darkness, where he committed the vilest acts against the most innocent. His plan was to rear his ugly face briefly for the purposes of capturing his next victim. This monster sought to add another suffering to his countless number of victims. His satanic hunger would not go unsatiated. He was among the devil-possessed or demon incarnates addicted to acts vomited from festered minds of demented wicked pleasures.

The thrill this gruesome evil spirit derived from witnessing pain was what filled him with life and purpose in a way only one perverse like him could honor and understand. All else would throw him into a pit to burn for eternity if they were wise—if they, in the first place, could detect the demon's true nature. His numbers logged already exceeded the denomination needed to guarantee him his gateway to hell, yet this fiend had no desire to cease his bile sport of snatching souls; instead, each instance further enticed his ghoulish needs for his next feeding frenzy on innocent flesh. Vile thoughts sadistically needled his wicked mind, setting his piercing eyes on his perceived next target. Right now, the monster's binoculars were magnified on Little Anna.

Hopefully, Yucky Monster is so scary ugly that other kids will stay away from him. I know he is bad, but will the others? Pipsqueak Yellow Hair better watch it. He could trick her. She'd be sorry.

Suddenly, Yucky Monster grabbed Anna's arm. His yellowish-brown stained teeth were ghoulish, and his parted, chapped lips released a vapor from a recently relished tortured soul crying aimlessly to be released. Anna intently tuned in to her own inner connecting voice for strength.

"Get what you want. Get out. Get away from this bad man," All Knowing spoke in a direct, demanding tone—a tone she hadn't heard him use before and one that emphasized danger.

"I remember when I bought half a pound of candy for a penny," Yucky Monster said.

You not only look old, you are an old, old man, Anna thought.

He said something. Anna cut him off. "You're a stranger, and strangers aren't supposed to be talking to little kids," she stated, wisely omitting but thinking, *unless they think bad things.*

He kept yapping, doing his best to engage her. Anna noticed he turned his body in an attempt to trap her. Anna pushed her way free, stepped up on a foot-rest, and maneuvered up onto a stool that had just become vacant. She stood on her knees and waved at the black-mustached man working the counter. He was busy answering questions from a bunch of others placing their candy orders, and Anna desperately waved more fervently. Still unnoticed and increasingly nervous, Anna shouted to gain the shopkeeper's notice.

"Help me over here, sir! I don't want this man bothering me; all I want is five pretzels!"

For a second, the place went dead silent, all eyes looking at her. The handle-bar-mustached man, appearing more like a saloon tender in a cowboy flick, finally shot his attention her way. "Yes, kid, you got me! Bang, bang, right back at ya. What can I do ya for?"

Yucky interjected in a sloppy spray of words, "Joe, get her whatever she wants. I got the tab."

Little Anna turned around to look at the imposing Yucky Monster, pushed her hand in his direction, and said, "I don't want anything from you."

"Okay, kid, what'd ya want? Soda, cake, pie, a burger, you name it, Joe got it."

"How much is a pretzel, sir?"

"I don't got us the street pretzels in here, kid. I just got the penny pretzels behind me. "

"Where? Are they the long stick kind for one penny?"

"Na kid, what's your name, kid? You don't want that!" Yucky Monster interjected.

"Cake, burgers, kid? Come on, what's your name, what's your game?" Joe said.

"I ain't got no name when it comes to strangers. I don't want nothing from this man here. I just want my pretzels; I got five pennies."

"Okay, listen, No Name, it's your first time here. Get a burger. Next time you come in, you pay me."

"I ain't wanting no burger. I'm wanting five pretzels, no disrespect, Mr. Joe sir," she leaned up over the counter to tell the man something out of the old man's earshot. "I just wanna get outta here, away from this scary old man!"

"All right, kid, he's in here every day. He's harmless. Here are five pretzels."

"What's she getting, Joe?" Yucky asked.

"Don't worry 'bout it, it's on me," Joe said.

"No thanks, Mr. Joe. Here's my five cents. Just give me the pretzels I paid for."

She plopped down the five pennies—two shiny, the others not—snatching her well-deserved trophy for her efforts. Descending the barstool, she turned to head out the door, pretending to be the Statue of Liberty, holding the pretzels high above her head like a torch representing her beacon shining her way out of the joint.

"Why didn't you let me buy you something?" Yucky asked, grabbing Anna's arm.

The child couldn't remember if she ever saw *a more ugly* human.

"Get out, away from him," All Knowing urged Anna.

Anna kept her composure as she held her scream inside. All she wanted to do was run from this fearful man.

"No thank you. I have a nickel to spend if I want to."

Winking at the proprietor, Yucky Monster called out, "Tell her I'm all right, Joe!"

Anna paid close attention just in case her hunches were wrong about him, but her goal was to get away.

"Come on, Glow Ball, I need help! I don't know what to say to get away!"

"Why don't you let me get you a hamburger?" Yucky asked.

"I will get myself what I want."

"Well ... ain't you a smart one."

Alarms, all kinds, sounded. Ambulances, fire truck sirens, fire alarms, burglar alarms, police in pursuit, alarm clocks. *Alarm clocks!*

"What time is it?" Anna blurted.

Oh boy, I'm nervous! But that's a good question. I know what to do now. She was smarter than he could ever imagine. Anna's mind replayed All Knowing's advice:

You're never alone. You are connected to Me, and through Me you have all the answers you need.

Right! And what I hear now is I gotta get outta here!

"What time is it?" she said again more forcefully to Yucky Monster.

To whatever he said, she answered, "My family is expecting me ten minutes ago. They're looking for me right now!"

Once again, she held her pretzels high, extending her ability to be seen. "Move it, people!" she repeated until she pushed her way to freedom on the other side of the exit door.

ON ANOTHER BOREDOM-FILLED DAY, the pretzels beckoned Anna to reenter the store. *What are the chances Yucky Monster will be here again? He is in jail or squished like a roach by now.*

This time, when Little Anna opened the door and stepped inside, she quickly stepped back outside, overwhelmed by the unexpected lack of people. Inhaling a deep breath with clear intentions of acquiring her yummy salty sticks, Anna walked back inside and headed to the back since the only store patrons were seated at the soda fountain counter.

"Hey kid, you're back?"

"Hello, Joe Sir, yes, I wish to buy two pretzels, that's two cents, right?"

"You remembered my name, I'm impressed," he said. Handing Anna the requested items, he added, "Still got no name?"

"No name is as good as any, thanks Joe," Anna said with a smile and thought, *Nice try.*

She put her two cents down. On her way to the door, Yucky Monster unexpectedly grabbed Anna's hand. "Look what I have!"

Besides shaking, spotted hands? Anna thought, disgusted by his touch.

The devil managed to sit on his spiked tail and pulled out a little box from his pants pocket. "SUCRETS" was printed on the top. Anna didn't recognize the name as any candy name she knew, so her mind photographed it. Yucky opened the tin and urged her indulgence.

"Pick one of the candies I have in here."

Quick to notice, Anna considered, *This guy thinks there are two suckers here.* Obviously, there was the one in the tin; the other he thought was the little girl. He was testing her out. Lucky for Anna, she wasn't an easy target. Anna recognized medicinal pills among his offerings, and she called him out on her findings.

"You have aspirin and other pills in there!"

"Oh, these two are aspirins."

"No, these two are aspirins, and the other ones are medicines. There's only one candy in there, mister!"

"You really are a smart girl. How about you come back to where I live, and we play some games. I have new ones you have never played before."

Anna gave him a look that said he better let go of her or she would scream. "You're a stranger. You are not allowed to touch me!"

He let her go, and Anna sped to the door with her heart racing out of her chest. *That old fart was up to no good! Coppers ought to billy club him and drag him to jail. That's where bad guys like him go, at least in cartoons.*

From now on, no matter what, Anna decided that as good as the pretzels were, she would fight her urges and stay put on the stoop when no other kids were outside to join her in play.

21

A COUPLE OF WEEKS PASSED with Anna sitting alone on the stoop. One day, heading to do more of the same, *nothing,* Anna did a double-take. Pretty Yellow Hair was already sitting in the spot where Anna had first introduced herself.

"Still playing with Barbie dolls?" Anna asked, thinking how stupid they were. She then plopped herself beside the girl. Yellow Hair was someone Anna could show off her pretty locket to, although she still didn't have a picture to place inside. They conversed about nonsense girlie stuff, and Anna didn't have a clue what the girl was talking about. When Anna asked a question, Yellow Hair went on tangents without answering the question. *Why do I bother listening to her? Argh!*

"*Let her talk. Listen to what she has to say. Something happened. Listen,*" All Knowing whispered into Anna's right ear.

"*Oh, you're here with me. It's good you're here. She is so boring. Okay good, I don't have to always talk, I can listen ...*"

"*Shhh! Listen!*" All Knowing interjected.

Oh? What could have happened to her? I bet Yellow Hair met Yucky Monster! Is that it? The pit of Anna's stomach dropped. *I bet that's it! I am gonna listen real good now.*

"Here, you dress this Barbie," Yellow Hair said.

Anna heeded His advice and told Yellow Hair, "No, I'm just gonna sit and listen to what you have to say."

Yellow Hair chattered. Anna boomeranged her companion's question with a question, making sure Yellow Hair spoke.

"What do you think first?"

Anna couldn't care less what Yellow Hair ran her mouth off about; her speed of monologue sounded like a freight train gone out of control, blowing bells and whistles and flashing lights, warning everyone to stay out of danger. She was irritating, and Anna's head was hurting already. Heck, Anna hoped the girl tired herself out, and then maybe she'd reveal if something happened with Yucky Monster.

So to whatever the girl said, Anna followed a momentary silence with an affirmative, "Yeah yup, sounds good."

This worked well. The girl did not catch on. Finally, the conversation grew in beef stew consistency. Anna finally got served the spicy dish pieces of meat and potato chunks she had been waiting to bite her teeth into.

"As mad as I was at you for being mean to my Barbie dolls, I don't … not like you. At least … you never made me do things in a game I didn't want to do."

Ooh, that's what I'm waiting for! "You made a new friend? Anyone I know?"

"My mommy told me not to talk about it to anyone. So, I can't talk about it, but I got to talk about it. Do you swear, swear not to tell anyone what I gotta say?"

"I swear."

"I don't believe you. How can I trust you? Do you cross your heart and hope to die if you lie?"

"No, but I will swear on a short pancake stack of bibles, and that's good," Anna said, keeping her legs crossed. "See, I don't have any fingers crossed."

"I don't know."

"Well, then don't tell me. It doesn't make any difference to me."

Yellow Hair started talking. She mentioned some monster man that was real yucky.

"Huh? You said monster and yucky, like Yucky Monster?"

"With big brown spots all over and the games he played."

YUP! It's Yucky Monster! Who else could it be?

"Yes, it's him," All Knowing affirmed to Anna.

Miss Barbie didn't know what the games were about, but she didn't care. She believed she was allowed to eat all the candy she wanted, to which she did admit, "Not all of it tasted good." Yellow Hair went into further detail about what the yucky man said, none of which made any sense to either child. In any case, Yellow Hair's secret was safe with Anna; she wasn't going to tell a soul. Anna was glad she saved herself, and as much as she found Yellow Hair quirky, she felt compassion for what had happened to her.

"Mr. Yucky told me there was no Santa Claus," Yellow Hair said sadly. "How could anybody be so cruel to take Santa Claus away from me?"

The whole world turned into a massive lie for Anna. "Why do adults lie to kids like that?"

The girls' conversation was suddenly interrupted. Out of Mama Koss's normal character, the old woman made a special trip to take Anna indoors. "Thank God, child, I find you here! Come on, dear," the old lady instructed and yanked Anna in unusual urgency, by the armpit, to pull her up from the stoop.

"What time is it, Mama Koss? Is Mommy coming?"

"Okay, child, let us be going now."

"Cross my heart, hope to die," Anna said before being hastily led away. "Bye, Yellow Hair."

Little did Anna know that was the last time she would ever see her Barbie-loving friend.

"Okay, my dear," Mama Koss spoke in an uncommon hushed and stern voice. "You won't be playing with the likes of her anymore, child."

"Huh, why not? You told me to play with her. Mr. Yucky Monster is the bad guy, not her."

"Some things are best left unsaid."

"Is it because Mr. Yucky Monster made Yellow Hair play games for candy?"

Anna got a sharp tug on her arm. "How you been hearing such talk?"

"Ouch! Mama Koss, I saw that Yucky Monster. You want me to show him to you? He needs to get the coppers called out on him. He's a very, very bad man. He wanted to hurt me. He hurt my friend Yellow Hair."

"There will be no more such talk. One of my neighbors told me about him. He is in God's hands now. Thank God you got the good sense to know better!"

"Yes right, I know that Yellow Hair, she's easy pickings. I told you she was a pipsqueak when you wanted me to be friends with her. Yucky Monster got ahold of my friend. Mother would call Yucky Monster a sick bastard. You see ..."

Mama Koss tugged on Anna to walk faster, as if Mama Koss knew something about the dark, looming area they now rushed through. *This area here is always spooky!* Anna thought.

"The superintendent still hasn't fixed that blasted light. It's so dark here, I could slip and fall for not being able to see where I be stepping."

"Hey, Mama Koss, I bet that Yucky Man lives over here behind the door," Anna said, pointing. "So that no one can see."

"How do you know that, child? You never been there before, have you? Good Lord, I hope not! That would be a whole kettle of worms we wouldn't want to be dealing with."

"No, but I can feel the bad; it's spooky right here. You feel it too. I know you do, Mama Koss."

With an even harder tug than the one before, they arrived at Mama Koss's door.

"Child, all this kind of talk stops right here and now! As soon as I unlock this stupid godforsaken door, the game is we forget this all, deal?"

"Mama Koss, *wowwy*, I know you're the good guy, but that's how that Yucky Monster was talking to Yellow Hair to make her do things."

Mama Koss's hands rattled so bad that she couldn't get the key in the door.

"Let me help you unlock the door," Anna offered, as she tried to wiggle her arm free without being noticed, but the woman wasn't letting go.

If Anna wasn't such a wee bit of child, Mama Koss might have expressed this to her: The filthy old man didn't care that the young lass he hurt cried as he did what he wished with her. He didn't care that she woke up with cold sweats and nightmares. He didn't care that he ruined her life. He didn't care that she was kept from her full potential. After a while, the sick bastard didn't even give her candy. But that was good for Yellow Hair's sake! Sweet and Innocent finally felt cheated and told her mommy about him.

Anna knew from Mama Koss's unusual behavior of dragging her off from the steps that Mama Koss had heard the full story of what that Yucky Monster did to Yellow Hair. And Anna had further proof when she asked Mama Koss about the door that was hidden in looming darkness. Anna also knew that Mama Koss loved Anna or at least cared enough to keep her safe. Anna didn't need to know the details of what was done to Yellow Hair. She would learn with time that Yellow Hair had encountered a person labeled a child molester. For the moment, it was enough to know that what happened was a bad thing, and Mama Koss wanted to protect Anna by sparing her the details she didn't need to be told. *Mama Koss might be the first person who cares for me,* Anna thought with glassy eyes.

Whatever that voice was, it taught Anna a lesson: *I'm gonna listen to All Knowing. His warning kept me safe!*

ANNA HATED THE IDEA of going to Suni's apartment because his mother was crazy, and she didn't want Mother to start sending her there again. The few times Anna did see Suni, it was always in his apartment. He wasn't allowed to go to the park with her. Both times, Suni was either being yelled at and getting beaten or having that cold spoon from the freezer pushed into a welt "to keep it from growing bigger," Lili or her boyfriend, Les, who she married, would say.

Knowing that her mother did the same thing to her with the spoon, Anna wondered, *Who learned this from who? Did Lili teach Mother, or did Mother teach Lili? Sheesh, my friend Suni has two people beating on him now.*

Oh God! I have to tell Suni there's no Santa Claus. Might as well get it over with. What are best friends for? Best friend? I mean only friend.

Even though Anna had never experienced Santa Claus, except through the movie *Rudolph, the Red-Nosed Reindeer*, she didn't want other children in the world in the know, including her, while her friend, Suni, was in the dark. She didn't want him to be the object of ridicule after she saw how kids treated Timothy. Anna tied on her imaginary superhero cape, fully aware of the backlash she was about to face for voluntarily educating him.

Of course, Anna battled with the right thing to do—to tell or not to tell there is or isn't a Santa Claus. After much contemplation, Anna questioned the intentions of parents and adults everywhere. *What's the purpose of the big lie? Didn't parents think of the harm they were setting up for their children? Christmas spirit was great with better Christmas shows, but why can't us kids be taught about Santa the same way we read or watch Pinocchio or Cinderella—as just a story? How are adults to be trusted if what they say is a big lie? That Yucky Monster told Yellow Hair to keep "their secret." He must have said: The same way your mommy keeps a secret with your daddy that Santa Claus is not real, you and I will keep "our secret" about these games.*

Anna expressed all that to prove her case against Santa to both mothers, Lili and Ann. As expected, Little Anna was handed more than a walloping can of whoop ass for her heroic move.

"How can you *bust* Suni's view of the world? You, of all people. You're his best friend; you're supposed to protect him. I would expect this from anyone but you!"

Ann and Lili went on and on. One picked up where the other left off, like snapping Siamese turtle twins. Anna wanted to tell the angry, raving, lunatic mothers how she learned what she knew, but she swore on a short pancake stack of bibles she wouldn't tell Yellow Hair's story.

The ranting and rage demonstrated by the two mothers bothered Suni, now absent in stare and wildly rocking himself back and forth on the couch, trying to comfort himself.

"You bust his bubble," Lili screamed, stomping her foot and slamming dresser drawers shut after she pulled them open.

That was just a moment of what continued for nearly an hour. Anna was amazed at the adult stupidity surrounding her; there was nothing she could say to teach these insensitive people. The adults carried on with their tantrums, screaming and thrashing themselves about, while Anna, detached, stood there observing.

Anna considered whether she could bust bubbles. The only thing that got busted here was Suni's head every day, like a piñata at a birthday party. Anna knew Lili beer-bottle-fed her son. Lili was the one who had just been released from Bellevue Hospital's mental ward. Lili was booked for rude, lascivious behavior and obstructing the peace. She walked New York City streets naked, yelling obscenities at people. In the same month as Lili, a drug-addict whore, sat in a padded cell in Bellevue, Les was taking up address in his own government-issued cell, serving time in the New York Penitentiary for aggravated assault and domestic violence.

Not having anywhere for Suni to go, Child Services of Manhattan stepped in and declared him in their custody. They misappropriated him into Juvenile Delinquency Hall. When Suni first arrived, he was so frightened that he hid for two whole days. When staff members located him, they sodomized, beat, and mentally abused him. The physical black-and-blues and tears disappeared with time, but Suni's behavior indicated that either he was suffering from the effects of fetal alcohol syndrome or severe trauma as a result of his physical and verbal abuse.

The young child who'd been released back into the custody of his mother now rocked back and forth vigorously. Most times, he no longer spoke a word, cracked a smile, or made eye contact. But Lili just considered his behavior as Suni intentionally being bad. Lili's genius comment to her son, who was rocking himself after she'd whacked him on the back of his head, was: "Why are you acting like an idiot moron?"

Anna's heart hurt to see how Suni was treated and spoken to. Although Lili said she loved her Suni Muni, Anna did not believe her. Lili's behavior did not show love or caring for Anna's friend.

These adults in Anna's world, who were wrongly defined as parents, were frustrating. Lili was Suni's worst enemy. How could she claim to love him? And Mother Ann never claimed to love Anna. Instead, she turned her head and gagged no different than her daughter did at the presentation of her mother's meal.

"No, you bust his bubble!" Lili screamed.

Pointing one finger at the well-meaning Anna was far simpler than looking at the three fingers pointing back at themselves.

"You apologize to him!"

"No! I am not sorry for telling the truth," Anna said, knowing she was right and about to pay the cost. It was only a question of *how soon.*

"Anna! You apologize right now, or I will beat the sh*t out of you!" Anna's mother said.

"I'm sorry Santa Claus is not real, and the Boogie Man is not real too," Anna said.

The only boogies I know are the ones from noses and the mothers pointing at me as if I'm the bad guy. Personally, Anna was glad because, at least for this short while, Mother and Lili busily pointed and were not yet slapping.

"Look who dares to open her mouth to us, Lili? Tell Suni you're sorry for lying."

"Mommy, why are *you* lying? You don't believe in Santa Claus, do you?"

Anna was dropped to her knees and beaten. She remembered nothing after that.

ANNA GOT BEAT FOR DOING the right thing. Her intentions were good—to save her friend from possible ridicule in the future. *Suni, Timothy, Yellow Hair, and I—we all get hurt by the monsters.*

Anna never saw Yellow Hair again, but what happened to Yellow Hair stayed in Anna's mind forever. Anna understood more as she got older. Anna now and then struggled to understand, *How are there so many monsters in the world?* Anna lived with a monster, her mother, and then she met Yucky Monster, the monster whose clutches she escaped. Then there were Les and Lili and the Irish gang kids who impacted Anna indirectly.

Anna didn't understand how one person enjoyed hurting another, how one person could think it was okay to make another cry and to pull out someone's heart and stomp all over it like a cockroach. *Where did these monsters come from? Why did monsters have to live with good people? Why can't monsters go bother each other and leave the good people alone? Why is it monsters do what they want, and the good guys, like Timothy, Yellow Hair, Suni, and me, get hurt?*

In her intense contemplation, All Knowing replied, *"We need the bad to know what's good."*

"Why?"

"There is no good without bad."

"I can't be bad. I never want to be bad."

"In that same way, some who are bad are so bad that they can't be good."

22

THE WEEKEND WAS OVER. *Thank God for Mondays!* Luckily, this Monday, Mama Koss planned something special. It was a chilly day, and she was already dressed in her one winter tweed coat, scarf, and gloves, ready to jig the both of them on their first day trip. All was great.

They climbed down a bunch of stairs into the belly of New York City. Anna hadn't stood on a subway platform before. Suddenly, a blast of wind and the growing screech from the oncoming train plastered the child's face with fear. Anna's grimace grew into a fright-filled scream but was drowned out by flying sparks from the friction of metal wheels that roared like a crazed lion as the train came to a menacing, screeching halt.

The thunderous wailing of the incoming train felt too uncomfortably similar to the overall sensation of an unwanted beating from Mother. Mama Koss saw the fear plastered on Anna's face and quickly opened her coat and wrapped the child tightly inside. "This little piggy is wrapped in a blanket," Mama Koss lovingly said. No one had ever held Anna close like that before. It was a special feeling of safety that the small, frightened child welcomed.

They finally boarded a train. Her first clue to where they were heading came as they walked up gray concrete steps that led to the heavy front doors of St.

Patrick's Cathedral on Fifth Avenue between 50th and 51st Streets. St. Patrick's Cathedral was worth the moments of struggle during their trip. The place was magnificent! Mama Koss taught Anna step by step the correct protocol for entering the church from the moment she set foot inside.

"Bless yourself with the holy water, and repeat the words, "Father, Son, Holy Ghost." Mama Koss was particular about the order in which the right hand went up to touch the forehead, down to the heart, and side to side, ending in a tiny humble curtsy. Anna concentrated hard and followed Mama Koss's every move. At the pews, Anna was to cross herself again, curtsy, and take a seat. Then she was to cross herself again, kneel on the wood before her, and pray.

"Don't forget, child, thank the Good Lord for giving you the good sense not to talk to strangers. And child, don't forget to pray for that little miss who didn't know better than be taken by the greed for candy. Do pray hard, child, pray hard."

Anna kept one eye open. Through her prayer hands placed over her eyes, her broken pinky left ample space for her to watch Mama Koss. Mama Koss rubbed her rosary beads in a fury and winced a few times. Her thin, mustached, quivering, moving lips did not utter a decipherable sound until her finale, "Amen."

Anna slid her hands in prayer position over her nose, which she rested on the back of the wooden bench in front of her so she could marvel at her surroundings. The vast space, the high ceilings, the statues, and all the candles intrigued Anna.

She whispered, "Ahem ... Mama Koss, what's this place?"

"It be the Lord's House, child."

"God did good for himself, right Mama Koss?"

"God does well for everyone!" Mama Koss replied.

"Yes, I see. He has a lot of visitors today. When do we meet him?"

"What, child?"

"Haha, Mama Koss! No one sees Him. I know He is with me. I'm asking He bless you for bringing me here."

ANNA FELL IN LOVE WITH St. Patrick's Cathedral. After visiting the cathedral with Mrs. Koss, she also loved when she was able to attend Catholic nursery school. Although she wouldn't be with Mrs. Koss, the nursery school reminded her of Mrs. Koss's precious church, and that was exciting for Anna.

Now that Anna was five, she could have started kindergarten in the public school, which would have saved Mother Ann a whole bunch of money and trouble. But Mother Ann didn't know that was possible. Since it was the same expense to send Anna to Catholic nursery school as what Mother paid to Mama Koss, Mother Ann decided to send her there. Anna didn't understand anything more than she was glad to attend Catholic school. The child had been baptized at nine months old, so there was no problem with her admittance.

Describing Anna's baptism, Mother Ann stated what Mutter Clara used to say: "If money can take care of a situation, there is no problem. She said it when she bought my baptism papers from the priest at the Basilica. Sadly, no amount of money could buy Clara papers because she was too old, according to the priest."

Mother Ann then added, "Anyway, how the hell am I supposed to make this money? I don't know! I just have to wait on tables, run errands for people, and work at that peasant Katy's cash register at the beauty shop."

Country Katy was Little Anna's godmother, and one of Katy's boyfriends was Little Anna's godfather. After a while, no one could keep track of Katy's personal escapades. Katy would have fourteen abortions before she was forty and seven husbands by the age of fifty-five. The only other ditty Little Anna ever heard about her baptismal ceremony was that she had outgrown the baptismal gown that Mother had bought for her when she was one month old. That, too, seemed to be Anna's fault.

In Catholic school, young Anna became infatuated with all the nuns wearing rosary beads and the same black lace-up shoes as Mama Koss. *I'd like some of those*, Anna thought. *They probably work like ruby slippers. Only ruby slippers take you home if you live in Kansas, and these nun shoes help make you a saint.* When it came to saints, there were an overwhelming number of them to learn about, including all their names, and too many words to the plethora of prayers to recite.

Anna compensated by silently mimicking words to prayer songs until they got to the chorus, which was the loudest part. Her favorite chorus line to bellow from the depths of her newly found diaphragm was: "King of Kings, Lord of Lords."

Anna practiced projecting her voice in the places where she found that the acoustics worked best. Hands down, that meant the bathrooms at church, the park, and at home. And, ah yes, she boldly sang in the church's stairwells as well.

"King of Kings, Lord of Lords."

The words *rushed* a special majestic feeling over her, much like an electric current traveled through a hot wire. The bravado of the words empowered her skinny, scrawny body with a thrust of warmth. They made her feel like there was something more than just her alone in the big, overwhelming world, perhaps a connection to All Knowing.

Goodness filled her thoughts. "King of Kings, Lord of Lords," the special lexis, rang better than Oreos and milk. It fortified Anna with its vitamin strength of peaceful, loving comfort.

ANNA LIVED AT 409 East 84th Street, which was on First Avenue, and she transported herself to the Catholic school she attended on 82nd Street and Second Avenue. Consciously, Anna's day first began with lunch and was followed by a mandatory nap and ended with story time. To the best of Anna's recollection, her mind did not anticipate any special event until the nuns repeatedly stressed the nearing importance of "the vows of silence." This meant all children needed to strictly adhere to "on-time pickup" on the one designated day that year. In simpler words, Anna interpreted this for her inquiring classmates and mother, "Mommies can't be late for pickup on that day, or hell will break loose!"

Anna learned that nuns were strict. They firmly did not permit any nursery-school-age child, including Anna, to enter or depart their institution without an adult escort. Mother Ann didn't adhere to the regulation for the simple fact it complicated her life. "How the hell am I supposed to pick up the little sh*t if I am waitressing a table? They think all women have the luxury of staying at home?" A month later, Mother Ann added, "They are not just checking names at the front door. They are stopping and directing those like me who haven't paid to the office. So, little sh*t, just slip in and out past the whore nuns before and after school because I don't have this money they want! They are no different than whores! Everybody's a whore! Everybody just wants money, including me."

Slipping past the nuns at the door was not easy. Anna had to wait to see which nun at the door turned their back at just the right angle for her to dodge between the nun and the open door. Days rolled into months of Anna answering her name at roll call in class without her name having been checked off the list of names entering the school. This caused "Superior Mother" to write a formal letter to Mrs. Anna Nagy. It was hand-delivered by Little Anna and needed to be signed and returned immediately.

The letter expressed clear instructions for parental drop-off and pickup. In response, Mother Ann sent Anna back with a handwritten note addressed to Mother Superior, issuing the nuns permission to allow her daughter to walk herself to and from school without escort. In reply, the school mailed a letter for Mother Ann to sign, specifically, a liability release in the event harm fell upon the child after Anna's release from school grounds. The signed form was mailed back to Mother Superior's attention. The fact that Mother showed no concern after she was made aware of the impending dangers of a child left unsupervised in New York City alerted Mother Superior: Anna was in uncaring hands! Enraged, Mother Superior rightfully placed her staff on the attentive lookout for this irresponsible mother, instructing, "I wish to speak to such a mother personally."

That same day, Mother Superior summoned the child to her sparsely deco-rated, foreboding office via nun escort. They walked up a rickety boarded stair-case not frequented for any other purpose but to access the tucked-away Mother Superior. The nun stayed on Anna's heels the whole time. They stood outside Mother Superior's door until they were permitted by another monitoring nun to knock. Anna was directed to step inside the Great Mother's private chambers. The accompanying nun stepped inside as well. Mother Superior redirected the nun to remain at the door. Anna thought, *This is like Simon Says. Whoever is more important becomes Simon. Only no one ever says Simon. They say Sister.*

Mother Superior made her salutations known through a strange, quick wave of her hand. She then simultaneously motioned for Anna to sit in the chair directly in front of her desk and ordered, "Sit." Sister was told with a gesticulating thumb to remain by the doorway located behind Anna.

Mother Superior would make a good traffic cop or a deaf interpreter with all the signals she gives.

The nun started to pull over a chair. "You're to stand, Sister." Sister did not look too happy about that and noisily dragged the chair back. "Sister!" Mother Superior's scolding eyes said more than her snap.

Mother Superior then pushed her chair on wheels away from her confining desk and walked away, allowing her rosary beads to dangle alongside her long black reverential ensemble. She excused herself. "I will return shortly."

Anna did not know that Mother Superior was testing her to see how she would act when Mother Superior was out of the room. Would Anna be fidgety, get up and walk around, or sit properly? Anna thought Mother Superior was juggling tasks. *She is the most important person in the school, with a lot to do.* Anna sat still and obedient; she'd had good practice instilled in her at home to do so. While sitting in her chair with her hands folded in her lap, she thought: *Mother Superior's face was much less wrinkled than expected for someone so High Holy.* Anna noticed her face because everything else on Mother Superior was covered. *I bet she doesn't draw funny faces on her body like Mother does.*

A memory flashed into her mind of her mother standing in front of the mirror and drawing a red lipstick circle around her nipples and a big lipstick smile below her belly button while she laughed at her image. *I don't think she knew I saw.*

Anna looked up from her lap and realized Mother Superior had quietly slipped behind her desk and was still wearing her habit. *She looks like the Flying Nun played by Sally Field.* Indeed, her larger and more elaborate habit gave the illusion of appearing more regal and commanding than all the other nuns. Anna was observing the Superior as much as the queen nun was keenly observing Anna. The cloaked reverence divinely sat behind a wooden school desk on matching mahogany wooden polished floors. Behind her, directly above her head on the wall, an impressive depiction of the "Lord Jesus Christ Our Savior" hung on his holy cross as a reminder of His suffering. Anna had as much of a hard time looking at the oversized crucified wooden figure as she did away. She wondered, *Is this what happens to people who don't pay? Is this a way of scaring people to behave? I don't get it.*

"We will commence in a moment. I am waiting on the paper your mother signed," Mother Superior stated before she was handed a paper by another nun while Her Grace sat behind her desk. Her face said she was all business. She reserved her calm voice as if it were a high-priced commodity. Every word Mother Superior spoke was intentionally meaningful, unlike the words of Anna's mother, who shouted insults.

Looking straight at Anna, Mother Superior asked, "Who takes you and picks you up from school?"

Wow, she doesn't scare me. That thing above her scares me, but she doesn't.

Anna then quickly recalled what she'd been instructed to do by the teaching nuns in class: "When adults question you, children, give them your full attention. This means you stop everything you're doing, any dilly-dallying and the like, and look us in the eye. Listen when spoken to and answer the question we ask you to answer. And, children, if by chance, you are honored to meet the Mother Superior, be, above all else, in your best form. If she asks you for your name, you state your name in full, first and last."

Anna sat up straight. "Mother Superior, Anna Nagy speaking. My mommy wants me to tell you she does, but I take myself. I don't want to get in trouble. I just want to come to this nice school."

"Her mother's actions are despicable," the standing nun behind Anna interjected.

"Sister! You have spoken out of turn! Now on the subject ... we are as much to blame for allowing this child to leave on her own recognizance without noticing there to be an issue. I understand the door is your responsibility, Sister."

Whatever Sister tried to say was cut short by Mother Superior. "I'm not hearing it. I am watching this child sitting perfectly still in front of me. I do not see her to be a bother. She sits well-mannered and looks attentive. She answers when spoken to and knows to pretend she understands. Perhaps she should be teaching you. Do you not understand me, Sister? Anna, do you go anywhere else by yourself?" Mother Superior inquired.

"Mother Superior, yes."

"Where might that be, dear?"

"Mother Superior, I take myself to the park. I took myself to the photographer once, and I used to take myself to Pauli's and to Mama Koss's. I take myself to Lili's, too, but that's nothing. She lives in the same building."

"Does your mother know you go to these places?"

"Mother Superior, yes. I follow the rule: Get out when the sun is up and don't return until it's turning dark."

"Anna, are you afraid when you are alone?"

"Mother Superior, I don't like it, but it is bad to be in the house."

"Anna dear, why is it bad? What's bad?"

Anna's eyes teared up. *I have a bad mommy who hates me. Mommy hits me all the time. I can't say that. I don't want to get a beating for telling on her.* Anna looked down, pretending to look at her hands while she blinked her stubborn tears away. She looked up again, remembering to respect Queen Mother.

Mother Superior's eyes softened and also filled with tears. She took a hard gulp, stood up, and adjourned the meeting by saying, "I had a mother like that. Okay, my dear Anna. I understand all I need to here. I will be sure to say hello and check on you when I see you around school. In the meantime, dear Anna, pray, pray hard you do not become your mother."

Wow, geez! Mother Superior had a mother like I got, and she is a saint!

WALKING HERSELF HOME that day and back to school in the days that followed, Anna contemplated, *Why are they so worried about me walking to and from school by myself?* She was, after all, a well-established veteran of Manhattan streets for a good square mile radius from her house in all directions. *It must be what Mother said—that the nuns want money. I remember Mother paying to get me in. I don't know if she paid them again. If they would ask me, I would tell them the same thing Mother told me to say to Mama Koss, "You gotta talk that stuff with my mommy."*

It became harder than ever for Anna to slip in and out of school. At the entrance door, nuns were keeping a stern "lookout for Mrs. Anna Nagy, mother to the child of same name." Mother Superior's orders: "I wish to speak to such a mother!" were now extended to all the nuns in the school.

Ever since the day Anna met Mother Superior in her office, Her Grace customarily took a moment out of her hectic schedule to kindly approach Anna when she spotted her in the hallways on her way to lunch with her class. Reverend Mother hunched over Anna and laid her saintly hand on the child's shoulder as if silently blessing her.

"Now dear, Anna, right?"

"Yes, Mother Superior, Anna Nagy," the small child responded to Mother Superior, standing as straight as she could, projecting her voice, and repeating her answer just in case she stumbled the first time. "Anna Nagy is my name, Queen Mother."

"If I can ever do something for you, my child, just give word to one of my sisters."

The saintly woman with softened eyes during their exchange then returned to her take-charge persona as Mother Superior. In transformation, Reverend Mother reconfigured her posture, cleared her throat, and announced her return, "Yes, back to business." Mother Superior motioned upward waves with her hands, a coded gesture to her subordinates, meaning, "Keep them in line, really!"

"WHAT'S ALL THIS, CHILDREN?" The nun teacher clapped her hands to stop the loud chattering. Anna didn't know why her classmates hemmed and hawed when Mother Superior stopped to visit her or called her privately aside. Only after Anna elbowed the loudest heckling kid next to her and said, "Hey, what's your problem?" did Anna find out.

"Only bad kids get sent to the head nun."

"That's not my case. Queen Mother likes me."

Only God knows how close they were to the Day of the Vows of Silence. What the day meant or what it entailed was not explained, at least not explained well enough to the children for Anna to know what that day meant. The nuns only said, "Vows of silence is what the words say it is."

All Anna knew was to follow orders, which she did, handing Mother the flyer sent home with her every day in the final week prior to the special day. She tried to impress upon her mother the importance of what was coming by saying, "On-time pickup is no joke. Nuns are locking the front doors when school closes. Read the note. It's important."

Consistently, Mother's shoulder shrugged as she responded, "Who cares. Throw that sh*t in the garbage."

"Superior Mother said it's the school rule that you drop me off and take me to school."

"The old head bitch always has her hand out for money, like every other whore. Her wizard outfit only gives her cause no different than a bad whore wearing fishnet stockings."

"I saw her up close. She's not old, Mommy."

"Well, don't tell me she isn't more puckered than a prune, never having a man!"

Nothing ever changed. Anna walked herself to and from school every day. And now, the day stressed for "on-time pickup" due to vows of silence, had arrived. *Will Mother remember to pick me up on time? I can't imagine what will happen if she doesn't.*

Anna made a mad dash to be the first to sit on the church lobby bench when the dismissal bell rang. From there, she watched the school flood with children happily greeted by smiling mothers and nuns crossing off the children's names on their clipboards. *There is no way for me to leave unnoticed today. There are two nuns posted back-to-back at each side of those two doors.*

Strict enforcement was instilled because Mother Superior wanted a word with Mrs. Anna Nagy.

I told my mother to come for me! Why can't she just do something right? For weeks, the message was constant and clear, "On-time pickup is mandatory, no exceptions!" *I reminded her every day this past week.*

Anna nervously chewed the callous inside her mouth, wondering, *Will Mother show on time?* The dismissal crowd dwindled to three other children on Anna's bench. Then she was alone. Anna sat on the hard bench like *garbage* on its assigned trash day, placed on the curb to be collected, except no one was coming to remove her. The nuns noticed that out of an entire school, Anna was the last remaining child's name to be crossed off their clipboard.

Mother Superior, the closest woman to being a tangible God, angelically transported herself to the worried-sick child. Reverend Mother's long black flowing gown never allowed her nun shoes to be seen, as if she devoted herself to be a nun just so she could show off her perfected art of floating across the floor.

"Anna Nagy, Queen Mother. What time is it? I know, I know, vows of silence. I am sorry. Mommy will come. It's not me. I do everything right. I still get in trouble."

Queen Mother occupied the bench next to her and rubbed her back. "Your mother has but little time, but it seems I don't need to tell you."

Ten minutes later, Mother Superior stood in front of Anna for a second time. Anna could tell Mother Superior was agitated. The holy woman nervously strummed invisible organ keys on the side of her thigh. Then she held her head. Anna knew she had a headache.

"Mother Superior, I know what that means. I get headaches too."

Mother Superior leaned in, way down into the child's face, "The vow of silence is scheduled to commence in an hour, child. We are now locking the doors."

Jesus Christ! I can't say Jesus Christ, but Jesus Christ!

Another hour passed, and Queen Mother skated by anxiously quite a few more times. Each time, Queen Mother's silent gestures became more demonstrative. She would walk into the lobby, stop and lock eyes with Anna, and tilt her head to one side. With an upward jerk of her chin, she mouthed, "She is late," pointing to her watch. Anna simply returned her sad, puppy-dog eyes with a worried, half-strained grimace to accompany the holding of her pained head.

"I don't know," Anna mouthed. Anna's head throbbed in pain; she wished she had a better response for the Great Patient One. Again, Anna felt she was the cause of a problem. *Should I try to push the doors open and go? They look too heavy. Oh, and they are locked now. I can't be bad. I don't want trouble. I am not the bad one.* Anna then recalled leaving the thrift store when her mother told her to sit and wait. She decided, *I better wait. I don't need more beatings.* Anna saw no choice but to sit on the hard wooden bench as she visualized herself stewing like discarded, stinking rubbish.

Worried sick, not certain of what she was supposed to do and thinking she was getting a beating from her mother for not choosing the right thing to do, Anna felt the room spin. "I don't feel so good," Anna voiced to the next nun who passed by.

"Oh, dear child, let me see if I can get Sister Josephine Ellen Catherine to fetch you some water."

From the look of most nuns in the school, especially the last one, Anna agreed with Mother. "Most of these women became nuns because no man could stomach kissing them. They were "godforsaken ugly." Anna really must not have been feeling well to agree with Mother on that.

Ten minutes prior to the biggest occasion of the year, Anna was removed to a room she did not recognize.

"Dear child, the time has come. There will not be a word spoken for the duration of an hour; you are not to move from your desk. Sit there and be still. If your mother comes, she will not be spoken to. We are forbidden to communicate with anyone. We must obey our vows of silence. I hope you understand. Use this time to pray. God is watching."

No sweat off my back, Sister, Anna thought as she complied sweetly with a smile. This was a piece of cake, peace and quiet, sit still for an hour. *I can do that hanging upside down on a monkey bar!*

While Anna sat, she contemplated the notion of committing her life as a nun. *Mother Superior had a mother like I do, and look at her.* Two minutes into the commencement of the vow of silence, the front doors were wildly flung open with brute force and clamor. The organ pipe music seemed to drop a few deep octaves, as in a Bela Lugosi movie introducing a feature villain. On cue, Mother Ann stormed in as if the Heavenly Father thrust her inside with a mighty punishing wallop for messing up ceremonies honoring Him. All scornful, angry eyes fell upon her. Ann rapidly noticed her daughter was not obediently waiting on the hard bench vacant before her.

Safely tucked away, Little Anna figured Mother was getting her money's worth at all costs, squeezing an extra hour of paid daycare. Anna had heard it a ton of times: "This nursery school is worse than an expensive whore, so I squeeze an extra hour out of them so I don't feel so bad."

Ann, an unrefined, impatient woman, approached every nun passing her in their procession into the chapel. No one could explain the vows of silence to Ann *now*!

"You saw my daughter, Anna? I am her mother here for pickup."

Naturally, Mother Ann received no response. The procession continued passing through the lobby and in through the double doors to the chapel. Next, clergymen carrying their bibles, dressed in white ceremonial robes, entered under the spell of the beckoning organ. They marched right past Mother Ann as if she were invisible, from one door into another, without replying to her frantic pleas.

"What's wrong with you people? What did you do with my daughter?"

Mother Ann was in hysterics. Still, the doors closed behind them. Mother, left in the lobby alone, screamed every profanity she knew, acrimoniously cursing everyone she knew. Another set of doors opened, and another long line of nuns proceeded to the opened doors to the chapel. Mother Ann tugged on the nuns and asked without shame, "Where is my daughter, Anna?" Still, no one answered her approach.

Perplexed, Mother Ann made quite a stir. She cried out, *"What could be so horrible that you can't answer me? Is she dead?"*

The clergy and nuns were certainly tested that day by the out-of-control Mother Ann. They successfully kept to their mandatory deep, silent prayer.

In the time Little Anna sat by herself in the expansive and otherwise empty room, she thought of how bored she would be wearing the same clothes every day if she were a nun. Later in her adult years, Anna understood how the devout dedication was termed "being committed to an institution." For now, Anna understood that there must be a happy in between that of constantly changing clothes like a Barbie doll and that of living like a nun. Nuns couldn't have but one man in their lives—the invisible Holy Father. She knew she wanted children and a father for her children, something her mother didn't have and didn't give Anna. As a nun, there was just so little she could do contained inside the church. *Look how nervous they are about me walking myself to the park. Maybe it's not about the money like Mother says. Maybe they are afraid to step out of the church.* Prayer was good, but the walls confined the sheltered nuns. So, Anna decided that, ultimately, life as a grown-up would be good *if I had prayer and kids and lived outside of a church with more than one outfit.*

When the religious ceremonies ended, Mother Ann was reunited with her child. Mother Superior watched the two from a distance. From the corner of her eye, Anna noticed Queen Superior doing her best to maintain her superior composure as she closed in on Mother Ann. Mother Ann clumsily backed onto Mother Superior's foot. In true Ann fashion, she did not apologize. She elbowed Mother Superior and hastily said, "Move back. *Hey! What are you doing?"*

"Yes, I was hoping to meet you under better circumstances. Step aside."

Anna watched Mother being reprimanded with a steady stream of disdain for her unacceptable, unladylike behavior.

"Mrs. Nagy, this exhibition of ungodly behavior will not be tolerated in my church; you are to take this stern warning seriously! There will be no next time! And woman, hug your child tight, for if it were not for my liking her, I'd have a good mind to dispense with you from my institution!"

"Yes, yes, I don't understand ... the child, where she is ... I don't understand ..."

"Exactly, that is the problem. You best be out of my sight before I shut these doors on you for good. Learn to bite your tongue, woman!"

All the way home, Mother Ann was nice to her daughter, engaging her in conversation. "I don't see what everyone sees in you and why they like you."

"Thank you, Mommy." *That's the second time she said that, and once she told me I was a good judge of people.* Anna appreciated this moment. *Whatever Mother Superior said, it worked!*

Mother behaving better at home allowed Anna to become more comfortable in her skin and, therefore, more aware of her surroundings. Anna was like a hermit crab stepping out of her shell.

Nursery school with the nuns was great. Even the food was great to Anna, no matter what others said.

"The spaghetti wasn't that good today, was it, children?" the nun asked before reading to class.

"The spaghetti here is great!" Anna shouted gleefully.

"Eeewww! *No!*" everyone else said.

No matter, Anna loved it. And she always accepted a leftover carton of milk the nuns offered at lunch and snack time. The nuns knew not to ask, "Who wants milk?" without first offering, "Anna, here, more milk."

Without fail, a chunky wax flake from the carton broke loose into her mouth and caused her to gag. She removed herself to the window so no one noticed. Anna did not like milk, but subconsciously, Mother's yelling voice overpowered her with, "Take everything they give you. Those whore nuns charge me enough!"

The nuns inducted Anna into a safe haven with discipline and education. Anna stayed the full year. As much as she liked the nursery school, though, Anna missed Mama Koss and hadn't seen her since starting school. Anna thought about the woman, especially when the nuns served spaghetti and meatballs. *Mama Koss taught me about this yummy stuff. But I can't go visit her if I don't have a check. Can't get Mother in more money trouble.*

23

PUBLIC SCHOOL 190 introduced Anna, now six years old, to Mrs. Brown, the kindergarten teacher. Mother Ann anticipated Anna starting her new school as much as her daughter did. Public education meant a freebie. The one-hundred-year-old building with separate entrances for girls and boys was located catty-corner from her Catholic nursery school and a block closer to Anna's tenement. On the first day, most of her new classmates shed tears when they were dropped off at the classroom door, worried their mothers weren't returning after drop-off. Anna was upset, too, but only at the end of the day—she didn't want to go home.

Anna was the emaciated, stick-figured child wearing the blue satin sash that belonged around the waist of her velvet-and-taffeta dress from the thrift store as an oversized bow in her tightly pulled-back chestnut brown hair. Nothing mattered to the child once Mrs. Brown set Anna up at an easel with paint. Anna immersed herself in a novel world filled with endless creative possibilities involving colors and shapes.

After the first day of school, Anna navigated her way to and from school alone. The quiet child preferred solitaire to torture, especially in the morning. As it was, her irritable mother had a great way of ruining each and every day before Anna left the apartment. At least once Anna closed that door, she slowly resumed some self-composure as she descended the six flights of stairs and counted to ten before opening the door to the outside world. *Thank you, I'm better alone.* Although, admittedly, Anna did wish a companion shared her route so she wouldn't be so lonely.

Rain, sleet, and snowy days wreaked havoc on Anna's one pair of shoes that she owned. The growing girl only received another pair when she outgrew the old one, so she was forced to wear her shoes even after they developed holes. On bad weather days when her hole-filled shoes got soaked on the way to school, her feet had to uncomfortably endure them for the duration of the day. She hoped they would dry overnight. In winter, Anna placed her shoes by the home radiator to ensure they would be dry before she left in the morning. In summer, Anna's shoes sat on the kitchen sill by the open window.

The harsh Northeast weather caused Anna to feel sick more frequently than she felt healthy. Anna felt better on some days, but they were still filled with non-ending headaches. Nevertheless, she never missed school. School was her safe haven.

On windy, wintry days, the cold winds hurt her unprotected ears. She suffered from perpetual earaches, a stuffed nose, and a sore throat. If Anna could have had someone dress and nourish her properly, as opposed to rant and rave like a crazy lunatic before she left the apartment, not to mention if someone drove or walked her with an umbrella to shelter her from the wet, Anna wouldn't have been the nuisance Mother claimed she was, stating, "You're a constantly ill pain in the ass." But Anna didn't complain, especially since she didn't have anyone to complain to about being neglected.

The weather outside was as frigid as Anna's relationship with Mother. Bad, torturous days blurred endlessly one into another. At the time, society dictated that all mothers be addressed as Mommy. Anna obliged her mother properly when speaking and when writing letters to her mother. Despising her mother, Anna wrote "Dearest Mommy" while she mentally pictured spitting on her. As a child who was beaten daily, Anna saw no other recourse than to not lie to herself. In the child's mind, she made a strong distinction between Ann as Mother and the Mommy Anna would become when her turn in life came to love and protect her own children. As far as Anna was concerned, "I have no Mommy."

It was horrible for Anna to fear Mother and frustratingly miserable not to be able to reach out to tell anyone how much she feared Mother. There wasn't a day Mother saw Anna without tormenting her with physical and verbal beatings. There was no method to Mother's madness other than that the sight of her child triggered her outrage. This perpetual action became a bad habit Mother couldn't break. Living in these pristine, lily-white, pressed-cotton-glove-wearing days, Mother didn't have to report to any governmental authority since family matters were left as such. And because Mother Ann was her only family, Mother only had herself to account to. This left little Anna running in unending vicious circles, *having to kiss the hand that slapped her.*

Anna understood she was an obstacle in Mother's way and strongly wished Mother had taken the abortion money and spent it the way her father—the man listed on her birth certificate—ordered, "Get rid of it!" *Mother beat it into me as far back as since forever. Mother even showed me the black-and-white picture where I am two months old, crying in my "father's" fumbling arms as he is smiling, and my mother is on the opposite end of the couch looking at me with hate. Why did Mother have to tell me that story other than to hurt me?*

Heartless, Mother relished in making *sure* Anna knew she was isolated and abandoned. There was nothing Anna could do or say to keep from being unjustly punished. Suddenly, she would get zapped by stinging words that burned forever.

"I will start to be nice to you when you are old enough to remember."

Dearest Mommy was a long way from warm and fuzzy, even when Anna responded and declared her admiration toward her sole parent.

"I love you, Mommy. I am so glad to be with you today!"

"I can't wait until you're an adult and out of my sight! Who the hell needs you around?" Then Mother slapped Anna so hard she fell to the ground. Mother left her there and walked away.

Remembering what she wore and where she was helped Anna singe that moment into her "Sad Memories" photo album alongside the next snippet:

"Mommy, you are the most beautiful Mommy in the whole world."

"*Drop dead, you piece of sh*t!*" *Smack!* Anna's head was knocked to the ground. How quickly devil-horned Mother with spiked tongue stole the child's sunshine. *I hate Mother. I wish she were dead.* But the reactive thought was not feasible because echoing fears of *then what?* rattled in her head. *What would happen to me alone? I have no one, no father, older brother, sister, aunties, or uncles."* Having Mother removed from Anna's life wasn't the solution. Anna saw what happened to Suni Muni after his parents were thrown into government hands. Anna didn't like her situation at home, but she also knew she had no better option.

Anna's headaches were every-single-day, all-the-time occurrences. She woke up with a headache and went to bed with a headache and lived with a headache all day in between. She figured her heart hurt so much that the pain traveled upward through her body to her head. Worst of all, it seemed times weren't changing to hold a glimmer of promise.

Outreaching an extended agonized arm for help, Anna asked All Knowing, *"Why do I need to experience all this pain, again and again?"*

He replied, *"Learn what to do by learning what not to do. By knowing the pain your mother causes you, you learn you have the choice to do differently. You are right, she is not right, but all will be all right, if you stay right. Right is to stay strong. Don't change!"*

Thankfully, Anna had been in contact with her All Knowing for as far back as she could remember. Mama Koss taught the clasping of her hands in front of her as she knelt on the floor before her bed as the correct protocol used to summon her All Knowing. Anna prayed and connected with Him without pomp and circumstance; she didn't need to get in trouble for yet another thing Mother didn't understand.

Anna prayed to fight off the evil words her mother spewed at her at least once a day: "You know what you are? You are a good-for-nothing little whore, an asshole, a piece of garbage. You are a good-for-nothing that should drop dead, but not without rotting. No one likes you. No one needs you. You are only one thing, and that is in the way. No one cares about you. You are so ugly. You have teeth and gums like a horse. You have a long, stupid face like a horse. You make a face like a stupid jackass, your big gums show when you smile, your stupid smile with your ugly yellow horse teeth. You have a nose like a pig. You are a pig—a dirty, rotten, good-for-nothing pig. You should drop dead! Your skin changes color from piss yellow to frog green. Your eyes bulge out of your head like a stupid fish. I just want to step and squash you. You keep your mouth open like a jackass, showing everyone how stupid you are. I hate you. I wish you were dead. Why don't you just rot and die already? You are too ugly with your large, protruding forehead. What the hell is wrong with you? You are a moron; I had to cover up that head when you were born; half your head was missing. That's why you have bangs to cover up your ugly forehead."

"Please, send me *help*!" Anna begged.

The critically damaging Mother didn't tire, not until Anna was passed out from the beatings or somehow exited the door. Beatings lasted a minimum of three hours. Mother reenergized as she filled herself with her daughter's grief, sucking her life force from her. Anna dared not glance away; she was better off seeing the blows as they came. Trapped by circumstance, Mother beat her, swinging at her with open slaps, clenched fists, shoes, books, and whatever was in her reach. The child, in turn, was forbidden to flinch, to put an arm up for protection, to whimper or speak up, which would lead to accelerated repercussions.

Sadly indeed, Anna was Mother's punching bag, her psychiatric couch, her means of medication, her sport, her outlet, and her secret-keeper of enduring punishment. Anna didn't want to be part of this sick world; even if Anna were useless, Anna was harmless. Mother Ann was cruel for harming Anna, her own flesh and blood.

"*Oh Father, who art in heaven,* hollow *be thy name,*" Anna mentally crossed herself. "*Father, Son, Holy Ghost, I will not be like my mother, I promise.*"

ALTHOUGH ANNA TOOK HER LIFE in her hands to approach Mother, Anna had to direct the question where it belonged. The topic of religion was buzzing about. Anna's classmates were taught by their parents to separate "us" from "them" according to their religious beliefs. She didn't know which they were.

Anna asked first thing one morning, saying, "I have school and can't be late. But I have a question."

"Go ahead," Mother replied from behind the newspaper she was reading in bed.

"What religion am I, Mommy?"

"Nah, so we are going to talk of something with substance," Mother said as she set her newspaper curtain to the side of her in bed. "Pick one you like, and be whatever you want."

The indefinite answer was puzzling.

"So, Anna, what did you come up with?" Mother asked.

I can't say, "I don't know"; that'll wind her up.

"I am thinking."

"If you are with Catholics, tell them you are Catholic; if you are with Jews or atheists, tell them you are Jewish or atheist."

"How's that, Mommy?"

"You have rights to both. You and I are both baptized Roman Catholic, and your father is Catholic. You are also Jewish. I am atheist, so you are not lying no matter what you say. God has yet to prove he exists to me."

Anna interpreted Mother's point: *Being what you are is not as important as what you say you are. White lies are okay to play safe.*

"These baptism papers saved my life," Mother said.

Mother Ann showed her daughter a piece of paper she pulled out from among other important papers under her pillow and her bankroll kept in a family heirloom, hand-embroidered satchel. "This used to be Regina's. One day it will be yours." After a pause, Mother continued, "My good Lord, look at the size of these feet on your birth certificate. I gave birth to a horse, not even a pony, well maybe a large jackass as ugly as you are! Jesus! Look at what God gave me!"

Then Mother Ann drilled a round of tricky questions before she reached her point. "See these papers? See this money? Which out of these two do you think is more important in life?"

Afraid of making the wrong choice, Anna thought hard before answering, "This paper!"

"How did you know that?"

"You just said the paper saved your life."

"Yes, and these are your baptism papers. We, Country Katy and I, had you baptized. This way, you don't have to worry about anti-Semitism, meaning people want to kill you just for being Jewish."

"Kill me?" *It is enough that Mother wants to kill me. What?*

Mother continued, "Another thing I don't understand is why Jews wear Jewish symbols like the Star of David."

Oh boy, Mother's raising her voice.

"There's no way anyone can tell me these people are normal! Why wear a symbol that says, 'I'm Jewish'? People in the Holocaust were forced to wear the Star of David; here, they want to! Are they crazy? Why do they have to attract hate-mongers? Don't they know people hate Jews?"

Ann didn't own one piece of religious symbolic jewelry, not crosses or stars of any kind, except for the Nazi cross, the swastika. She pulled the swastika from the satchel. "See this? This is off a dead Nazi bastard; I took it off the soldier myself. The Russians must have shot him, and he was just lying there in the street. I keep it to remind me just what kind of people there are in this world. It is my proof that what I lived through wasn't just a nightmare."

Sometimes the right people die, Anna thought.

Mother fell into a moment of eerie silence. Then she started again. "People still hate. Hate isn't turned off like a light switch, and if it is, it takes nothing to flip the switch to spark the stream of electricity waiting on standby. Just because the war is declared over doesn't mean people's harbored feelings are instantly dropped."

People hate Jews.

"Thanks to God we are given a chance!"

"Yes, Mommy, thank God, Amen."

"There were two sets of rules, one for the Jews and another for the gentiles, non-Jews. It's unfortunate but true: Jewish people were ostracized. Thousands of years ago, Jews were blamed for killing their worshipped God, Jesus."

Surely, the adults don't know what they're doing again. For the first time, Anna thought Mother made sense. *Who cares what religion someone is! What happened to everyone shaking hands and sitting down for a meal like they taught at school that the Indians did with the Pilgrims?*

Anna didn't feel any different being Jewish; she only knew she wasn't going to tell her classmates. In the predominantly German-Irish neighborhood with 97 percent of her classmates and teachers' names beginning with O' (as in O'Neil, O'Hare, O'Malley) and Mc (as in McCormick, McBride) or even Mac (as in Macintosh), no one was anything but Catholic or Christian, except for a few Chinese, and they weren't Jewish either.

As a Jew, Mother observed no Jewish tradition; there were no Shabbat candles lit on Friday nights. On the other hand, Anna knew when it was Good Friday in school. Fish sticks were served for lunch, and the calendars indicated it was so, just in case the teachers in school had the fact slip their minds.

One such Friday, Mother announced, "That peasant Katy is coming over. You remember her?"

"She used to be with Pauli, and you said she is my godmother." Anna omitted mentioning, *Katy was the one who told Mother I was "deaf" when she came into the room and I didn't respond to all her clapping.*

"Yes, that's right. Religion is a money-making business, *a business to control people by fear.* Your baptism papers are just to protect you, like mine did me. Religion is garbage. Why is one God better than someone else's God? I worry you were indoctrinated with all that Catholic garbage because I sent you to Catholic school. Anna, how old are you again, five?"

"February 20, 1959, I was born, so I am six, this many," Anna said, holding up her right hand and left thumb.

"You're impressionable—don't believe what they say, that Jews killed Jesus.

I don't know what that has to do with anything when it happened a thousand years ago."

"That's the man hanging over Mother Superior's desk?"

"Whatever, listen, remember people will tell us all kinds of things to our faces when they don't know we're Jewish. We will know a lot of things other Jews will not, all because we don't look Jewish. Keep your eyes and ears open and your mouth shut. Now that you are aware, you will see Katy expose herself."

"Okay, Mommy. I have to leave now. I can't be late for school."

Anna had plenty to think about; the least importantly was, *When did I see Katy last?* Katy had a beauty parlor catty-corner to the Carl Schurz Park entrance on East End Avenue and 84th Street. Mother took Anna there to get her hair cut. Katy would sit Anna up on two *Yellow Pages* phonebooks, then place a bowl on Anna's head upside down and cut around the lip of the bowl. The results: Mo's haircut from *The Three Stooges*. Anna recalled that Katy would have her sweep the entire beauty salon with a broom and dustpan, starting at age three.

Thinking back, Anna remembered when Mother took her to the beauty salon. Little Anna would ask the customers, "Ya want an English muffin or tea or coffee?" She would then go down the block to the diner and climb up onto the stools to place the order at the counter. The store clerk would offer her a free 7-Up, but Anna didn't take what she couldn't pay for. She returned to the East End Beauty Salon with the customer's order and then told them the price. It was "a quarter for a coffee and an English muffin." She held out her hand and pointed to her palm, saying, "I get a tip." Then she would walk over to her mother, who was watching the financial transaction with one hand on her hip, and place the nickel or dime she had earned into her mother's open palm.

In Anna's later years, Katy would braid Anna's hair or pull it back in a pony-tail, after which Katy cut Anna's hair above the rubber band. Mother sadistically accumulated the braids and ponytails and kept them in a plastic bag all the way up to the time Anna attended college.

THAT AFTERNOON, when Anna walked home after the school day and opened the apartment door with the key she wore on a shoestring around her neck, Mother and Country Katy were sitting on the couch in the living room.

"Come here, Anna," Mother called her to her side. "Come, darling, now what were you saying, Katy dear?"

"I can't talk in front of the child."

"Oh her, she is no ordinary child. She is an eighty-year-old lady in disguise. There's nothing you can't say in front of her."

"What?" Katy was perplexed.

"Well, how else is she going to learn?" Mother said.

"Jews are a bunch of lowlife dogs!"

"Really? Educate us, Katy."

"They should have all been cremated. It's a shame any one of them lived!"

"What did they do to you?" Mother wanted her *companion* fully exposed.

"All those Jew bastard children going to private schools in all their fancy clothes, one uglier than the other. All their parents are doctors and lawyers. They make more goddamned Jewish doctors and lawyers. They suck the life out of us."

"Really now?" Ann looked at her daughter with eyes that said *you hear this!*

"Yes, I would have been more than happy to have shoved them into the crematorium and lit the match at Auschwitz myself!" Katy said with total hate.

Ann turned to her daughter. In the right-coded words, she said, "You see why you have to listen to this? You would never believe me half as much if you only heard me tell you this. You have to hear it for yourself."

This lesson was repeated over Anna's lifetime. Later, at age thirteen, Mother's friend, a Holocaust survivor, told of her own experiences at the mercy of the Nazis. With time, Anna understood more and more that there really were people who hated blindly, believing what they were taught, never questioning what they were taught, and never searching for their own truth.

"Kinky black hair, big hooked noses ... book-smart people ... all Jews," Katy kept going.

"Since when is book smarts a deformation of character?" Mother said, looking at Anna.

Mother, a clandestine *Jewess, has nothing compared to complaining Katy. But Mother is saving up money to move up, as soon as she is better at reading* The New York Times.

Mother continued educating Anna after Katy left. "These people like Katy are just as dangerous as Hitler! After all, Hitler couldn't rise to power if it weren't for goddamn heel-clicking closet Nazi bastards like this. People have two faces."

"Two faces? You mean like not looking Jewish and having baptism papers?"

"I'm talking about one face they show while the other is hidden behind your back."

"Oh, like the way you stuck your tongue out behind Katy's back when you hugged her after you smiled in her face?"

"Sure. How can I not do that, knowing who she is? Look at what she said, pouring her disgusting soul out to us. Katy told us what she thought of our people, not knowing we were part of them. If she knew we were Jewish, she would have spit on me and cursed me to hell, but this way, she feels sorry for us and helps out. Unbelievable, heh?"

I like Mommy when she explains smart stuff to me.

Mother Ann sighed and stopped for a moment before she spoke again. She was slipping away into a flash from her past.

"Watch your ass, little girl. Promise me you will be a smart little girl and watch your ass."

As if a switch had turned, Mother fell into a distant, immobile stare into space. Daughter Anna watched, confused and concerned, as Mother babbled indecipherably. Anna had to balance listening with not making a peep or a movement. Even her breath would send Mother into a tizzy of rage. Through the years, the child grew this comprehension from repeated beatings.

Mother slipped back to being twelve-year-old Anci in the ghetto. *Emaciated, skeletal dead bodies were piled so high that Anci had a difficult time walking over them. Anci did her best not to allow herself to stumble and fall on top of decaying human carcasses.*

"They were all over in the stairways and the hallways; they were spread to the enormous courtyard," Mother said out loud before slipping away again.

No flower grew there for the dead; there was no room on the grass for the sun to shine through. The corpses lay on every patch of dirt. No one came looking for them. There was no one left to go to respect the dead. They were dead.

"The courtyard to the building I lived in was where the Nazis ordered the dead bodies be thrown. The bodies were everywhere, everywhere," Mother said.

The stories of a betrayed life stolen by illegitimacy, depression, war, death, bombings, revolution, and escape would prove too much for most people's lives, spoiling their irreparable core. This was, perhaps, not the case for Mother Ann. Her psychological or genetic makeup may have been created in defense of such a harsh world. There was a benefit in being heartless. After all, being a triumphant survivor, able to endure more than heroine-like characteristics to battle inhumanity, worked to Ann's victorious advantage. Anna felt Mother was the one to watch out for and not the other way around.

Anna knew "do not interrupt" these frozen, stared-off-into-space ramblings with a word, let alone a question. And so, Anna strained to listen, to absorb as much as her young mind feasibly could.

Ann's mind skipped to her friend Joszi, a grown man twice her age. He was assigned to carry dead bodies to the empty stores in the ghetto for storage. How gruesome that the store with the former purpose of a "BUTCHER HOUSE" was ironically showcasing human carcasses in the window as the store's ghoulish sign hung above.

"The stench from summer heat decaying maggot-ridden, rotting bodies with hovering flies buzzing was a strange sight. Think about it: each one of those grimly grinning carcasses was once someone's baby."

Joszi taught Anci how to differentiate between the rich Jew corpses and the poor Jew corpses.

"The rich ones had fewer teeth in their mouths. Rich Jews had their gold teeth *removed with crude pliers while they were alive and without the use of Novocain because Nazi sympathizers found the screams of a Jew amusing."*

Ann's demeanor quieted, and her eyes stared vacantly, stuck in time.

Hairs on the back of Anna's neck rose up, and in another split second, it would be too late. *What time is it? I'm nervous.* Anna knew. *It's time I leave.* There was a point at which Mother's quiet would light like a match, bursting into a blazing fire of unleashed Hades. Anna did love Mother when she shared intelligent insights but not to the point of self-sacrifice. Anna didn't deserve to play catalyst to Mother's "healing" through another beating. Anna silently prayed to her trusted and true connection.

"Dear All Knowing, won't you send someone. Help me!"

With that, Anna realized she hadn't seen Mama Koss in a very, very long time. In a state of stifling fear, she knew Mother would kick her ass around the apartment and then kick her ass out to the city streets.

Anna decided to hit the cold, uncaring pavement of the streets to resolve her question, *Where is Mama Koss?* Recently, an Irish street rat exchanged words with her while they were in line at the A&P. Anna remembered the scene as if it were yesterday and not months ago.

"You ain't never gonna see Mrs. Koss again!"

The obnoxious kid was too gleeful for Anna's comfort. "What yous talking about?"

Anna retorted, talking like these street kids to avoid further brutality.

"Yeah, yo Mama ain't no more!"

The gutter rats snickered like liquored pirates dominating a ship. They then barreled Anna with a heavy load and fired, "Mama Koss dropped dead!"

Yikes! Mother said she curses Mama Koss for charging her. Mother's curse worked! Mother's an evil witch!

Dropped dead? Anna didn't believe these good-for-nothing ratbags. *I need proof.* Surely, Mother would have told her. She would have laughed, glad she got away with not paying what she owed. That thought made Anna realize that *Mother doesn't know Mama Koss died. Mother would love to hurt me with that news.*

"I'll look everywhere; I gotta bump into her. I gotta know if Mama Koss is dead or alive!" Anna walked to Mama Koss's brownstone and looked everywhere in the neighborhood where she knew Mama Koss went on foot. After a few days, Anna accepted that Mama Koss had passed. Melancholic Anna, in conclusion, wished she'd given her Mama Koss one more loving bear hug and said, "I love you."

There's to be no more, "This little piggy is going to the stoop, or this little piggy is in a blanket" because Mama Koss piggy died. There was to be no more of Mama Koss's spaghetti and meatballs, Oreo cookies, peanut butter and Flintstone jelly sandwiches. No more Pepto-Bismol or Mama Koss's cats, and certainly no more trips to her favorite place: St. Patrick's Cathedral, where Mama Koss took her once. Anna couldn't brave the subways to go there by herself. She needed Mama Koss to pull her small frame in close, into her billowy softness, to silence her soaring, crying nerves from the horrendous howling noises of the trains melding with her loudest screams of terror.

Anna hadn't seen Mama Koss since she started Catholic nursery school, but the woman was often on her mind, especially when she followed Mama Koss's proper protocol, through imagery, while lying in bed before slumber. Pretending to use St. Patrick's holy water when she used her spit, Anna said, "Father, Son, and Holy Ghost," crossing herself.

"Mama Koss, you're the first mother-like person who loved me, whether you got money or not." Just like Mother said, "Hate is not turned off like a light switch."

Anna believed that *love isn't turned off like a light switch. Good night, Mama Koss, rest in peace.*

God bless you! I love you, and I miss you!

P.S. Watch over Timothy.

Pssst ... tell the big guy up there to send me help!"

24

IT SEEMED SCHOOL HOLIDAYS MEANT fun for her classmates, from the cheers they made upon their announcement. But to six-year-old Anna, that meant another day contending with the streets.

One such unwanted day, Anna rushed out of her tenement and suddenly found herself across the street, wondering, *What now?* Exhausted, she looked around, dreading everything about her NYC concrete jungle. Anna wished she could retreat to a warm, cozy place. *Timothy and Mama Koss gone makes life hard.* The young miss didn't want to deal with another person in the world as cold as crystallized popsicles outside. Rather, the child's heart panged to be whisked away from the city's harshness. As easily as the thought came, Anna mentally disconnected from her surroundings, transporting herself into the deep reaches of her rich, imaginative mind. There, Anna escaped to where she could not otherwise survive.

Anna's mind floated her away to racing bumblebees as her hair played kite to the wind. She imagined glorious beams of a sunshine halo above her head. The healing rays entered her body through the crown of her soft, flowing hair. In the process of being fortified with the benefiting qualities of goodness from the sun, Anna simultaneously expelled the dark, heavy gloom weighing her down with each deep exhalation.

Staying in this powerful moment of bliss, Anna employed her sense of smell to overcompensate the noxious toxins of carbon exhaust emitted into the stinky world of the street by cantankerous metal monsters passing her by. Anna, with determination, permeated her mind with an imagined gift bestowed to her from Mother Nature. Aromatic fields, plentiful in rose and lavender flowers, perfumed Anna's mind, bringing splendid pleasure. Anna saw herself in her escaped place of heaven. She skipped, jumped, twirled, and ran with thankful outstretched arms, heading toward never-reaching, glistening, snowcapped mountains. Incorporating her ears to churn the cacophony of the wild metal beasts, wheeling on all fours picking up garbage in the neighborhood, into less-formidable, trivial sounds, Anna boomeranged a slew of giggling echoes into her mental imagery.

Not to forget to address her loneliness, she added into this daydreaming wistfulness frolicking children beckoning her to join them at play. She filled her lungs with a deep breath of wonderfulness and noticed on the golden horizon where she stood that the sunflowers were taller than her and a circle of trees stood in the distance before the far-off mountains. But, of course, because the scene unfolded in Anna's mind, the trees extended their friendly branches in the same way children interlock clasping hands in a singing game of "Ring Around the Rosie."

Easily emotional, Anna's eyes swelled with a small ocean of saltwater. A loudly racketing garbage truck that she referred to as the metal hippopotamus turned the corner and jostled Anna away from her vision of heaven and back into her despised concrete jungle reality. To ease assimilation, Anna clicked her *Wizard of Oz* Dorothy heels three times. Once again, Anna was left to test her creative devices and asked herself, *What time is it? What the hell am I supposed to do all day? It's bad enough we have weekends off. I hate these school holidays.*

Anna unconsciously worked her fingers to perform Braille magic. They nimbly identified a couple of copper-bearded Abraham coins sharing common space in her jacket pocket. Thought of any other denomination was senseless.

Good luck pennies were all anyone found on the street. With an empty belly, Anna automatically licked her weather-chapped lips. *Yum, maybe there's a sweet shop selling candy close by. I still got a full day to figure out. I hate this!*

Her ingenuity popped a golden idea into her head no different than she figured a small-time miner sifted a golden nugget out of a heap of sand. Her question that led her out of her boredom: *What would I do if it were my birthday?*

As great as the question was, Anna shrugged her shoulders, not knowing. Just like her entire body, they, too, were sore. *Mother's right. I really am like an eighty-year-old woman.*

Chilled by the winter air from standing in the same spot while the sun played peek-a-boo behind the clouds, Anna acted like a lizard and soaked in the rays of the warming sun coming out to say hello. Anna wished she had a second mitt and had worn warmer clothes. *At least a pair of tights under these pants!* But Anna could not return home, even if the tenement where she lived was almost within arms' reach, due to the "sunup to sundown rule." Those were the hours Anna had to be out of the house unless it was raining or snowing.

She'd had two mittens in her jacket pockets the last she remembered, but now she could only retrieve one. *Great. Hope Mother doesn't find out, or that's another beating.* Angry with herself, Anna retied her scarf to better cover her ears and then tucked her hands into her springtime short coat pockets. *I got my hands in my pockets and my pockets in my jacket and my jacket's got two Abrahams. Whoops, step on a crack, break my momma's back.*

Anna began making her way to the park where she wound up regularly. In her own unique style, depending on which muscle group hurt least, *This little piggy can't skip or run. I will hop, shuffle, and scoot to the park.* Today, feeling a need for variety, Anna was determined not to play on the swings or the monkey bars, and she certainly wasn't mounting another seesaw. *Not ever, as in never!*

No, not after she tore the pink frilly dress that Mother bought her for her fifth birthday at the neighborhood thrift store. *Nope, I broke that bone that would have grown a tail if I were a monkey. That's why it's called a tailbone.* On days Anna forgot, her back reminded her to never trust a new kid again.

Her mind drifted back to that fateful day. Anna sat on one end of a large seesaw, waiting for a new playmate to abracadabra form from thin air.

"Hey, ya wanna get on the other end?" she asked any kid walking by.

"Only if you play Dare."

Somebody finally! "Fine. Get on."

"Close your eyes," he said before he jumped off and ran away. Anna let out a hurt-filled cry. She was flat on her back, squirming in agony. No one came to help her. As usual, she was on her own. Anna could hardly drag her body home, let alone up the excruciating six flights of stairs, but she had to push onward. She had to be on time for her birthday party. None of this birthday "celebration" in the summer made any sense, though, since Anna's birthday was in February. While Anna scratched her head to make sense of what she knew, she realized, *Oh boy, I'm gonna get it. I ripped my dress.*

Anna didn't get to tell Mother about the incident when she got home.

"Why are you late?" *Smack!*

"I'm hurt. This boy ..."

Her mother pushed her past the kitchen and down their long hallway.

"Please, you're hurting me. That's where I hurt."

"Shut up," was preempted and followed by countless pushes, right where it hurt, through the family room and into Mother's bedroom. Then Mother picked up Anna and slammed her down on the bed, right where Suni Muni was sitting alongside some other girl she had never met before.

Her words for her mother to stop hurting her only fell onto her one true, trusty listener, Suni. He was all ears because he was still continually beaten senseless and given that brown water to drink on a daily basis. *He does nothing but sit staring ahead. Well, at least he won't get beat as much by keeping quiet.*

Mother picked up a camera and said, "I will be right back. First, I am taking pictures of the party in the kitchen."

Anna could hear the commotion in the kitchen. *Maybe that's why Mother pushed me past the kitchen.* Anna looked at Suni and complained about her boo-boo. Even though he stared straight ahead without any reaction, Anna knew he understood her pain. And knowing Suni couldn't protect her, Anna had to survive what her mother would do next.

"Okay, you kids, smile with faces looking like ugly pumpkins. I am taking photos quicker than yesterday and getting my ugly duckling daughter out of my sight. She is so ugly she better not break the camera." *Mother is making fun of me in front of others my age. She doesn't care that birthdays are to make the birthday person happy. This is not fun.*

"Okay, now, you two take turns hitting Anna five times and one more time for good luck. The harder you hit her, the better her luck will be! I will start," Mother announced.

"My back hurts, so punch my arm," Anna said, preempting blows to her back just as her mother lifted her by the arm and then smacked her in the back six times and threw her down, saying, "Your turn" to Suni and the girl Anna didn't know.

Mother is like no Mom I've seen on television. Indeed, a simple, loving cuddle or a hug from Mother never happened outside of the occasional public eye. Sidney wasn't at the party in the kitchen. *He would have come over and said hello. Hmmm ... I haven't seen Sidney in a while,* Anna considered.

That thought preempted Mother Ann's next move. She was incapable of embracing another person without extending her tongue in a gag behind her embracer's back. There were different variations of this lovely move; none reflected well on Ann as a mother. The more someone guided Mother to refrain from rolling her eyes while hugging, or to not stick her finger down her throat as if inducing her gag reflex, or to not make obscene sexual gestures, the more Ann accelerated her shockingly inappropriate behavior.

Anna's mind wandered on purpose to distract her from the hitting phase of the birthday. Her mind then snapped back with a smack to the back of her head from Mother. With that, she found Mother's furious eyes warning the birthday girl, "There's *hell* to pay for ripping that dress, but later, now we're in company." As if her day hadn't been ruined enough by being treated like a bad dog in front of her peers, having her favorite pink dress torn, and her non-ending back pain from falling so hard, she'd have more punishment coming later from her mother.

The big birthday bash consisted of the three kids. There was no food or drink or cake, but there was alcohol in the kitchen for the adults. Lili walked out of the kitchen with a stupid smile and pointed to her tumbler glass, saying, "Hey Ann, we need more ice and tea."

Anna knew Lili didn't drink tea. *Click!* Mother blindingly clicked a camera with the flash ten more times. The entire ceremonious event, including her whacks, smacks, and punches, consisted of no more than ten minutes. *There are blue and yellow spots wherever I look. They're like the stars I see pop up when Mother beats me.*

Suni was the first to point out, "The circles are in color and not white stars."

Anna knew all too well what Suni was referring to. "Yeah, Suni, I get those too. I don't think it's a good thing."

The birthday picture Mother Ann shared with the birthday girl developed weeks later and captured three jack-o'-lantern toothless children pitifully wearing recycled birthday dunce hats from who knows whose past birthday. In a month's time, the finished black-and white party photo with shades of gray was swallowed up by the pit of a drawer of forgettable clutter. Yet somehow, the photo managed to etch into Anna's memory album. Perhaps Mother's condescending comments as the camera flashed brandished the event to forever sear into Anna's brain.

"You think *donkey ears* at age five is smart enough of a jackass to remember whether she had a party or not?" Mother Ann elbowed Lili, standing next to her, in her side. Further humiliating her daughter, Mother Ann laughed and pointed, performing for her small audience. "Hey you, donkey, sit over there before I kick the remainder of your stupid teeth into that moron head of yours. Okay, smile! What's your problem, donkey head? Why don't you smile? Stop looking at me with those stupid donkey eyes and give me your retard donkey smile."

"My head and body hurt, Mommy."

"Smile or don't smile, happy birthday. You'll see with a face like yours ... in later life, you will realize how much I sacrificed. Good you didn't smile. Now I have proof. Okay, five more minutes and everybody out. That's enough stupid sh*t for one day."

Suni understood. His mother, Lili, shared the same philosophy as Mother Ann's. *They don't remember anyway. Take a picture, put it out, make up a story. It's all good enough.*

THAT WAS THEN. "Shuffle, shuffle, off to Buffalo ..." Anna switched her strut as she was still making her way to the park, compensating for the pull she felt in her back—all because she fell off the seesaw and her mother favored hitting her there.

Another quick adjustment to her scarf, and Anna kept moving along. *Careful, step on a crack, and I break my mama's back. I must have stepped on so many cracks that I broke my own back.* The sun once again played peek-a-boo behind tall NYC steel-metal skyscrapers, making its grand appearance again.

Every morning, Anna was prompted, "Get your ass out of the stinking apartment!" If she rose before her alarm clock, the yelling went on in her head; otherwise, the yelling came directly from her mother when the alarm rang. No matter how the day began, in those seconds, overwhelming panic flushed through the child.

Once down the flights of stairs and on the street, Anna reversed her long-held breaths with a deep inhalation and then consciously tried to get her breathing into a normal rhythm. The cool air in her lungs pierced her slightly, and she coughed. *I better not be sick again!*

"That's right!" Anna heard her mother's yelling pop out of nowhere again. "You better not get sick, or I will beat the sh*t out of you, you good-for-nothing bother. I ought to get paid for all the times I got to take you, you ignoramus, to the hospital," she screamed, referencing the many times she flagged down police in the middle of the night to get a ride to the hospital for sickly Anna. "Next time I go, I'll check if the hospital's made me a punch card!"

Oh Jesus, Mother Mary Ann Joseph, breathe deep. An inner shift came with self-assigned deep breaths, so Anna took some more, alternating which eye she kept open and which she closed since she didn't stop walking. With persistence,

Anna's deep inner calm finally rescued her. Anna disconnected from her over-whelming physical life, and there, in a peaceful space, she reached out to her All Knowing:

"No school today because of a stupid national holiday. So what can we do that would be different?"

"Get walking to the park," He said.

Once at her targeted entrance, the gates of Carl Schurz Park on East End Avenue, a couple of avenues down from First Avenue where she resided, Anna heard All Knowing guiding her again. *"No playground today."*

She walked until she reached a paved walkway where green park benches lined up on opposite sides like jade beads waiting to be strung into a necklace. She stood quietly, waiting for a sign to tell her which direction to take. Her eyes perused hungrily to locate the right trail.

"Which way do I go?" Anna asked.

"Out of the ordinary path," All Knowing directed Anna.

"Over here!" a child shouted before darting away.

Oh, that's a sign for me to go there. Anna twirled about-face like a pink tutu ballerina.

She shuffled to the odd place behind the row of benches, as opposed to the paved pathway where the benches faced each other. Where the kid went after he pointed out that spot was not of importance. Anna had to focus intently on All Knowing's guidance. The kid led her to a new area of grass and trees to be explored. Magnetically pulled like a hooked fish being reeled in, Anna felt compelled to walk with the soft, cushiony grass underfoot.

Each cushioned step across the small terrain, All Knowing affirmed to Anna, *"You are on to something. Put your head down. Look for something special."*

"Like pennies for pretzels?" Anna asked, concentrating intensely. She didn't want to lose the connection. She didn't want to chance something distracting her. She had to balance both the real concrete world where she lived with whatever place All Knowing was from.

"Better, something different," All Knowing said.

Anna walked on.

"Stop. Pay attention to where you step," All Knowing emphasized.

Anna noticed a dog relieving itself in the area she was trampling. *"Great. Well, there are better ways of getting good luck than me stepping in puppy poop, aren't there? Okay so, what will make the spot I'm looking for perfect?"*

"It will feel right," All Knowing replied.

"What am I looking for?" Anna asked, somewhat agitated.

"You'll see," All Knowing said.

"This is not easy, ugh."

Even more intently than before, Anna focused on the ground. With a stick, she flicked through piles of leaves, pebbles, and twigs. Her determination as a diligent scavenger finally paid off. Anna found something small. To relieve the strain from her lower back, yet careful not to let her knees touch the ground, Anna knelt to inspect her discovery.

"Oh my God, this must be it!" Anna exclaimed.

No answer.

"Is this it?" she asked a few times.

"Trust yourself," He whispered.

"Found something!" Anna popped up like a skittish meerkat. *"What time is it?"* Struggling to curtail her excitement for the next part of her adventure to unfold, she paced about.

"Thank you, All Knowing, for this gift," she said and crossed herself several times with crosses and then hearts. Anna chuckled. *I must look like a troubled deaf person doing sign language.* She counted to ten, composed herself, squatted back down, and focused.

"Ahh!" Anna screeched when her brain registered that she had poked a creature.

In the way the hairless thing bounced back, Anna deduced it was once a living thing. In fact, because there were no bugs on it, the child-scientist determined that the animal had recently died. Left to decipher what this God's creature was, Anna wondered: *Did its mother have something to do with its condition?*

Wow, I guess compared to this, I can't complain. Anna found its unrecognizable hairless skin strange and its shut eyes tiny.

For better inspection, Anna needed to find an object to raise this grotesque and scary, yet alluring, intriguing thing. Intermittently, she scratched her head with her lost mitted hand, questioning, *"Why's this so special? I know it is, but why?"*

A few feet away, Anna resorted to rummaging through discarded treasures in the park's receptacle. Finding an empty matchbox, Anna plopped her discovery inside. The thud of the lifeless body into the box sprouted goosebumps along the gamut of Anna's body as the peach hairs on her face stood electrified. Anytime Anna had goosebumps, it was a sign of some extraordinary information coming in.

I got goosebumps when I knew there was a monster near me, and it was Yucky Monster. But these goosebumps are different. Goosebumps! What else has goosebumps? Goosebumps. Chickens have goosebump skin. I've seen them in cartoons, and I've seen chicken skin before it's cooked. I remember when Mama Koss took me to pick out a chicken at the butcher once. I said, "That's the lucky guy," to which the butcher said, "Maybe not so lucky when you see what happens to it," right before he chopped its head off. Wow! I forgot about that. Goosebumps—thanks for the hint! But I still don't know what this is.

Anna jumped and freaked out. With her back pain, she hopped from one leg to the other, appearing like a religious zealot in church, witnessing the coming of the Lord. Anna counted to ten again and regrouped her skittishness so she could set the makeshift coffin down to continue her inspection. She avoided sitting down in the dirt; she didn't need a beating for messing her clothes. She held the matchbox-casket up close to her face to inspect its newly placed resident.

What is this thing with no arms or feet or hands? Wow, All Knowing is not helping me.

All Anna recognized were its shut eyes. The skin looked like a miniature version of a packaged plucked chicken kept in the grocer's freezer case. *Skin not growing fur had to grow feathers.* There it was—first *goose pimples* and now *feathers*! Suddenly, its odd nose made sense as a beak. She now had the answer: It was a bird! *This thing is a bird, a baby bird!*

She asked a question, hoping All Knowing would answer. "*Did the bird get knocked out of the nest like I am out of the apartment every day, or like Timothy, to never be seen again?*"

"*This bird has a special meaning,*" All Knowing guided.

Anna exerted great intent in acquiring the special meaning. "*All Knowing, I know I'm to remember this moment. Help me make sense of this dead bird.*"

Anna removed herself to the bench, where she could sit and concentrate. She took deep, rhythmic breaths, calming herself.

A vision of her in another life came to the child as if she were in a dream. A man in an ankle-length brown robe tied with a rope in three knots around his waist, with a bowl haircut and a shaved scalp, was walking down a long path of cobbled stones in open-toe sandals. He was disappointed with his life. He'd given much of his life to spread the word of God, yet God never showed himself to him. Anna was given visions of the friar's vows of silence, his starvation, and his actions spreading the word of the gospel, yet God did not present himself.

Blindly kicking the cobblestones in disgruntled disdain, his foot bumped a fleshy thing. "What's this?" The friar discovered it was a dead bird. "There are no coincidences! I get the meaning! God is telling me to live my life! God showed Himself through this dead bird, a symbol of the Holy Spirit, just as I was drowning in feelings of worthlessness. I must be the best I can be and live my life. Be good, for goodness' sake, without expectation.

Anna jumped up and danced a Snoopy dance of joy. Be my best, *live my life!* For meaningful moments like this, Anna was glad to keep living. The meaning of this message gained weight with each inch Anna grew in her upcoming years.

Not clear about what her next action should be, Anna decided, *I will do as I want someone to do for me.* She performed a ceremonial burial for the bird out of respect. Anna became emotionally overwrought. Removing her one glove to wipe her tears off her face, again her mother's voice interrupted, "Piss is the same salt as tears, and it's easier."

Goodness' sakes, shoosh Mother! Anna set the one mitten under her knee to keep her pants from getting dirty and rebalanced her achy body from sitting further on her pained heels. Anna's legs screamed with poking pins and needles while her heart ached for this dead bird. *I'm a mess.*

Through this unexpected thrust into dealing with death, Anna realized the extent that she painfully missed her childhood friend Timothy, stricken with polio and his unexpected institutionalization. From Timothy, she learned: *It was good he lived his life playing when he could, cuz there came a day he couldn't.*

Grieving now, Anna couldn't turn off her faucet of tears. *I miss you, Timothy. I love you.* The more Anna tried to suppress the flow, the greater the stream of pressure from unresolved issues poured forth. And with this, Anna also faced the extent that she missed her loving, saint-like caretaker, Mama Koss, who the neighborhood street rats rudely pronounced had "dropped dead."

Anna gathered available small pebbles to ornament the altricial bird's burial spot. The child patted down a caressing blanket of Mother Earth to cover the matchbox-casket. Struggling to see past a hazy cloud of tears, Anna laid her meager offerings of pebbles and twigs and configured a stick-figured bird's foot inside a pebbled heart. The simplistic symbolism encompassed the funeral mound. Above that, she laid two twigs for a cross.

Limited by word mastery and experience at six years old, Anna ended her ceremonial loose ends, conveying loving regards toward the bird and the special departed persons in her life, and she especially thanked her silent guide, All Knowing. His wonderful, guided journey blessed Anna on this day, beginning with Him engaging the sun in a friendly game of peek-a-boo!

Hesitant to leave this powerful experience, the child hoped she'd received all its intended benefits. And to make sure, she mentally replayed her black-and-white-and-gray snapshots of this day's events, as she had done and would do with prior and future events to serve her correct recall in the future, when she was older and wiser, to decipher the intended messages.

Anna didn't question herself when she connected with All Knowing. He proved to be trustworthy. He was her *Father*, in essence, replacing the tangible father Anna had never known or had. In these moments, Anna was richer than most, even though her Father was everyone's. All anyone had to do was believe.

Dusk approached, and the chill warned Anna to heed the dangers of catching another cold. Anna's drenched and cold used hanky was mindfully retired to her subservient jacket pocket to join Anna's mitted hand. The un-mitted hand had enough to deal with—the cold—and her soaked sweater sleeve played backup to her soaked hanky. *I feel cheated. I could continue this good cry longer if I had more hankies, but it is a sign it's time to go.*

Standing and ready to leave, Anna looked down, gaining a new perspective of her creation. The heart with a bird's foot in the center had become a peace sign. *Sort of like how God sees His world.* Anna scratched her head as to why her symbolism also resembled a pretzel. Anna rubbed her growling belly and chalked it up as the answer.

25

TALK ABOUT CHANGING WINDS! Like a witch stirs brew in her cauldron or Merlin wands his way with magic, Mother Ann spit in mysticism's face, believing she had strengths unknown by all of humankind above and below ground. With added sputum, the sorceress whisked to alter lives in a rain of events.

Rattling leaves began to lightly rustle into clusters. Loose particles gladly joined in the strengthening whirling gusts, as so often is the case with the brink of a storm. Somehow, Ann held spellbound heaven, earth, and the underworld to meet her wants. Yes, Ann was no ordinary human—not to her daughter and not to anyone who knew her. Ann had Herculean strength ... when she finally decided to do something. Ann's energy accelerated from mostly nothing at all to all of most. Ann had plans. Her latest intent entailed migrating her mother, Mutter Clara, to America.

Through the years, Ann had been corresponding with Mutter Clara, still living in the old country, Hungary. Early on, Mother Ann busily mailed Clara rejected photographs she had paid to be taken, hoping to place her baby with a modeling agency. Scouts for modeling agencies returned Mother Ann's photo packages of baby Anna with a cowardice sheet insert, whereby a lazy checkmark indicated: "Your child falls under the 'nothing special' category."

Ann thought that sending one or two photos from a dossier she got suckered into buying to "place baby into money-earning commercials" would at least compensate for some of her wasted money. "Since I don't have a fireplace, sending Mutter the pictures is the next best thing to wiping my ass with them."

At least Anna didn't have to hear Mother's usual spiel. "Na, I look like a schmuck. They saw this immigrant as an easy target. People have no conscience; they promised the world until they got my money, and then they pissed on me. Why couldn't they tell me 'Your child looks like a retarded idiot' in the first place? Why did the no-good bastard take my money out of my mouth to kick me in the ass afterward?"

Clara returned the correspondence. She openly revealed that her life had spiraled downward. Her husband, Tibby, had died in 1964. His passing ushered a new beginning to a new end. Clara fell in love with a good-for-nothing gypsy who took cruel advantage of her vulnerability. Clara, known to be a foolhearted romantic, sadly never found a man deserving of her. Mother condescendingly called Mutter Clara "Sweet Clara," as in this case: "Sweet Clara's first mistake was inviting the conniving gypsy into her home. In a world where extended families live together in one room, a house was a tremendous luxury to own."

Poor Clara lived through raising her illegitimate child, Ann, as a hardworking laborer at age seventeen in a world and a time that scorned her. Then she worked in a Nazi labor camp. Clara's reward as a Holocaust survivor was to live a brutal life under communist rule. During the Red Star occupation, Clara kept company with a man who hated children and forced her to give up her child, Anci.

"I will marry you," Tibby said, "but on the condition you give up your child." Mother added to the story, saying, "Tibby paid for me to be boarded at the best Jewish school for rich children in Budapest."

Holding Clara's letter in hand, Mother Ann was educating her daughter. "What kind of a person was he? What kind of a person was she? I'll tell you! Mutter Clara was desperate to have a husband and a home. Times were terrible, but Clara should have known better. After all, she married her best friend's husband, Tibby. His dead wife used to complain: 'Tibby beat me. I gave a bite of chocolate to our son, and for this, he beat me.' Despite her friend's black raccoon eyes, all Clara saw was their big house; she wanted a house like that. Seemingly, she prayed hard enough because she got it. She got it, oh, but she got it good, that Clara."

Ann continued to tell Anna the story of Mutter Clara and Tibby. As Anna later recalled the story, it went something like this:

Tibby's first wife, Mootzy, and his second wife, Clara, first met each other while they both worked at the same bookbinding factory. Clara was thankful Mootzy talked to her; not too many people did since Clara was a scorned single mother with a bastard child. In fact, they did not exchange their initial "Hello, how do you do?" until Mootzy and Clara were formally introduced at Pataki's apartment. Clara and Pataki's relationship had been strictly a monetary exchange from Clara for Pataki's last name that she obtained through the marriage papers he signed, which then paid off his gambling debts. Mootzy, on the other hand, was at Pataki's apartment because she was cheating on her husband, Tibby. Mootzy and Clara built their foundations for a long-lasting friendship by each vowing an unspoken pledge to never reveal the other's secret.

Within a year, life betrayed both Clara and Mootzy. The two women were roused out of their separate homes and made to march in frost and snow as captives to a Nazi labor camp, where they were reunited. Under desperate times in a Nazi extermination camp, Mootzy and Clara became interdependent. Their bond was never more evident than when Clara fainted. Mootzy had a special way of catching Clara by wedging her body to fall in a sandwiching procession of others in roll call, saving Clara from falling to the floor and rescuing her from a bullet.

Out of the two women, Clara, for obvious reasons, seemed to be more dependent on Mootzy for survival. But, though Clara was weak, she was a great loyal asset to have in a horrible place where the notion of anything good was an oxymoron. Mootzy was half the size of the women, while Clara was twice the size of the women and protective of her friend. In a place where the daily food ration was a piece of bread, turning women animalistic, Clara, nicknamed the "*maci/*

teddy bear" was a great pal indeed. The strong companionship between Maci and Mootzy in the sadistic work camp literally saved each other's lives many times.

One day at roll call, Clara's body fell limp in a faint. Mootzy, as usual, used her body weight to hold Clara upright. Mootzy saved Clara, but it cost her. The bullet meant to shoot Clara only grazed her ear but shot a hole through Mootzy's head, killing her on the spot. Feeling indebted to Mootzy, Clara, when she was released from the work camp, returned home to Budapest and cared for Tibby. True to his dirtbag reputation, Tibby took full advantage of Clara, but at least he married her.

"Now Clara is homeless and roaming the streets, the goddamn gypsy bastard, two-bit whore, threw her out of her own house and into the cold streets! Watch what I do now. I might be saving all our lives with a little lick. No, never mind, you do it, Anna."

"But Mommy, didn't you say the part you lick on the envelope is made out of grinded animal bone?"

"Yeah, that's why I am having you lick it."

After being shown how, Anna sealed Mutter Clara's fate with a long lick along the gum of the envelope containing a ship's voyage ticket to America. Then Mother Ann stashed that envelope into the pocket of the same thick brown seal fur coat Mother Ann had worn from Hungary to the safe shores of America. Unlike most, Mother Ann operated better under war conditions and hard struggling times than the rest of the population. She kissed her seal coat—a luxury item she had earned working the black market under communism—sighed, and shoved the bulky coat into a box, saying, "See you soon. Work your magic. Go back home to keep Clara warm, and then see to it you escort her safely on her big journey to this great country, America. We can use her help."

Clara used the seal fur coat well. She voyaged the entire freezing month of February in the stirred seas within the deep belly of a frosty cauldron called the S.S. *United*. As the ship fought winter-brewed tides, Mother Ann prepared her daughter for Clara's impending arrival. Several times, Mother Ann sternly slammed her daughter into a sitting position at the foot of her bed. Holding a picture of Mutter Clara, Mother Ann chanted repetitively: "This Clara is your grandmother." Mother Ann, wearing her usual house attire, bra and panty, said this repeatedly as she pointed toward the picture with a stick of ash longer than the cigarette. "She is my mother," she explained, pointing to her naked torso. "I am your mother. She is Clara. She is my mother like I am your mother, and she is your grandmother."

Anna thought, *Mother thinks I really am a retarded idiot.* Anna couldn't take the cloud of smoke she was forced to sit in no more than Mother's repetitive words that never slowed down but instead, sped up with a voice that became louder rather than softer. Anna felt the rising tension from Mother becoming a heated, out-of-control steam locomotive getting ready to barrel down on her.

To save herself, Anna blurted, "Clara is my grandmother because you are my mother."

They both figured they knew it all at that point. More important was what went unsaid: Anna's hopes and prayers were being answered.

"Help is on its way!"

Hustle and flurry whirled in the air like leaves swirling before a big rain. Finally, the anticipated day arrived. Everyone was invited to greet Clara at the docks of the large ocean voyager steamship that had transported her. Mother Ann kept Sidney separated from Anna ever since that incident at the park where Mother threw Anna out of the car. Sidney was around, but Anna hadn't seen him in years. Although there was no babysitter for Anna, her mother would prance into Anna's bedroom in a fancy new dress with her hair all done and ask, "Anna, how do I look? Sidney is taking me to dinner and a show tonight."

"Very pretty, Mommy. I have the prettiest Mommy."

"That's right, ugly duckling. I don't know how I ended up with you."

"Ann, is that necessary? Let's go. We will be late," Sidney said through Anna's confining closed bedroom door as he stood in the adjacent family room—just as Ann had instructed him to do.

With Clara's arrival, Anna finally saw Sidney for the first time in two years. Anna observed, *He feels distant. No big hello.*

Sidney drove Mother and her to the ship dock. "He drives since he is the only one with a car," Mother said when all the car doors closed. Then Mother added, "That's what I liked about you, Sidney. You remember how we met? First, I saw your car, that Jaguar. Then you came up to me. We talked. What happened to that car, Sidney? This is a piece of sh*t compared to that."

Anna already knew the real story. Katy had introduced Mother to Sidney. Mother Ann's stories altered more than a seamstress fixes the closet of a woman on a yo-yo diet.

"Ann, doll, you said Arthur is bringing his wife, Rose?"

"Yes, I thought I should call him to come. He didn't sponsor me, and he is a real piece of sh*t. Never calls to ask how we are or if he could help us."

"That's terrible, doll, you ever met Rose?"

"No, but I saw a picture. Jesus Christos, ach! Well, I will let you see her for yourself."

After they parked, Ann weaved in and out of the densely crowded waiting dock in the lynx coat Sidney had bought for her. Pulling her daughter along, not caring that every lady's purse smacked Anna's head from all directions like a prize fighter hitting a boxing speed bag. Mother was running around like a cursing chicken escaping a farmer's wife who was waving a butcher's knife. Anna couldn't take it anymore. Punch-drunk and dizzy, she dared speak up in the sudden presence of her Great-Uncle Arthur, now looking like Lurch on *The Addams Family*, accompanied by his mean, hunched-over, ugly wife, Rose, looking like George Washington in a funeral dress.

"What are we doing, Mommy?" Anna asked. "Are we playing Chicken Little and the sky's falling?"

Ignoring Anna, Mother Ann grumbled to Arthur, "What took you so long to get here, Arthur?"

"We depend on the bus system. We are still early," Arthur replied, speaking like Lurch.

Thankfully, Mother passed Anna to Great-Uncle Arthur, who, in the nick of time, intervened. "Ann, may I speak alone with the child?"

"Yes, good, she is in my way. I can't maneuver with this sh*t hanging on me, pulling me back. Take her."

Stiffly robotic, yet demure, Arthur led Anna by the hand away from the crowd. *This is something new.* Mother Ann preferred to lead, holding Anna at the wrist—if she held her at all. Touch bothered Mother and served as a trigger of agitation.

"This is the first time I've met you, and the first time I am seeing my sister since I left Hungary," Arthur said. He locked eyes with Anna. "Now, I am too old to do this, so will you do me the favor?"

Anna tilted her head, not saying yes, not saying no, just playing it cool. He had to respect that. He was Mr. Cool as a Cucumber himself.

Plenty of times, Anna heard Mother refer to Uncle Arthur as "a complete retard, good-for-nothing bastard, a big stupid, cold dummy," when in reality, he was an undercover agent for the CIA. He had first served the British, handing them information from the Germans. Later, with changing political times during the Cold War, Arthur worked on the American side against the Russians. Arthur was the mole no one could ever find. No one thought of searching Washington Heights in New York City, where people did the dead man's walk from heroin and cars went stripped in seconds if they dared park there.

Needless to say, the child was no contention for Uncle Arthur. "Anna, you will do me this favor, and you will be happy you did. I want you to jump up into Clara's arms and say, 'I love you, Grandma!' You can do that."

The child looked at him with big eyes. "Mother will kill me."

"Yes, I want you to practice with me, 'I love you, Grandma!'"

"If I say that, I am dead."

"What are you afraid of, your mother?"

"Yes, she will kill me; she warned me that Clara is her mother, not my mother; she will not like this."

"If you keep your favor to me, I promise to make your mother happy."

"I love you, Grandma?" Trying to compromise her situation, Anna phrased the words in a question.

"No, you said you were a smart girl. That won't do! Do it like we practiced!"

Arthur's compliment won Anna's confidence, and she obeyed. "'Grandma, I love you!' Is that good?"

"Great, that will do."

Anna knew that Clara's arrival was a big deal. She felt the pressure, and she better perform. Anxiously waiting, in her best effort, she spent the idle time reviewing, rewinding, and replaying the information until suddenly, Arthur nudged her.

"She's here! The passengers are coming off the ship!"

Anna couldn't see anything but a sea of pants, stockings, trampling feet, and the dreaded slew of those dangerously dangling arm bags that wailed like lethal torpedoes to her head.

"I can't stand being little!" Anna cried out in frustration.

Arthur nudged her again, this time harder, and pointed. "There, there's a woman in a seal coat! Run for it! Go!"

"Hi, Grandma," Anna said, beating everyone to Clara. Anna jumped up and took hold as instructed. "I love you, Grandma! I love you, I love you."

Anna held on, but without assistance, she slid slowly down, down, down. Fighting gravity, Anna still hung on with a big, forced smile. *Have I got the right person?* This grandma managed to keep walking even though she was burdened by Anna's weight. Others then joined arms in a big huddle, like players who had just won a football game. Once each had their one-on-one time with Clara, it was time to go home. Grandma sat in the back seat of Sidney's car, next to the window, where Anna butted up next to her as close as possible, like a loyal dog.

Loving this new idea of being encouraged to display affection, during the ride home, Anna hugged her beautiful grandma, noticing she had a squishy, sugary middle, like an Oreo cookie—good enough to eat. Grandma smiled at Anna with love in her eyes. Anna couldn't get her arms around Clara the same way she couldn't get them around Mama Koss, reminding Anna of the love she felt for Mama Koss.

"Grandma, you are so squeezable!" Anna said, as Grandma hugged her back.

Anna busily snapped mental black-and-white and seal-brown photos to add to her journaling memory album. These were happy and heartwarming, a new kind of unforgettable. Snapshots were suddenly not just black, white, and gray.

Clara's sweetness reminded Anna of an older Snow White. This naturally made everyone else, in Anna's eyes, the seven dwarfs and Mother the wicked witch or the mean jealous queen, Anna wasn't sure. Grandma exuded genuine goodness. Halfway home, as Anna and Grandma continued to hug each other, Anna was surprised how someone she never knew before that day had seized her heart so quickly. Anna truly loved her Grandma and hoped she wouldn't change like the blowing-in-and-out seasons or soiled bed sheets.

Grandma was placed in Anna's old bedroom, the room closer to Mother; the child was glad and preferred the buffer. In no time at all, Clara found a job as a bookbinder, accepting the first job offered.

Mother Ann was rudely outspoken, and if she were prudent, she would not have offered any opinion. Ann should have praised Clara for landing a paying job within two weeks. But instead, Ann's big mouth said, "It was her trade back in the old country, but like a stupid dumb jelly sh*t, my mother goes to New Jersey to work, on the subway from Manhattan, when everyone else comes in from New Jersey to work in Manhattan. I can't understand this. This is stupid. Someone's got to speak the truth!"

No one answered Mother Ann back. The truth was that Mother was lucky to have Clara help with bills, cleaning, cooking, and Anna. There was no winning against Mother, though, who repeatedly said, "Crazy people got more strength than anyone."

Don't I know! Funny, only Mother's allowed to call herself crazy, Anna thought to herself.

As for Anna, she couldn't have been more thrilled for her good fortune; namely, Grandma Clara. To start, Grandma prepared Anna breakfast every morning. No more self-prepared, roach-stomped cereal; instead, Anna sat down to delicious toast and hot tea during the week and French toast or farina and tea on the weekends. *Yummy* farina was the child's favorite!

Grandma sat with her, or at least squirmed, while the child attempted to eat. However, more often than not, the girl's grandma left Anna to sit alone at the kitchen table. The patience needed to eat with Anna was immeasurable. With a language barrier between them, Grandma used the charade excuse, "Getting dressed and ready for work."

From everyone's previous comments, Anna knew why Grandma really left her side. Everyone agreed, "Anna is the worst eater! No one can eat at the same table with her."

On the rare occasion Anna was included in a group at mealtime, Anna pushed her food from one side of the plate to the other, and when she finally placed food in her mouth, she gagged. Eventually, everyone laid their forks on their plates and retired to the living room. The child knew she had a problem, but the problem controlled her because the more she tried to eat, the worse the issue became. The child knew she was a bother to grandmother, too, even though it was the last thing Anna wanted.

"Chew and drink, chew and drink. The tea will soften up the food and help wash it down. Chew and drink," was among the first sentences Clara learned to speak in English.

Clara had the best intentions, and Anna had the best intentions, but did it matter? Yes, now that Grandma was around, she brought Anna home real food and kept monstrous Mother at bay.

Every day, Anna stayed after school as long as she could, participating in all after-school activities for free daycare. At five o'clock, Anna walked home and waited for Grandma to come home, busying herself in her room with colored letter magnets on her easel, not understanding what was so great about them because she couldn't spell yet. Anna checked the clock above her, counting down the minutes until she'd kiss and hug her favorite person in the world. For the first time, Anna felt she had someone she belonged to, someone who cared for her in a healthy way. It had been a hard six years she had waited to feel loved, and now she was. Mama Koss had loved Anna, but Anna belonged to Grandma. There's a difference.

Six nights a week, Grandma cooked a Hungarian meal, alternating the menu items between blood sausages with a side of mashed potatoes, potato casserole, cabbage stew, chicken paprikash, or goulash with handmade noodles and leftovers. But nothing compared to the seventh night when Big Mama prepared a sixteen-ounce steak! In Hungarian, big and grand is the same word, which also happened to be Anna's last name, Nagy. Either way, when Anna addressed Clara as Nagy Mama, she thought of Clara as Big Mama because, in the child's mind, she was calling Clara her real mother since Anna thought of Mother Ann as a monster.

"Tonight's the big night!" Big Mama would declare. "I unwrap this prized meat from the butcher paper like a groom unwraps his virgin bride on their wedding night. This whole steak cost me five dollars. I worked three hours to earn this steak, before taxes, but you are worth every penny. This is for you, my angel; it will make you strong and healthy. Eat the whole thing if you can. Don't worry about me. I will find something else. If you leave any leftovers, then I will have that."

Big Mama couldn't believe the child ate the whole thing every time! "You poor darling, someone should feed you. You are nothing but skin and bones."

Indeed, it was true what all the Hungarians said: "That sorry-looking child looks like she is walking out of the concentration camps."

Mother chimed in, "You get all the dogs in the neighborhood barking at you because they spotted a walking bag of bones." Damaging her daughter's ego was never Mother Ann's concern. Gathering an audience where she was the center of her egocentric stage was.

Unwanted cruel memories were dismissed with Grandma's gentle smile, a loving pat on the back, and a big plate placed in front of Anna.

"Don't worry, trust me. Eat this so you grow."

"Thank God for you, Big Mama!" Anna exclaimed. She was a wild animal, left to eat without having been taught how to use silverware, so she utilized nature's forks, her hands, at mealtime.

"Madness!" Grandmother gasped. In shock, Grandmother ran to stand in front of the child to make sure her eyes didn't deceive her. "This food deserves better treatment. Treat it with dignity; eat like a princess!"

"What? How do I do that?"

Grandma demonstrated and promised, "I will not sit down to eat with you until you learn how to eat properly."

Adults are so strange. They expect me to know how to do things. Mother beat me instead of taught me. At least Big Mama was taking the time and effort.

ONE MORNING, while still at the ripe old age of six, Anna decided she needed to change her name. Anna clearly remembered the moment she dialed into the airwave frequencies of some mysterious radio dial in her mind and suddenly understood the Hungarian conversations between her mother and Big Mama. Both Mother and Clara were surprised, and from then on, a new rule was introduced: no more English spoken in the home. After that, this rule was never wavered from. Anna didn't see the big deal. It wasn't like it was hard to speak Hungarian.

For some unexplained reason, Mother began to refer to Mutter as Clara, and this became too confusing for the child, who would run as fast as she could to answer to her names Anna and Clara, only to be told when she got there, "Not you, the other one." So she decided on a school holiday, while her grandmother was working, that she would take her life in her hands and approach her mother about the topic since her mother was at home watching television in bed.

Yup, I am going to change my name. I gotta time out the right time to tell her. I am going to do my talking during commercials of Mother's favorite soap opera, The Edge of Night. *But I can't just tell her I want to be called Nancy because it's the pretty girl's name. I have to let her think she thought of the name. She might not let me have that name if I tell her. I just won't agree to any other name. I hope she is busy watching her show and agrees. In the same way I have to speak Hungarian in the home to be heard, I won't answer if I'm called anything else but Nancy.*

And so, that's how it went. Mother at first asked, "You want the name Katy or Lili?" to which Anna explained, "I have to have my own name. I don't want to be told 'not you, the other one.'" By the end of the show, speaking only during commercials because it was the only time the child was allowed to speak, Anna convinced Mother to call her Nancy.

Nancy felt a sense of accomplishment, especially after she told Big Mama how and why she changed her name. "You are how old?" Big Mama asked, smiling.

"I am this many, a whole hand and one of these," Nancy said, holding them up.

"Hmm, you are a smart girl, Nancy. Maybe you should become a lawyer with a brain like that."

"I love you, Big Mama!" Nancy said, with a huge grin on her face and her arms around her human teddy bear, Grandma.

LIFE CHANGED WITH BIG MAMA around, not just the pages of the calendar whisking by days into months but months into years. Big Mama indoctrinated traditions from the Old Country into their everyday lives from the time Anna was six until she was eleven. The consistency was welcome.

One such crazy fun ritual was when Big Mama sponge-bathed naked Nancy while she stood in a tin tub placed on the kitchen table. Colder nights were harder to handle than the warmer ones, and naked Nancy in the metal tub with her friend Suni Muni, the neighbor boy, added more laughter. Suni had been out of the picture for a long time but would be back sporadically. Lucky for him, Grandma said she would take care of him whenever his parents were incarcerated throughout the upcoming years. Suni's stepdad was continually in and out of the pokey for aggravated assault, while Lili was sent to Bellevue Mental Hospital "for God knows what, like walking the streets of Manhattan naked and yelling at people. None of it the fault of the child," Grandma would compassionately say. Nancy watched enough cartoons to have images of Lili in a straitjacket in a padded cell with her eyeballs swirling around in her head.

"Yea, Big Mama, poor Suni."

When it was time to be washed with Suni, Nancy made light of his situation, singing, "Les stuck one foot in, he stuck one foot out, he did the hokey pokey and turned himself about. You see, Suni, Les will be fine; he will turn himself from bad to good. That's what 'turn yourself around' means. Sing with me." The two kids giggled as Nancy carefully turned Suni as they stood in the metal wash bin on the kitchen table.

Overall, Nancy preferred alone time in a bathtub, especially as they reached a certain age where being washed was strange in her underwear in front of a boy. Baths were safe now that Mother wasn't around to beat Nancy and make her sit in a scalding bath. Mother even yelled at Anna a few times, saying, "I got fired because I burned a couple of old biddies giving them a bath. This isn't hot. You're all just weak sh*ts!" But now with Big Mama around, being submerged in warm, running water for hours became Nancy's sacred practice with the door closed. Once a week, Big Mama rinsed Anna's hair with hot water and vinegar "to make the hair shine." But more importantly, Big Mama would say, "If soap and water is the solution, there is no problem," and even better, "Cleanliness is next to Godliness."

AMONG THE GIRL'S PLEASANT MEMORIES, Nancy loved washing Big Mama's back. She also loved sharing Big Mama's cherries, Hershey's chocolate bars, lemon wafers, and peanuts, after which the child joyously sang along with Big Mama to the albums Sidney brought. *My Fair Lady,* in particular, had the two rolling in stitches. Big Mama did her best to pronounce the English words and overexaggerated each enunciation. The two got along famously; they were both healing for one another.

When Nancy went somewhere with Mother and Big Mama, people didn't just say, "You don't look anything like your mother," like they used to. Instead, they stated: "You look just like your Grandma Clara, and you are just as sweet. Everyone loves her." The words fed Nancy a new sense of identity, one so much better than Mother's degrading comeback in the past, "Right, Anna looks nothing like me. She is a jackass." Not only did she have a new name, Nancy, but she was beginning to see herself in a whole new way.

Big Mama took her growing girl, now at eleven years old, shoulder height with Clara's five feet six inches, on an excursion across town to Central Park, as they had done together since Nancy was six. They skipped from their favorite animals, the seals, to the penguins at the free zoo. Since it was winter, Big Mama had worn her seal fur coat. She stopped to comment to the seals as if she were Dr. Dolittle. "Don't hate me; I am wearing one of your relatives. If it makes you feel better, this coat is most special to me." Turning to Nancy, she asked, "Do you think they can tell, my girl?"

Swinging their invisible canes and twitching their mustaches, the two "Charlie Chaplins" walked over to sit on a park bench. While chomping Cracker Jacks, they giggled about what they imagined the surrounding umbrella of trees planned for that evening. Suddenly, Grandma had a hot flash. She draped her seal coat around her shoulders and pulled up her sleeves. Nancy noticed some numbers.

"Big Mama, you're trying to learn our phone number? But our phone number starts with YUK ..."

"Okay, my girl," Grandma said, choking up as a tear rolled down her cheek. "These numbers are from something I survived in the past. Don't ever tell your mother, Anci, that you saw these numbers on me. We don't talk about it until you're older."

"I promise. You survived what?"

"Actually, I survived twice. One I can't talk about. The other was the typhoid. I was dying; an American soldier saved my life. He wanted to marry me."

"Why didn't you marry?"

"Ach, I had to return to Anci and the family. I just managed to find Anci as she was rolling away with a truck full of orphans to the land of Zion. I spotted her. I called out, "Anci," and she jumped off as the truck kicked up dust, pulling away. Everyone else in our family was gone." Grandma utilized her hanky, cleared her throat, and continued, "Remember, my girl, you can learn the easy way or the hard way. Easy way is to learn from people's mistakes. Hard way is to learn through your own experience. If I could do my life over, I would do things the easy way. Unfortunately, I wish I had learned that sooner so I wouldn't have lived such a hard life. 'One little mistake affected my whole life,' my Mama Regina used to say all the time because she married her Leo."

"I learn how not to be a mommy by learning what not to do from what Mommy does to me."

"That's good, my girl. You are taking a hurtful thing and turning it to your advantage. Now I will tell you what I wish I would have listened to when I was told. The truth about life. Life is hard. Even when doing our very best and listening to others' warnings, we will still encounter uncomfortable, hard situations in life. This is life and why it is a good idea to not look for trouble, since trouble will still find us. When it does, remember, we aren't to beat ourselves up for it since we've been doing our best. And instead of complaining, we must use our energies to pull ourselves out of it. Results may not be immediate, but then this teaches patience. Your comment about you not wanting to become like your mother shows me you see this challenge you have for a mother as an opportunity to better yourself. If we are smart like this, we can conquer the hard times that provide hidden lessons. No matter what, look for the good in people and in everything. We have to be thankful to your mother, for example. She birthed you in America, and she brought me out to this great country. That's priceless! Remember, you and I are the same. Instead of turning bitter and mean and crazy from hard times, we will grow, learn how to survive, forgive, and gain compassion."

Nancy thought, *Thank goodness, I have You, too, All Knowing. I can trust everything You say, and You sent me Big Mama when I cried for help.*

Just then, All Knowing whispered into Nancy's right ear: *"It's good you appreciate all that you have."*

Big Mama gently raised Nancy's face to lock into eye contact with the child looking down, who was concentrating on All Knowing's whispers, before she continued. "Nancy, this is a lot to understand, I know, but listen. There are monsters and then there are sinners. Monsters are bad people who bother people like themselves. Sinners harm the innocent and the angelic. Remember, everything has a cost. But there is no greater suffering than straying away from being good. This is a huge challenge, but the merits will pay off in another lifetime, if not in this one."

Nancy's mind didn't have time to register His words. She was now caught up in Big Mama's huddling embrace inside her coat. The older explaining her past; the younger listening as sparrows joined them to share their Cracker Jacks.

"Look, Big Mama, your favorite birds."

"Nancy, these birds are not worth much, yet look how God deeply cares for them. They remind us to be the best we can be. We all matter."

"Yes, Big Mama, be the best we can be and *live life!*"

"You really are smart like an eighty-year-old woman."

Nancy squeezed her Big Mama tight, and Big Mama reciprocated.

"Nancy, we don't understand things at the time, but everything is for a good reason. I mean, look! You are the reason I didn't die when so many did. God gave me you, the little girl I always wanted."

"Big Mama, you are God-sent too! I prayed really hard and really long, and you've been heaven-sent. So, you must be a saint."

Both their noses were red from crying joyful tears. Then Big Mama said, "Stick your nose in my cheek, and then I will stick my nose in your cheek. You know how we do."

They did so, giggling.

"Hold it right there, Big Mama. I have to take a mental photograph of us right now. *Click!* This one is in full color!"

Every one of Big Mama's healing hugs released endured abuse and tragic memories for both of them. In letting go, laughter replaced sorrow, which then enabled new eyes to look to the sky and see the wonderful gifts of the world— where birds don't merely fly overhead but applaud from above the transformed people below.

"Wait! Why did You say? 'Appreciate all you have now'?" Nancy asked All Knowing telepathically.

The hairs on the back of my neck are electrified, and my body has head-to-toe goosebumps. I have to pay attention!

"All Knowing, what do you mean?"

"Nothing lasts forever," All Knowing whispered.

"Right, All Knowing, like you sent me Big Mama and made everything so much better!"

With the biggest smile, Nancy hugged her Big Mama even tighter. In this moment on the park bench, the glowing happiness from Big Mama's presence exemplified how Nancy felt in her heart. It was the same as when she first realized All Knowing was by her side and she experienced him as Glow Ball. His goodness, His luminescence, shined through and around her to not only prove to Nancy her acknowledgment that His magical, powerful omniscience was real but to heal her. Nancy would not forget either of the highly healing moments with All Knowing or her Big Mama. She would need to call on these moments in the years to come.

Invite Nancy to Your Book Club!

As a special gift to readers of Whispers, Sinners, and Saints, Nancy would love to visit your book club either via video conferencing or in person.

Please contact Nancy directly through her website, nancyheart.com, to schedule her appearance at your next book club meeting.

Acknowledgments

SPECIAL THANKS to the omniscient by my side since before my earthly existence in this lifetime. If it were not for the *whispers* of the divine, I would not be alive today to share my story. Mother's slander and abuse is what consistently pushed me into the invisible intangible—to the divine presence who guided, supported, uplifted, and carried me.

The accounts I share are the proven reason for how I stayed with the divine. And yes, I even thank all who played a part in my life, whether good, bad, or ugly. We have a special cosmic contract between us, and I have learned from each of them, even if I do admit I hope our karmic circles never intersect again on any dimension.

Lovingly, my heart thanks my daughter and son. I hope by publishing this book, I continually inspire them to feel that any dream is possible. They alone know how many decades this project took to bring to fruition.

On a professional note, I wish to give a shout-out to my editor, Donna Mazzitelli, with whom I gel very well and hope to work with on all my upcoming books.

About the Author

NANCY'S RECIPE FOR HAPPINESS is to share ideas and deep thoughts and avoid wasting time in superficial conversations and gossip. She has traveled six out of the seven continents. Having grown up in Manhattan and South Florida, she is a xenophile—preferring exposure to various cultures of the world over sand and sun. She graduated with  a Bachelor of Arts in Psychology from the University of Miami, studied Art Appreciation in Europe, attended the Fashion Institute of Technology, studied Kabbalah and Buddhism, and traveled the perimeters of the United States.

Nancy's philosophy is: "One who laughs loudest, masters pain the best." Pain offers the opportunity to discover one's true self and greatest strengths.

Nancy now lives in Colorado. She is an ambivert, and when not writing with her Maltese-poodle "Cookie-Cake" by her side, she enjoys urban hikes, mahjong, scrabble, reiki as a master, and meditation. Above all else, Nancy appreciates quality time with friends and her adult children.

Made in United States
Troutdale, OR
04/15/2024